Punk

Punk

The Definitive Guide to the Blank Generation and Beyond

RICH WEIDMAN

Backbeat Books

Essex, Connecticut

An imprint of Globe Pequot, the trade division of
The Rowman & Littlefield Publishing Group, Inc.
4501 Forbes Blvd., Ste. 200
Lanham, MD 20706
www.rowman.com

Distributed by NATIONAL BOOK NETWORK

British Library Cataloguing in Publication Information available

Library of Congress Cataloging-in-Publication Data
Names: Weidman, Rich, author.
Title: Punk : the definitive guide to the blank generation and beyond / Rich
    Weidman.
Description: Essex, Connecticut : Backbeat, 2023. | Includes bibliographical
    references and index.
Identifiers: LCCN 2022023235 (print) | LCCN 2022023236 (ebook) | ISBN
    9781493062409 (paperback) | ISBN 9781493062416 (ebook)
Subjects: LCSH: Punk rock music—History and criticism. | Punk culture.
Classification: LCC ML3534 .W433 2023 (print) | LCC ML3534 (ebook) |
    DDC 781.6609—dc23/eng/20220517
LC record available at https://lccn.loc.gov/2022023235
LC ebook record available at https://lccn.loc.gov/2022023236

Dedicated to the memory of legendary Times Square hustler, junkie, storyteller, and Beat Generation muse Herbert Huncke (1915–1996), the original punk.

Contents

Acknowledgments

First of all, I would like to thank my wife, Nadine, and kids, Hailey and Dylan—none of whom have any interest in punk rock whatsoever! However, they provided encouragement and patience as I spent countless hours at my desk working on this book. A special thanks as always to my family—Mom, Dad, Boyd, and Tracy and her family (Cliff, Emma, Jack, and Chris)—for all your support and enthusiasm during my punk rock odyssey over the past year and a half. Thanks also to the McAuley clan—Jan; David, Kathy, and Kennedy; and Dan, Carrie, Joey, Kyle, and Caiden.

A big thanks as always to Jack Thompson, who has collaborated with me on some truly incredible internet projects over the years such as Alternative Reel, Forgotten Movie Classics, and Pro Wrestlers: Dead or Alive. Jack also introduced me to the Gainesville punk scene via legendary local band the Doldrums ("All That Shimmers"). In addition, for a very brief period in 2008–2009, I experienced what it was like to be a "rock journalist" as we covered a handful of Central Florida concerts by the likes of Seether, Staind, and Papa Roach, as well as Doors tribute band Peace Frog.

I'm truly grateful to Chris Chappell, Laurel Myers, and Barbara Claire from Rowman & Littlefield for their assistance throughout all the production stages related to this book and for tolerating my frequent delays. Thanks as always to Robert Lecker of the Robert Lecker Agency for his persistence and assistance.

A special mention goes to Matt and Pam Weber of ROAR! Internet Marketing, as well as legendary music promoter Jim Faherty and founder of Figurehead Records, who gave me a great insider's overview of the entire punk scene. For their ongoing inspiration, a special shout out to Jim Foley, Art "Barfly" Spackle, Bill Chinaski, Ben Parker, John Nixdorf, John "Hooch" Lewis, John Mills, Alex Velazquez, Robert Rodriguez, Jim Cherry, Robert Ray (who introduced me to the Situationist International), Tony Fernandez, and Michael McCloud. This book is dedicated to the memory of James Ketchen, Michael Raymond, and C. Carter Colwell.

Introduction

Punk rock was the tsunami that threatened to drown us all in 1977. —Pete Townshend of the Who

Everything that is true is inappropriate. —Oscar Wilde

Where there is a stink of shit there is a smell of being. —Antonin Artaud

Did you know . . .

- Considered one of the most influential rock bands of all time, the Ramones never even scored a top 40 single on the Billboard Hot 100 (their highest charting single, "Rockaway Beach," peaked at no. 66)?
- John Lydon (Rotten) of Sex Pistols fame once dismissed Nirvana as "a dismal folk band with some squalling thrown in to bump up the revenue"?
- English grindcore band Napalm Death holds the record for the shortest song of all time—the 1.316-second "You Suffer" from the band's debut studio album *Scum* (1987)?
- Los Angeles punk band the Dickies performed "Hideous" on a 1978 episode of the TV comedy show *C.P.O Sharkey*, which starred Don Rickles?

- The slogan for the Sex Pistols' 1996 Filthy Lucre tour was "Fat, Forty, and Back"?

These are just a few of the tidbits to be found in this exploration of the world of punk rock. In addition to the music, *Punk: The Definitive Guide to the Blank Generation and Beyond* focuses on the significant impact of punk on culture more generally in terms of attitude, ideology, fashion and style, film, literature, art, and more. The book has been designed for casual browsing, so you can simply open it up at any spot and start perusing or, if you prefer, read it from cover to cover.

How did I become interested in punk rock? It was a long and rewarding process indeed! As a fifteen-year-old high school student in 1980, I completely missed the punk rock movement, and my musical interests lay elsewhere. The first album I ever purchased was the Cars' 1978 self-titled debut album, which featured such new-wave classics as "Just What I Needed," "Good Times Roll," "You're All I've Got Tonight," and "All Mixed Up." Around this time, I also got caught up in the first major renaissance of interest in the psychedelic music of the Doors when I came across a copy of the Jim Morrison biography, *No One Here Gets Out Alive*, then bought *The Doors: Greatest Hits* and became hooked on the band.

That's why my first exposure to punk rock was through an unlikely source: the 1984 cult film *Repo Man*, which was directed by Alex Cox and starred Emilio Estevez and Harry Dean Stanton. Not only did I find the movie offbeat and hilarious, but I also totally freaked out over the film's music—I had never heard anything like that ever before! So I picked up a copy of the soundtrack on cassette and played it to death. I thrilled to such songs as Black Flag's "TV Party," the Circle Jerks' "When the Shit Hits the Fan," Fear's "Let's Have a War," Iggy Pop's "Repo Man," Suicidal Tendencies' "Institutionalized," Burning Sensations' cover of Jonathan Richman's "Pablo Picasso," and the Plugz' "El Clavo y la Cruz."

When the 1986 biopic *Sid and Nancy* came out in the local movie theater, I sought it out even though I had no knowledge about the Sex Pistols at all—simply because I discovered it was directed by none other than Alex Cox of *Repo Man* fame! I marveled at Gary

Oldman's mesmerizing performance as Sid Vicious, and I really got into some of the songs from the film's soundtrack, especially "Haunted" by the Pogues and "Love Kills" by the Circle Jerks, as well as "I Wanna Be Your Dog" and "My Way" sung by Oldman. So I went out and bought the Pogues' landmark album *Rum Sodomy & the Lash* (1985) and became a big fan of the Celtic punk band as well.

You get the idea. One thing led to another, and I began a lengthy process of discovering all the great punk albums I missed the first time around—from not only such legendary bands as the Sex Pistols and the Ramones but also proto-punk bands like MC5, the Stooges, and the New York Dolls. However, I didn't delve too deeply into some of the more obscure punk bands at that point. That all changed during my research for a book on Guns N' Roses that was published by Backbeat Books in 2017. I knew *Appetite for Destruction*, *Use Your Illusion I*, and *Use Your Illusion II* inside and out, but I had never listened to the band's unfairly maligned 1993 album of covers, *The Spaghetti Incident*. This album opened a new world for me with the likes of the Damned's "New Rose," UK Subs' "Down on the Farm," Misfits' "Attitude," the Professionals' "Black Leather," Johnny Thunders' "You Can't Put Your Arms Around a Memory," and especially the Dead Boys' "Ain't It Fun." So I sought out the original versions of these songs, which led me to other punk bands, and so on, and the rest is history.

I continue to make new discoveries by excavating the punk rock genre and making valuable connections that lead to more and more hidden treasures. I encourage you to read up and seek out any music listed in this book you've never heard before. Hopefully, everyone from the casual punk-rock listener to the hardcore-punk fan will find plenty of interesting nuggets within these pages. Happy exploring!

1

Search and Destroy
Defining Characteristics of Punk

Rock 'n' roll is about attitude. I couldn't care less about
technique. —Johnny Thunders

According to the *Treble Zine*, "Punk is fairly easy to define: It's
played fast and loud, it's anti-authority and anti-status quo and it
doesn't give a shit what you think." By these standards, Henry David
Thoreau was a punk when he stated in his famous 1849 essay, *On
the Duty of Civil Disobedience*, "Let your life be a counter-friction
to stop the machine." Despite the diversity of its scope, punk rock
features the following overarching characteristics that have helped
define the movement over the years:

DO-IT-YOURSELF ETHIC One of the essential components that fueled
the punk subculture outside of its pure rebellious stance is the
concept of a powerful and all-encompassing do-it-yourself, or DIY,
ethic. This took shape in the form of independent record labels,
fanzines, venues, promotions, and strong social networking that
allowed punk to thrive and spread rapidly beyond its initial origins
in New York City and London. The DIY ethic is most notable
in the countless independent record labels that sprouted up to
bypass the corporate record industry such as Stiff Records, Epitaph, Alternative Tentacles, SST, Fat Wreck Chords, Dischord
Records, and many others. Flyers also served as an integral part of

DIY to promote upcoming punk shows in the days before internet and social media. According to John Lydon in *Punk Rock: An Oral History*, "Some great things came from punk. The do-it-yourself aspect—don't rely on others, don't wait for a movement, get out there and start your own!"

ANTI-CONSUMERISM   Especially in its earliest incarnations, punk rock ideology featured a strong stance against the continual buying and consuming of material possessions. For example, X-Ray Spex railed against mass consumption in several tracks on the band's 1978 debut album, *Germfree Adolescents*, including "I Live Off You," "Plastic Bag," and "Warrior in Woolworths." Shane Mac-Gowan of the Pogues highlighted the anti-consumerist nature of punk in his 2001 memoir:

> To make great music, you gotta have no interest in houses of any description. You don't care if you sleep in the fucking street, as long as they're playing my music. . . . That's the attitude you have to have. Like, you can't think about a house, or a car, or fucking anything. . . . You've just got to be fucking overwhelmed by the idea of getting your music on to a piece of fucking vinyl.

MINIMALISM   With punk, less is more. The Ramones and other punk bands stripped music down to its essence. According to Nicholas Rombes in *A Cultural Dictionary of Punk*, "The Ramones were the consummate minimalist American band; Wire the consummate minimalist UK band. . . . Rather than abundance, punk celebrated reduction."

NOSTALGIA FOR THE 1950S   The Ramones deliberately adopted a 1950s style in the form of motorcycle jackets, T-shirts, torn-up jeans, and sneakers that recalled Marlon Brando's Johnny character in *The Wild One* (1953). In addition, the teenage angst and rebellion inherent in punk served as a direct descendant of such classic 1950s teen flicks as *Rebel Without a Cause* and *Blackboard Jungle*, both of which were released in 1955, just a year before Elvis Presley skyrocketed to stardom with the release of "Heartbreak Hotel."

Considered to be the original outlaw biker film, *The Wild One* (1953) heavily influenced later punk style exemplified by artists like the Ramones and Joan Jett. COLUMBIA/PHOTOFEST

AMATEURISM *Sideburns* fanzine famously declared, "This is a chord. This is another. This is a third. Now form a band." In fact, all you really needed to form a punk band was a desire to express your individualism. Many punk bands learned their instruments while playing gigs. Sid Vicious of the Sex Pistols didn't know the first thing about playing bass guitar, but he had the look and attitude that fit the role. Joey Ramone advised, "Play before you get good, because by the time you get good, you're too old to play." In his 2006 memoir, *Amped*, Jon Resh of Gainesville punk band Spoke remarked, "We weren't good at all. But the music we played was music we put every ounce of ourselves into, music that pulled us to our emotional core, music that made us feel *alive*. Our sole aim was to express ourselves as clearly and intensely as possible, to bring the simple melodies playing in our heads to life."

REJECTION OF STADIUM/CORPORATE ROCK A major shift in the music industry began in the 1970s when large multinational corporations with no previous experience in music started purchasing major record labels. Meanwhile, rock 'n' roll in general had become bloated and self-indulgent. According to Joey Ramone, "There was no spirit left, no challenge, no fun, and so many artists had become so full of themselves." Bands like Led Zeppelin flew in private jets

Punk rock served as a rejection of the corporate rock of the 1970s personified by
Peter Frampton, whose *Frampton Comes Alive!* (1976) sold more than thirteen million
copies. A&M RECORDS/PHOTOFEST

and rode in limousines to gigs. With his 1976 album, *Frampton
Comes Alive!* which sold more than thirteen million copies, Peter
Frampton became the unwitting poster boy for "corporate rock"
as he played for huge sellout crowds. In contrast, punk fans could
completely interact with their favorite bands at such dives as New
York City's legendary CBGBs. In the words of Pete Townshend of
the Who, "Punk rock was the tsunami that threatened to drown us
all in 1977."

2

Beginning to See the Light

Punk Origins and Influences

> Plagiarism is what the world's about. If you didn't start
> seeing things and stealing because you were so inspired
> by them, you'd be stupid. —Malcolm McLaren

Legendary architect and philosopher Buckminster Fuller once remarked, "You can never change things by fighting the existing reality. To change something, build a new model that makes the existing model obsolete." Punk rock attempted to recover authenticity in the face of bland corporate rock culture by destroying the existing norms and starting over in a new direction like a phoenix rising from the ashes.

However, punk rock did not simply arise in a vacuum. Punk is evident in the French symbolism of Arthur Rimbaud, the absurdist literature of Alfred Jarry, the philosophy of Dadaism, the spontaneity and rebelliousness of the Beat Generation, the precepts of the Situationist International, the raw minimalism of garage rock, and even the nihilism of Stanley Kubrick's 1971 dystopian masterpiece, *A Clockwork Orange*. All these distinct types of influences and many others would make themselves evident in punk culture in one way or another, consciously or subconsciously.

ARTHUR RIMBAUD   None other than French novelist and philosopher Albert Camus (*The Stranger*) called Arthur Rimbaud "the poet

5

Pioneering punk rock artist Patti Smith was influenced by both French symbolist poet Arthur Rimbaud and Beat Generation icon William S. Burroughs. BY DOUG ANDERSON/ WIKIMEDIA COMMONS

of revolt, and the greatest." A visionary poet and self-destructive genius who influenced the work of pioneering punk-rock artists—especially Patti Smith, Richard Hell, and Tom Verlaine—Jean Nicholas Arthur Rimbaud was born on October 20, 1854, in Charleville, France. His father, a career military officer, abandoned the family when he was just seven years old. As a rebellious teenager, Rimbaud sought out experience and actively embraced anarchism and mind-altering substances. An encounter with the works of acclaimed French poet Charles Baudelaire (*Flowers of Evil*) led Rimbaud to embark on a literary career, which lasted just four years. After Rimbaud started a correspondence with symbolist poet Paul Verlaine, the two writers engaged in a short, turbulent affair that ended abruptly after Verlaine shot Rimbaud in the left wrist and was sentenced to two years in prison.

At the age of nineteen, Rimbaud completed his masterpiece, *Une saison en enfer* (*A Season in Hell*), in which he exclaimed,

"Boredom is no longer my love. Rage, debauchery, madness—I know all their aspirations and disasters—all my burden is laid aside." He then embarked on a reckless career as a trader and gun runner in Africa. On November 10, 1891, Rimbaud died of bone cancer in the Hospital of the Immaculate Conception in Marseille at the age of thirty-seven. He is buried in Charleville-Mezieres Cemetery, and his epitaph reads, "Priez pour lui" ("Pray for him").

In 1973, Patti Smith organized the first of her Rock 'n' Rimbaud events at the Le Jardin disco in the Hotel Diplomat in Manhattan. According to rock historian Jon Savage in *England's Dreaming*, "From the days when Richard Hell and Tom Verlaine transformed themselves, Punk was infected by a Rimbaldian script: live fast, disorder your senses, flame brightly before self-immolation."

ALFRED JARRY   Best known for his 1896 absurdist play *Ubu Roi*, French dramatist and satirist Alfred Jarry was born on September 8, 1873. Full of obscenity and violence, *Ubu Roi*, a parody of Shakespeare's *Macbeth*, was first performed in Paris in 1896 and has since been acknowledged as a precursor of Dadaism, Surrealism, and the Theatre of the Absurd. A heavy drinker, Jarry was known to knock off a couple of bottles of wine and five to ten absinthes ("the Green Goddess" he called it) every day.

Jarry died of tuberculosis aggravated by drug and alcohol abuse at the age of thirty-four on November 1, 1907. His last words, directed to a priest, were, "I'm dying. Please . . . bring me a toothpick." *Flashbak* has dubbed *Ubu Roi* "the most punk play of all time." Cleveland, Ohio–based avant-garde proto-punk band Pere Ubu, which formed in 1975, took their name from *Ubu Roi*. In 2009, the band released an album titled *Long Live Pere Ubu!* which served as a soundtrack to a musical adaptation of *Ubu Roi*.

DADAISM   Centered around the Cabaret Voltaire in Zurich, Switzerland, Dadaism served as a European avant-garde art movement of the early twentieth century. *Dada*, which means "hobby horse," was allegedly pulled out randomly from a dictionary, according to legend. Reacting to the brutality and insanity of World War I, the Dadaists utilized a variety of artistic techniques such as collage, cut-up writing, poetry, and sculpture to express their outrage against the absurdity of modern society.

Key adherents of Dadaism included Hugo Ball, Max Ernst, George Grosz, Richard Huelsenbeck, Marcel Duchamp, Hannah Hoch, Francis Picabia, Man Ray, Hans Richter, Sophie Taeuber-Arp, Beatrice Wood, Kurt Schwitters, Raoul Hausmann, Tristan Tzara, Jean Arp, Elsa von Freytag-Loringhoven, Emmy Hennings, and Johannes Baader, among others. According to Grosz, the whole concept of Dadaism was the "organized use of insanity to express contempt for a bankrupt world," while Tzara stated, "The beginnings of Dada were not the beginnings of art, but of disgust," and Huelsenbeck declared, "Dada means nothing. We want to change the world with nothing."

The influential English band Cabaret Voltaire, which formed in 1973, took its name from the Zurich nightclub that served as the center of early Dada activities. In addition, Los Angeles punk band the Weirdos, which formed in 1976, evoked Dadaist tendencies and proclaimed admiration for Duchamp and his pioneering conceptual art. Known for their classic punk anthem, "We Got the Neutron Bomb," the band featured lead singer John Denney, his guitarist brother Dix Denney, guitarist Cliff Roman, bassist Dave Trout, and drummer Nickey "Beat" Alexander. Proponents of their own eclectic do-it-yourself ethic known as "weirdoism," the band created their own logos, flyers, record sleeves, bumper stickers, T-shirts, and other merchandise.

BEAT GENERATION   Born out of disillusionment with the conformity and repression that pervaded post–World War II life in the United States, the Beats pursued more creative alternatives to the mind-numbing banality of modern culture. Beat Generation writers were no strangers to controversy: both Allen Ginsberg's prophetic poem "Howl" (1956) and William S. Burroughs's apocalyptic novel *Naked Lunch* (1959) led to obscenity trials, while Jack Kerouac's classic novel of freedom and the search for authenticity, *On the Road* (1957), was blamed by the establishment for corrupting the nation's youth. "Howl" itself helped set the tone of the Beat movement with its powerful opening lines: "I saw the best minds of my generation/

destroyed by madness, starving hysterical naked." Ginsberg
would later make a cameo on
the Clash song "Ghetto Defendant" from *Combat Rock* (1982).

William Blake, Charles
Baudelaire, and Edgar Allan
Poe all served as inspiration for
Kerouac. According to legend,
he wrote *On the Road*, which
detailed his wanderings across
the United States between
1947 and 1950, on a 120-foot
roll of teletype paper without
margins or page breaks during
three Benzedrine-fueled weeks
in 1951. Kerouac advocated for
a theory of spontaneous prose,
where the novelist wrote whatever comes to mind, "all first-
person, fast, mad, confessional,"
much like the improvisation evident in jazz music.

Beat Generation icon William S. Burroughs, who revolutionized literature
with the publication of *Naked Lunch*
in 1959, inspired the early NYC punk
rock scene in the mid-1970s centered
around CBGBs. PHOTOFEST

According to Burroughs, it was Kerouac who suggested the
title for *Naked Lunch*: "A frozen moment when everyone sees what
is on the end of every fork." Critics over the years have described
this groundbreaking novel, which documents an unrepentant
drug addict's Boschian descent into a personal hell, as "brutal,"
"obscene," "disgusting," and "immoral." *Naked Lunch* was banned
for obscenity by Boston courts in 1962, but the Massachusetts
Supreme Judicial Court reversed the decision in 1966.

Known variously as the "Godfather of Punk," "Elvis of American
Letters," and "Cosmonaut of Inner Space," Burroughs, a longtime
heroin addict, once described himself as "an unaffiliated conservative anarchist." A countercultural icon, Burroughs appeared on the
cover of the Beatles' *Sgt. Pepper's Lonely Hearts Club Band* 1967
album. According to Burroughs's biographer, Ted Morgan, in *Literary Outlaw*, "Although the rock musicians adopted Burroughs as

one of their own, he had absolutely no interest in their music and would go to considerable lengths to avoid listening to it." In fact, Burroughs remarked in the punk oral history *Please Kill Me*, "I always thought a punk was somebody that took it up the ass."

SITUATIONIST INTERNATIONAL   First organized in 1952 as the Lettrist International and re-formed as the Situationist International in 1957, this groundbreaking movement launched by an international group of political artists and activists offered a playful critique of Western consumer capitalism that culminated with the French student revolt of May 1968. The Situationists were in turn highly influenced by the Dadaists and Surrealists.

Situationist International founding member Guy Debord, a renowned French poet and filmmaker, wrote the highly influential 1967 book *Society of the Spectacle*, in which he declared, "In societies where modern conditions of production prevail, all of life presents itself as an immense accumulation of spectacles. Everything that was directly lived has moved away into a representation." Another highly influential book in the Situationist movement was *The Revolution of Everyday Life* (1967) by Belgian author Raoul Vaneigem, who produced such highly digestible slogans as "Down with a world in which the guarantee that we will not die of starvation has been purchased with the guarantee that we will die of boredom."

Malcolm McLaren, Vivienne Westwood, and Jamie Reid were all influenced by Situationist thought, which they utilized to perfectly shape the attitude and theatrics of the Sex Pistols. In his outstanding 1989 treatise, *Lipstick Traces: A Secret History of the Twentieth Century*, Greil Marcus thoroughly explores the connection between the Situationists and punk rock. However, former Sex Pistol John Lydon (Rotten) dismissed any connection between the Situationist movement and the punks in his 1994 autobiography: "All the talk about the French Situationists being associated with punk is bollocks. . . . We didn't sit around and wax Situationist philosophy."

GARAGE ROCK Sometimes referred to simply as "garage punk," garage rock was a raw, gritty, and raucous form of back-to-basics rock 'n' roll that flourished mostly in the United States and Canada during the mid-1960s. Although many garage-rock bands simply faded into obscurity, the most memorable groups such as the Troggs ("Wild Thing"), Count Five ("Psychotic Reaction"), the Standells ("Dirty Water"), Strawberry Alarm Clock ("Incense and Peppermints"), Question Mark and the Mysterians ("96 Tears"), and Blues Magoos ("We Ain't Got Nothin' Yet") proved to be highly influential to the burgeoning punk scene of the mid-1970s.

According to John Holmstrom in *Punk: The Best of Punk Magazine*, "To us, all those fast, loud, arrogant, obnoxious teenage bands made the best music of the twentieth century. To us, *they* were the 1960s—and the hippie bands produced music that needed to be wiped off the face of the Earth."

Lenny Kaye, who would later become the lead guitarist of the Patti Smith Group, collected some of the best garage-rock band singles for Elektra Records to create the highly influential 1972 album *Nuggets: Original Artyfacts from the First Psychedelic Era*, such as "Dirty Water" by the Standells, "Pushin' Too Hard" by the Seeds, "You're Gonna Miss Me" by the 13th Floor Elevators, "Night Time" by the Strangeloves, and "Let's Talk about Girls" by Chocolate Watch Band, among many others. According to Kaye, in the liner notes of the fortieth anniversary Rhino reissue of *Nuggets* from 2012, "It's the songs in the end that make *Nuggets* so memorable, the lightning strikes of brilliance that move a record past genre into the realm of classic." *Nuggets* later ranked no. 405 on the *Rolling Stone* list of the "500 Greatest Albums of All Time."

In addition, many garage-rock band classics have been covered by proto-punk and punk bands such as Question Mark and the Mysterians' "96 Tears" (the Stranglers), the Kingsmen's "Louie Louie" (the Stooges), Chocolate Watch Band's "Let's Talk about Girls" (the Undertones), and the Sonics' "Strychnine" (the Fall), among many others.

POP ART Utilizing imagery from popular culture to break down the wall between art and everyday life, pop art first emerged in the mid- to late 1950s. Defining characteristics of pop art were the use of recognizable images, bright colors, irony and satire, mixed media, and collage. In addition, pop art's use of found objects and images recalled Dadaism.

Artists associated with the pop art movement include Andy Warhol, Robert Rauschenberg, Jasper Johns, Roy Lichtenstein, Larry Rivers, James Rosenquist, Robert Indiana, Richard Hamilton, and Eduardo Paolozzi. Among the most famous pop art works are *Campbell's Soup Cans* (Warhol), *LOVE* (Indiana), *Just What Is It That Makes Today's Homes So Different, So Appealing?* (Hamilton), *Three Flags* (Johns), and *Drowning Girl* (Litchtenstein).

Of all the artists connected to the pop art movement, none had more impact on punk rock than Warhol and his Factory Studio, which played an essential role in setting up what would become the New York punk scene in the 1970s. Warhol discovered the Velvet Underground, made the group a crucial element of his Exploding Plastic Inevitable multimedia performance art shows, and put forth the money to finance the band's debut album, *The Velvet Underground & Nico*, in 1967. Most famously, he designed the peelable banana album cover! Although it sold just thirty thousand copies, *The Velvet Underground & Nico* has over time been recognized as one of the most influential albums of all time.

A CLOCKWORK ORANGE   Based on the 1962 novel of the same name by Anthony Burgess, Stanley Kubrick's 1971 terrifying dystopian film is set in England in the near future and features Malcolm McDowell as the Beethoven-loving Alex, who leads a gang of thugs (known as "droogs") on a spree of rape and "ultraviolence." After getting arrested and sent to prison, Alex undergoes a conditioning process that makes him detest violence, and then he is released to the streets with horrific results. The tagline for the film reads, "Being the adventures of a young man whose principal interests are rape, ultra-violence, and Beethoven."

Several punk-rock groups were heavily influenced by *A Clockwork Orange*, such as the Adicts, a British band formed in 1977 known for their clown makeup, bowler hats, and black boots, similar to Alex and his gang of droogs. In 1981, the Adicts released their

Stanley Kubrick's 1971 dystopian masterpiece, *A Clockwork Orange*, served as the inspiration for several punk rock bands such as the Adicts, who dressed in the style of the film's so-called "droogs." WARNER BROS./PHOTOFEST

debut album, *Songs of Praise*, which the *Encyclopedia of Popular Music* called "something of a cult-classic in punk record-collecting circles." In addition, Johnny Rotten once claimed Alex as a role model, and Sex Pistols bandmate Paul Cook said *A Clockwork Orange* was one of only two books he had ever read in his life (the other being a biography of the notorious Kray twins). The Ramones even referenced the movie on the cover of their 1984 album, *Too Tough to Die*, which was taken by photographer George DuBose in a tunnel in Central Park.

Burgess, who had drawn specific inspiration for his book from the desolate, bleak atmosphere of his hometown of Manchester, had nothing positive to say about the punk movement, remarking in a 1977 issue of *Psychology Today* that "all the punk singers can bring to the presentations of their songs is the gesture of sexual obscenity or of impotent rage. There is a lot of caged simian gibber. . . . British youth, like American and French and Upper Slobovian youth, needs a good kick in the pants and a lot of solid education."

GLAM ROCK   Originating in the United Kingdom in the early 1970s, glam rock served as a short-lived rock genre that would have a tremendous impact on the punk-rock scene, as well as heavy metal in the 1980s. Glam rock featured a heavy guitar sound, and its adherents donned outrageous gender-bending costumes, makeup, hairstyles, platform shoes, and glitter.

In the United States, Rodney Bingenheimer's English Disco at 7561 Sunset Boulevard in Hollywood, California, served as the center of the glam-rock scene. A legendary DJ and later proponent of punk rock, Bingenheimer was known as the "Mayor of Sunset Strip." The English Disco hosted the likes of Iggy Pop, David Bowie, T. Rex, the New York Dolls, Lou Reed, Andy Warhol, Elton John, Keith Moon, and Led Zeppelin, as well as scores of underage groupies such as Sable Starr and Lori Mattix.

According to John Holmstrom in *Punk: The Best of Punk Magazine*,

> Glam rock created the first break from the tedium of "rock," becoming an inspiration for most punk bands. But it was also silly, self-serious, and over-produced. It brought attention to some great rock 'n' roll bands, like the Stooges, Mott the Hoople, the Alice Cooper Band, the New York Dolls, T. Rex, Brownsville Station, even Slade, and some obscure bands like the Modern Lovers and the Sonics.

Notable glam rock songs include "Hot Love" by T. Rex, "Queen Bitch" and "Ziggy Stardust" by David Bowie, "School's Out" by Alice Cooper, "Virginia Plain" by Roxy Music, "All the Young Dudes" by Mott the Hoople, "Vicious" by Lou Reed, "Ballroom Blitz" by Sweet (which heavily influenced the Ramones' "Blitzkrieg Bop"), "Personality Crisis" by the New York Dolls, and "Cum on Feel the Noize" by Slade.

REGGAE   Originating in Jamaica in the late 1960s, reggae proved to be a tremendous influence on punk, with bands ranging from the Clash and the Ruts to the Members and the Slits playing many reggae-influenced songs. Other punk and new-wave bands inspired by reggae included Public Image Ltd, Bad Brains (whose members even converted to Rastafarianism), Generation X, Operation Ivy, Rancid, and NOFX, among others.

The 1973 cult film *The Harder They Come* helped to spread the popularity of reggae worldwide. It starred reggae superstar Jimmy Cliff as Ivan, a Jamaican musician/gangster. The film's powerful soundtrack features such classics as "You Can Get It If You Really Want," "Many Rivers to Cross," and "The Harder They Come" by Cliff, as well as "Rivers of Babylon" by the Melodians, "Pressure Drop" by the Maytals, and "Johnny Too Bad" by the Slickers, among others.

The Clash were among the first punk bands to establish a reggae-punk connection when they recorded "Police and Thieves" by Junior Murvin for their self-titled debut album in 1977. The band later recorded "Pressure Drop" by Toots and the Maytals. As a positive response to hearing the Clash's version of "Police and Thieves," Bob Marley recorded "Punky Reggae Party" in 1977 as a B-side to the "Jamming" single with the lyrics: "The Wailers will be there/the Damned, the Jam, the Clash/Maytals will be there/Dr. Feelgood too." In a 1977 interview with *Sounds* magazine, Marley remarked, "Punks are outcasts from society. So are the Rastas."

Last but certainly not least, the French record label Guerilla Asso created an intriguing Bob Marley–Ramones mashup album called *Rocket to Kingston* in 2021 credited to "Bobby Ramone" and featuring such tracks as "I Don't Wanna Stand Up," "Stirring in My Room," "Today One Love, Tomorrow the World," "Kaya Bop," "Glad to See You Cry," and "Is This Love Kills."

3

I'll Be Your Mirror
The Best Proto-Punk Bands

I'm a street-walking cheetah with a heart full of napalm/
The runaway son of the nuclear A-Bomb. —Iggy Pop

Proto-punk retroactively encompasses any groundbreaking rock band active in the 1960s or early 1970s that laid the foundation for the punk-rock movement. These range from pioneering garage-rock bands like the psychedelic 13th Floor Elevators and the experimental avant-garde Monks to loud, raucous, and revolutionary bands such as MC5 and the Stooges, quintessential glam rockers like the New York Dolls, and art-rock bands such as the Velvet Underground, among many other musical styles. Here are some of the most notable bands that paved the way for the punk-rock explosion soon to follow.

13TH FLOOR ELEVATORS   Formed in Austin, Texas, in 1965, the 13th Floor Elevators are a leading candidate for being the first full-fledged psychedelic rock band. The lineup featured lead singer and guitarist Roky Erickson, guitarist Stacy Sutherland, and electric jug player Tommy Hall (not kidding!). The band released their best-known single, "You're Gonna Miss Me," in 1966, and it reached no. 55 on the U.S. charts. The song appeared on the band's 1966 debut album, *The Psychedelic Sounds of the 13th Floor Elevators*, as well as the highly influential collection of garage-band classics compiled by Lenny Kaye titled *Nuggets: Original Artyfacts from the First Psychedelic Era 1965–1968* (1972).

The 13th Floor Elevators chose their unique name because *m* (for *marijuana*) was the thirteenth letter of the alphabet, and the band allegedly handed out free LSD to their audiences: a truly psychedelic rock band, the Elevators truly believed that their fans could reach a new level of consciousness by listening to their music. The fascinating 2005 documentary *You're Gonna Miss Me* documents Erickson's strange life and struggles with mental illness.

Essential Listening: *The Psychedelic Sounds of the 13th Floor Elevators* (1966)

ALICE COOPER   According to cultural historian Nicholas Rombes in *A Cultural Dictionary of Punk*, "Alice Cooper was the missing link between glam rock and what came to be known as punk rock." Known as the "Godfather of Shock Rock," Alice Cooper (Vincent Damon Furnier) was the son of a preacher from Detroit, Michigan. The family moved to Phoenix, Arizona, when Furnier was just three years old. In high school, Furnier and some friends formed a band called the Earwigs, which soon became the Spiders, then morphed into the Nazz, and later Alice Cooper. The band featured Furnier on vocals, lead guitarist Glen Buxton, rhythm guitarist/keyboardist Michael Bruce, bassist Dennis Dunaway, and drummer Neal Smith. Furnier soon adopted the band's name as his own.

During the late 1960s, the Alice Cooper Band earned a justifiable reputation as "the worst band in Los Angeles." They eventually signed with Frank Zappa's Straight Records label and released two albums: *Pretties for You* (which the *Rolling Stone Album Guide* called "strictly inept psychedelia") and *Easy Action* in 1970. Unable to gain any momentum in Los Angeles, the Alice Cooper Band decided to head to Detroit, where they received a better reception and befriended local bands such as the Stooges and MC5. In 1971, the band released *Love It to Death*, which spawned the hit single "I'm Eighteen"—an instant teen anthem that reached no. 21 on the U.S. charts. The Ramones' song "I Don't Care" was based on the chords of the main riff in "I'm Eighteen," while Johnny Rotten wrote the song "Seventeen" in response to the song. In addition,

Rotten auditioned for the Pistols by singing "I'm Eighteen" along with a jukebox at SEX, Malcolm McLaren and Vivienne Westwood's London boutique.

By the early 1970s, the Alice Cooper Band started indulging in rock theatrics and incorporating elaborate stage props into their live shows such as black makeup, fake blood, guillotines and electric chairs, amputated dolls, live boa constrictors, and six-foot-long inflatable phalluses. Cooper's first solo effort, *Welcome to My Nightmare* (1975), featured narration by Vincent Price and the ballad "Only Women Bleed." Alice Cooper was inducted into the Rock and Roll Hall of Fame in 2011.

Essential Listening: *Love It to Death* (1971), *Killer* (1971), *School's Out* (1972), *Billion Dollar Babies* (1973), *Welcome to My Nightmare* (1975)

THE DICTATORS   Formed in New York City in 1974, the Dictators were one of the most influential proto-punk bands. Mired in trash culture, the band sang of such topics as pro wrestling, TV, fast food, cars, and girls. However, since the band hailed from the Bronx, they always felt like outsiders to the burgeoning CBGB's scene during the mid-1970s.

The classic Dictators lineup featured lead singer "Handsome" Dick Manitoba (Richard Blum), guitarist Ross "The Boss" Friedman, bassist/keyboardist Andy Shernoff, bassist Scott "Top Ten" Kempner, and drummer Stu Boy King. The band's loud, fast, and satirical brand of rock 'n' roll was directly influenced by 1960s garage rock. They started out playing gigs at notorious dives like Popeye's Spinach Factory in Brooklyn.

In 1975, the band released their debut album, *Go Girl Crazy!* which featured such memorable tracks as "Teengenerate," "The Next Big Thing," and "(I Live for) Cars and Girls," as well as an unlikely cover of Sonny & Cher's "I Got You Babe." *Trouser Press* described the album as "a wickedly funny, brilliantly played and hopelessly naïve masterpiece of self-indulgent smartass rock 'n' roll."

Essential Listening: *Go Girl Crazy!* (1975)

EDDIE AND THE HOT RODS   Founded in 1975, this high-energy pub-rock band from Essex in southeast England scored a top 10 hit in the UK with their 1977 song "Do Anything You Wanna Do." The classic Eddie and the Hot Rods lineup featured lead singer Barrie Masters, guitarist Dave Higgs, bassist Rob Steele, and drummer Steve Nicol. Known for their amazing live performances, the band released their debut album, *Teenage Depression*, in 1976. It reached no. 43 on the UK charts. The 2000 reissue of the album featured several covers such as "The Kids Are Alright" by the Who, "Shake" by Sam Cooke, "Wooly Bully" by Sam the Sham and the Pharaohs, "96 Tears" by Question Mark and the Mysterians, and "Get Out of Denver" by Bob Seger. In addition, "Teenage Depression" appeared on the soundtrack for the 1979 cult film *Rock 'n' Roll High School*, which starred the Ramones.

The Sex Pistols opened for Eddie and the Hot Rods at the Marquee Club in London on February 12, 1976. The following year, Eddie and the Hot Rods accompanied the Ramones and Talking Heads on a U.S. tour.

Essential Listening: *Teenage Depression* (1976), *Life on the Line* (1977)

ELECTRIC EELS   A fixture of the early 1970s proto-punk scene in Cleveland, Ohio, the Electric Eels only performed publicly five or so times, but each show reportedly ended up being a disastrous drunken fiasco, as the band earned a notorious reputation for being confrontational and stirring up violence among themselves and with audiences. The Electric Eels lineup featured lead singer and sometimes clarinetist Dave E (McManus), guitarists John Morton and Brian McMahon, and drummer Nick Knox (who later joined the Cramps).

According to Nicholas Rombes in *The Cultural Dictionary of Punk*, the Eels "made music so shattering and ridiculously alive that it made even the rawest post-1975 punk sound tame by comparison." The band's sound has been described as "art terrorism," which was achieved through various eclectic means like banging a sheet of metal with a sledgehammer or running a lawn mower on stage.

Essential Listening: *Having a Philosophical Investigation with the Electric Eels* (1989)

THE KINGSMEN   Recorded for $50 in a small studio in Portland, Oregon, the Kingsmen's version of "Louie Louie" (which was written and first recorded by Richard Berry in 1955) rose to no. 2 on the U.S. charts (behind "I Want to Hold Your Hand" by the Beatles) and appeared on the band's 1963 debut album, *The Kingsmen in Person*. The album remained on the Billboard charts for an astounding 131 weeks. Believe it or not, the FBI launched an investigation into "Louie Louie" to determine if the song had obscene lyrics. One of the most covered songs in rock history (most notably by John Belushi as Bluto in the 1978 comedy *Animal House*), "Louie Louie" ranked no. 156 on *Rolling Stone*'s list of the "500 Greatest Songs of All Time."

Essential Listening: *The Kingsmen in Person* (1963)

LOVE   One of the first racially mixed rock bands, Love skillfully blended garage rock, folk, and psychedelia. The original lineup featured highly eccentric singer-songwriter Arthur Lee, lead guitarist Johnny Echols, rhythm guitarist Bryan MacLean, bassist Ken Forssi, and drummer Alban "Snoopy" Pfisterer. Widely regarded as Love's masterpiece, the mesmerizing, psychedelic album *Forever Changes* (1967) only reached no. 154 on the U.S. charts but has proven highly influential. It has been since added to the Library of Congress's National Recording Registry. Over the years, Love has served as inspiration for such bands as the Jesus and Mary Chain, the Stone Roses, and Primal Scream, among others.

Essential Listening: *Love* (1966), *Da Capo* (1966), *Forever Changes* (1967)

MC5   A legendary proto-punk band that formed in Detroit, Michigan, in 1964, the MC5 (Motor City Five) are best known for their rallying anthem, "Kick Out the Jams" (which opened with the infamous introduction, "Kick out the jams, motherfucker!"). The band's signature song appeared on their debut album, *Kick Out the Jams* (1969).

MC5's classic lineup featured lead singer Rob Tyner, guitarists Fred "Sonic" Smith (who later married punk poetess Patti Smith) and Wayne Kramer, bassist Michael Davis, and drummer Dennis Thompson. The MC5 churned out two more albums—*Back in the USA* (1970) and *High Time* (1971)—before breaking up in 1972. MC5 has been nominated (yet to be inducted) for the Rock and Roll Hall of Fame in 2002, 2016, 2018, 2019, 2020, and 2022.

Essential Listening: *Kick Out the Jams* (1969), *Back in the USA* (1970), *High Time* (1971)

THE MODERN LOVERS   Led by eccentric Massachusetts native Jonathan Richman, the Modern Lovers also featured keyboardist Jerry Harrison (later of Talking Heads), bassist Ernie Brooks, and drummer David Robinson (later of the Cars). The band's unique sound owed a lot to the influence of the Velvet Underground. Recorded in 1972, the Modern Lovers' self-titled debut album wasn't released until 1976 and features such classics as "Roadrunner" and "Pablo Picasso," which has been covered by Iggy Pop, David Bowie, John Cale, and Television Personalities, as well as short-lived Los Angeles rock band Burning Sensations for the 1984 cult film *Repo Man*.

The band's signature song "Roadrunner" was reportedly inspired by Richman's childhood travels throughout Massachusetts with his father, who was a salesman. Covered by the Sex Pistols (and finally released on the 1979 album *The Great Rock 'n' Roll Swindle*), "Roadrunner" ranked no. 77 on *Rolling Stone*'s list of the "500 Greatest Songs of All Time." The song also has been covered by the likes of Wire, Joan Jett, and the Greg Kihn Band, among others. As for Richman, he later showed up as "The Singing Narrator" in the hit 1998 comedy *There's Something about Mary* and appears on the film's soundtrack singing the title track, as well as "True Love Is Not Nice," and "Let Her Go into the Darkness."

Essential Listening: *The Modern Lovers* (1976)

THE MONKS   A quintet of U.S. servicemen stationed in former West Germany formed the Monks in 1964. The truly eclectic rock band wore monk robes onstage and forged a highly experimental avant-garde sound. The band only released one studio album, *Black Monk Time* (1966), which Julian Cope of the Teardrop Explodes described as a "lost classic." Bands such as the Dead Kennedys, the Fall, Beastie Boys, White Stripes, and the Early Years have all acknowledged the Monks' influence.

Essential Listening: *Black Monk Time* (1966)

NEW YORK DOLLS   Formed in New York City in 1971, the New York Dolls evolved out of a band called Actress and were known for their outrageous stage presence, complete with lipstick, satin, leather, and high heels. The classic Dolls lineup featured David Johansen (lead singer), Johnny Thunders (lead guitar, originally known as "Johnny Volume"), Sylvain Sylvain (who replaced original guitarist Rick Rivets), Arthur "Killer" Kane (bass), and Billy Murcia (drums). In December 1971, the band scored their first gig at a flophouse called the Endicott Hotel.

Known for their outrageous stage presence and wardrobe, glam rockers New York Dolls served as a bridge between the garage rock of the 1960s and the NYC punk scene of the 1970s. PHOTOFEST

In 1972, the Dolls scored a breakthrough gig at the Mercer
Arts Center in Manhattan and started playing gigs in the facility's
Oscar Wilde Room regularly. Word started to spread. The New
York Dolls were the only band around, so "we didn't have to be that
good," according to Johansen. In fact, in a 1974 poll conducted
by *CREEM* magazine, the New York Dolls were named both the
"Best New Group of the Year" and the "Worst New Group of the
Year." Tragically, Murcia died at a post-gig bash on November 6,
1972, during the band's brief tour of England and was replaced by
Jerry Nolan, who later referred to the band as "the Dead End Kids
of today."

The Dolls released their self-titled debut album in 1973, which
was produced by Todd Rundgren. It only reached no. 116 on the
U.S. charts but had lasting impact. For example, one of the best
tracks on the album, "Personality Crisis," ranked no. 387 on *Rolling
Stone*'s list of the "500 Greatest Songs of All Time." The album also
features such classics as "Jet Boy" and "Trash." The Dolls released
their second album, with the appropriate title *Too Much Too Soon*,
in 1974. George "Shadow" Martin produced the album, which
peaked at a miserable no. 167 on the U.S. charts. By this time,
Thunders and Nolan were both full-blown heroin addicts, and Kane
had become a hopeless alcoholic.

In desperation, the New York Dolls enlisted the help of Malcolm McLaren to change the band's image. His solution was to
dress them in matching red leather suits and get "more political." It
didn't work. The band splintered apart. Thunders and Nolan soon
quit and formed the Heartbreakers with Richard Hell of Television. McLaren returned to London with the lessons he learned and
promptly formed the Sex Pistols (and the rest is history!).

Johansen later morphed into flamboyant lounge singer "Buster
Poindexter" and pursued an acting career (most notably as the
Ghost of Christmas Past in the 1988 film *Scrooged* opposite Bill
Murray). Kane somehow managed to sober up, relocated to Utah,
and joined the Mormon Church(!). In 2004, Morrissey of the
Smiths organized a reunion of the three surviving band mem-
bers—Johansen, Kane, and Sylvain—at the Meltdown Festival in
London. Just three weeks after the show, Kane died of leukemia

(his fascinating life story was depicted in the 2005 documentary *New York Doll*).

The New York Dolls influenced a host of rock bands such as the Sex Pistols, the Ramones, the Damned, KISS, Hanoi Rocks, the Replacements, the Smiths, and Guns N' Roses, among others. In *Satisfaction: 10 Albums That Changed My Life*, Soul Asylum singer-songwriter Dave Pirner called the Dolls "fearless, full of energy and rock 'n' roll madness in all the right ways. Set aside the lipstick, eye shadow and platform boots, and they just rocked out without a bunch of bullshit." In a 1977 Hyde Park interview, Sid Vicious remarked, "I like the New York Dolls because they were nasty and mean and they wore makeup and they didn't give a shit and they played godawful rock 'n' roll and they had good names and good hairdos."

Essential Listening: *New York Dolls* (1973), *Too Much Too Soon* (1974)

QUESTION MARK AND THE MYSTERIANS   Formed in 1962 by the teen-age kids of migrant farmers who settled in Bay City and Saginaw, Michigan, Question Mark and the Mysterians (aka ? and the Mysterians) was the prototypical garage-rock band that forged a unique sound consisting of electric-organ-driven instrumentals. The band's extremely quirky name came from a 1957 Japanese science fiction film called *The Mysterians*.

The original Question Mark and the Mysterians lineup featured lead singer Rudy Martinez (who always wore sunglasses and eventually had his name legally changed to ?), guitarist Bobby Balderrama, keyboardist Frank Rodriguez, bassist Larry Borjas, and drummer Robert Martinez (Rudy's brother). After Borjas and Robert Martinez got drafted into the military, Frank Lugo and Eddie Serrato, respectively, replaced them.

The band's first single, "96 Tears," skyrocketed to no. 1 on the U.S. charts in 1966, followed by their debut album, also titled *96 Tears*, which reached a respectable no. 66 on the U.S. charts. The album included a quirky cover of T-Bone Walker's "Stormy Monday." The group broke up in 1969 but has re-formed several times over the years. However, they have never come close to replicating the success of "96 Tears." Cover versions of "96 Tears" have been recorded by the likes of Iggy Pop, Eddie and the Hot Rods, the Stranglers, the Texas Tornadoes, and even Aretha Franklin.

Essential Listening: *96 Tears* (1966), *Action* (1967)

ROCKET FROM THE TOMBS   "I can't think. I need a drink. Life stinks." Billing themselves as "The World's Only Dumb-Metal Mind-Death Rock and Roll Band," Cleveland, Ohio–based proto-punk band Rocket from the Tombs revealed the strong influences of the Velvet Underground, the Stooges, and the Troggs ("Wild Thing"). Formed in 1974, the band featured the classic lineup of Peter Laughner, David Thomas (aka Crocus Behemoth), Craig Willis Bell, Gene O'Connor (aka Cheetah Chrome), and Johnny "Madman" Madansky (aka Johnny Blitz).

Classic Rocket from the Tombs songs include "Ain't It Fun," "Sonic Reducer," "30 Seconds over Tokyo," "Down in Flames," "What Love Is," "Caught with the Meat in Your Mouth," "Final Solution," "Life Stinks," "Muckraker," and "Frustration." After breaking up in 1975, the band split off into the "young, loud and snotty" Dead Boys and the much more experimental "avant-garage" band Pere Ubu (named after Alfred Jarry's 1896 absurdist play, *Ubu Roi*). Tragically, Laughner died of acute pancreatitis on June 22, 1977, at the age of twenty-four. None other than renowned rock critic Lester Bangs dubbed Rocket from the Tombs as "the original legendary underground rock band."

Essential Listening: *The Day the Earth Met Rocket from the Tombs* (2002)

THE SEEDS   A truly bizarre southern California proto-punk garage band, the Seeds claimed to have coined the term *flower power*. One of the most popular acts during the peak years of the Sunset Strip scene, the Seeds were led by a true eccentric, Sky Saxon (real name: Richard Marsh), who was born a Mormon in Salt Lake City, Utah. Guitarist Jon Savage, keyboardist Daryl Hooper, and drummer Rick Andridge rounded out the band. The Seeds are best known for the hit song "Pushin' Too Hard," as well as such garage-rock classics as "Mr. Farmer" and "Can't Seem to Make You Mine." In 1972, "Pushin' Too Hard" appeared in Lenny Kaye's famous compilation album, *Nuggets: Original Artyfacts from the First Psychedelic Era 1965–1968*, along with a slew of other garage-rock-band classics.

According to the *Rolling Stone Album Guide*, "Compared to the Seeds, the Mothers of Invention seem labored, Arthur Lee [of Love] comes across as a logician, and the Troggs sound tame. The band virtually defines the term 'guilty pleasure.'" Early on, the Seeds could often be heard at funky Los Angeles nightclubs such as Turkey Joint West, Bido Lito's, and the Sea Witch. An early Bido Lito's ad for the band exclaimed, "Flower-Rock Sounds of the Seeds Five Nights a Week—It's Flower Music—It's Earthy—You'll Dig It!" In 1967, the Seeds released what was intended to be their psychedelic masterpiece, *Future*. For better or worse, the Seeds never caught on outside of Los Angeles and soon faded into obscurity. In the 1970s, Saxon joined a hippie spiritual cult called the Yahowha and proceeded to release several albums under various band names over the subsequent years. On June 25, 2009, he died of heart and renal failure at the age of seventy-one.

Essential Listening: *The Seeds* (1966), *A Web of Sound* (1966)

THE SONICS Formed in Tacoma, Washington, in 1960, the Sonics took their name from the sonic booms emanating from the nearby McChord U.S. Air Force Base. The classic Sonics lineup featured guitarist Larry Parypa, bassist Andy Parypa, vocalist/keyboardist Jerry Rosalie, saxophonist Rob Lind, and drummer Bob Bennett. In 1965, the band released their debut album, *Here Are the Sonics*, which featured such classics as "The Witch" (a regional hit that sold more than twenty-five thousand copies), "Psycho" (reportedly written in just fifteen minutes after a gig), "Strychnine" (about the pleasures of getting high on rat poison for kicks!), and "Boss Hoss." The Sonics influenced such musical acts as the Stooges, MC5, the Flesh Eaters, the Dead Boys, the Cramps (who covered "Strychnine"), the Bags, and Nirvana, among others.

Essential Listening: *Here Are the Sonics* (1965), *Boom* (1966)

THE STOOGES/IGGY POP   Acknowledged in some circles as the "Father of Punk Rock," James Newell Osterberg Jr. was born on April 21, 1947, and grew up in a trailer park in Ypsilanti, Michigan. Embarking on his musical career as a professional drummer, Osterberg backed several Motown groups, such as the Four Tops, and later formed a band called Megaton Two, which morphed into the Iguanas (Osterberg by then rechristening himself "Iggy"). On March 3, 1968, the Stooges (originally known as the Psychedelic Stooges and named in honor of Moe, Larry, and Curly) performed their first gig opening for Blood, Sweat & Tears at Detroit's Grande Ballroom. Iggy soon took his stage antics to a new level—rubbing peanut butter, hamburger meat, and raw steaks all over his body; slicing his chest open with broken glass; and hurling himself into the audience.

In 1968, the Stooges landed a record deal with Elektra and recorded two classic proto-punk albums—*The Stooges* (1969),

Widely known as the "Father of Punk Rock," Iggy Pop formed the Stooges in 1967 and soon became known for his outrageous stage antics. BY RAPH_PH/ WIKIMEDIA COMMONS

which Velvet Underground's John Cale produced, and *Fun House* (1970)—that failed miserably but have since been acknowledged as true rock classics. In his memorable review of *Fun House* for *Rolling Stone*, Charlie Burton exclaimed, "Do you long to have your mind blown open so wide that it will take weeks for you to pick up the little, bitty pieces?"

Mired in drug addiction, the band broke up and later reformed as Iggy and the Stooges for their third studio album, *Raw Power* (1973), which has become recognized as one of the most influential rock albums of all time. Once again, the album failed to sell, the band broke up, and Iggy sank into the abyss of heroin addiction. Over the years, the Stooges' musical influence extended to such bands as Suicide, the New York Dolls, the Ramones, the Sex Pistols (who recorded "No Fun" in 1976), the Damned, the Germs, Black Flag, Sonic Youth (which covered "I Wanna Be Your Dog" on their 1983 debut album, *Confusion Is Sex*), and Nirvana (Kurt Cobain listed *Raw Power* as his favorite album of all time), among many others.

None other than Henry Rollins has called *Fun House* "the greatest rock album ever made." British rock critic Nick Kent referred to *Raw Power* as "the greatest, meanest-eyed, coldest-blooded hard rock tour de force ever summoned up on a recording studio." Critic Lester Bangs called Iggy the "most intense performer" he had ever seen. According to Bangs, "Iggy was just a fucked-up kid who took too many drugs and wanted to have the most fucked-up band in history so as to externalize his own inner turmoil."

Essential Listening: *The Stooges* (1969), *Fun House* (1970), *Raw Power* (1973)

VELVET UNDERGROUND　　Often referred to as the ultimate art-rock band, the Velvet Underground formed in New York City in 1964 with singer-songwriter Lou Reed, guitarist Sterling Morrison, multi-instrumentalist John Cale, and drummer Angus MacLise (who soon quit the band and was replaced by Maureen "Moe" Tucker). As a student at Syracuse University, Reed was mentored by none other than the acclaimed poet and short-story writer Delmore Schwartz.

Pop superstar Andy Warhol "discovered" the band at Café Bizarre. On December 11, 1965, the Velvet Underground made their inauspicious performing debut at the Summit High School auditorium in Summit, New Jersey. According to Cale, "The one reason we wore sunglasses on stage was because we couldn't stand the sight of the audience." The Velvet Underground released their debut album, *The Velvet Underground & Nico*, in 1967. The album features such notable tracks as "I'm Waiting for the Man," "Heroin," "Venus in Furs," and "There She Goes Again." Although initial sales were poor, it has since gone on to be recognized as one of the most influential rock albums of all time. Warhol's memorable

Lou Reed formed the Velvet Under-
ground in New York City in 1964 with
John Cale, Sterling Morrison, and
Angus MacLise (soon replaced by Mau-
reen Tucker). BY ANNULLA, BROOKLYN,
USA/WIKIMEDIA COMMONS

cover art for the album, a peelable yellow banana set against
a plain background, perfectly
exemplifies the pop art movement of the late 1960s. In fact,
the album became a traveling
sound and light show called the
Exploding Plastic Inevitable.

The Library of Congress
added *The Velvet Underground
& Nico* in its National Recording Registry with the following
dedication: "For decades this
album has cast a huge shadow
over nearly every sub-variety of
avant-garde rock, from '70s art-
rock to no wave, new wave, and
punk." In the liner notes for
the fiftieth-anniversary edition
of the album, Cale remarked, "I
wanted to cross-pollinate rock with the avant-garde, and then I met
Lou Reed and that was the solution."

The Velvet Underground were "basically psychedelic beatniks,"
according to Gerald Casale of Devo. Lester Bangs wrote, "Modern
music begins with the Velvets, and the implications and influence
of what they did seem to go on forever." Considered one of the most
influential bands in rock history, the Velvet Underground were
inducted into the Rock and Roll Hall of Fame in 1996. In addition,
Rolling Stone ranked the band at no. 19 on its list of the "100 Greatest Artists of All Time."

Essential Listening: *The Velvet Underground & Nico* (1967),
White Light/White Heat (1968), *The Velvet Underground* (1969),
Loaded (1970)

4

I Wanna Be Sedated

The Ramones and the
NYC Punk Scene

My life was as empty as the trail of beer cans I left behind me wherever I went. —Dee Dee Ramone

In a January 2007 interview with *Uncut* magazine, Tommy Ramone remarked, "In its initial form, a lot of [1960s rock] was innovative and exciting. Unfortunately, what happens is that people who could not hold a candle to the likes of Hendrix started noodling away. Soon you had endless solos that went nowhere. By 1973, I knew that what was need was some pure, stripped down, no bullshit rock 'n' roll."

The New York City punk scene exploded out of such legendary clubs as Max's Kansas City and CBGBs, where the Ramones first hit the stage in August 1974 with their three-chords, back-to-basics sound. Other NYC bands made their mark here, such as punk pioneers Television, Johnny Thunders and the Heartbreakers, Blondie, Patti Smith, and Talking Heads.

THE RAMONES The Ramones formed in Forest Hills, Queens, in 1974 with each band member adopting the pseudonym *Ramone* as their surname (allegedly inspired by a fake name Paul McCartney used for checking into hotels, "Paul Ramon"): lead singer Joey Ramone (Jeffrey Hyman), guitarist Johnny Ramone (John Cummings), bassist Dee Dee Ramone (Douglas Colvin), and drummer

None other than the Clash's Joe Strummer once referred to the Ramones as "the daddy of all punk bands." MAGNOLIA/PHOTOFEST

Tommy Ramone (Tommy Erdelyi). As they struggled to get gigs early on, Joey distributed flyers for massage parlors for $50 a week, and Dee Dee spent some time as a male hustler (as depicted in the Ramones song "53rd & 3rd").

In a 1975 press release about the band, Tommy stated, "The Ramones all originate from Forest Hills and kids who grew up there either became musicians, degenerates, or dentists. The Ramones are a little of each. Their sound is not unlike a fast drill or a rear molar." According to Joey Ramone, "We just weren't hearing any music we liked anymore, so we stripped it back down and put back the passion and energy and emotion that were missing from the music we were hearing at the time." The Ramones were "the daddy of all punk bands," according to the Clash's Joe Strummer.

Other Ramones band members over the subsequent years included Marky Ramone (Marc Bell), who replaced Tommy Ramone in 1978; Richie Ramone (Richie Beau), who replaced Marky Ramone in 1983; C. J. Ramone (Christopher Joseph Ward), who replaced Dee Dee Ramone in 1989; and Elvis Ramone (Clem

Burke of Blondie, who filled in for just two gigs). In 1979, the Ramones appeared in the cult movie *Rock 'n' Roll High School*, the highlight of which was footage of the band performing a medley at the Roxy in West Hollywood that featured "Blitzkrieg Bop," "Teenage Lobotomy," "California Sun," "Pinhead," and "She's the One." Dee Dee left the band in 1989 and embarked on a short-lived rap career under the alias "Dee Dee King" (the music video for "Funky Man" must be seen to be believed!). However, he also kept writing songs for the band.

The Ramones performed approximately 2,200 shows and released fourteen studio albums, from their celebrated 1976 debut *Ramones* to 1995's *Adios Amigos*, which rather appropriately included a cover of Tom Waits's "I Don't Want to Grow Up." The last Ramones concert took place at the Palace club in Hollywood on August 6, 1996. A typical Ramones set featured "Loudmouth," "Beat on the Brat," "Blitzkrieg Bop," "I Remember You," "Glad to See You Go," "Chain Saw," "53rd & 3rd," "I Wanna Be Your Boyfriend," "Havana Affair," "Listen to My Heart," "Judy Is a Punk," "I Don't Wanna Walk around with You," and "Today Your Love, and Tomorrow the World," along with encores "Now I Wanna Sniff Some Glue" and "Let's Dance."

In 2002, the four original band members and Marky Ramone were inducted into the Rock and Roll Hall of Fame. Sadly, all the original Ramones have passed away: Joey of lymphoma in 2001, Dee Dee of a heroin overdose in 2002, Johnny of prostate cancer in 2004, and Tommy of bile duct cancer in 2014. Although they never scored a hit single, the Ramones influenced countless rock bands such as the Sex Pistols, the Clash, the Damned, Generation X, Sham 69, Black Flag, Dead Kennedys, Social Distortion, Descendents, the Lurkers, the Undertones, the Zeros, the Dickies, and Green Day.

Produced and directed by Jim Fields and Michael Gramaglia, the definitive Ramones documentary *End of the Century: The Story of the Ramones* (2004) traces the band from their inauspicious beginnings as punk teenagers in Forest Hills, Queens, and early shows at CBGBs to their 2002 induction into the Rock and Roll Hall of Fame. The film premiered at the Slamdance Film Festival.

In 2011, the Ramones were awarded a Grammy Lifetime Achievement Award. *Spin* magazine has ranked the Ramones as the second greatest rock band of all time, behind the Beatles.

Essential Listening: *Ramones* (1976), *Leave Home* (1977), *Rocket to Russia* (1977), *Road to Ruin* (1978), *End of the Century* (1980)

BLONDIE   Formed by singer Debbie Harry and guitarist Chris Stein, who had played together previously in a band called the Stilettos, Blondie was briefly known as Angel and the Snake. Reportedly, the name *Blondie* came from what NYC construction workers yelled at Harry as she sauntered by. The band released their debut single, "X Offender" (originally titled "Sex Offender") in 1976, the same year as their self-titled debut album, which reached no. 75 on the UK charts but fizzled out in the United States.

The breakthrough 1978 album *Parallel Lines* gave Blondie its first no. 1 hit with "Heart of Glass," as well as such memorable tracks as "One Way or Another" and "Hanging on the Telephone." The album eventually sold twenty million copies. Other notable

Cofounded by Debbie Harry and Chris Stein, Blondie became regular performers at both CBGBs and Max's Kansas City in New York City during the mid-1970s.
PHOTOFEST

Blondie albums include *Eat to the Beat* (1979), which featured "Atomic," and *Autoamerican* (1980), which spawned "The Tide Is High" and "Rapture," the first no. 1 single to feature rap vocals. Over the years, Blondie has recorded ten studio albums and sold approximately forty million records worldwide.

Blondie broke up in 1982 after recording their fifth album, *The Hunter*, but has regrouped sporadically over the years. In a 1993 interview, Harry remarked, "I made my own image, then I was trapped by it." Blondie was inducted into the Rock and Roll Hall of Fame in 2006. The event caused quite a stir when former band members Frank Infante and Nigel Harrison (who had both several years earlier sued the group to prevent a reunion tour under the name *Blondie*) were denied the opportunity to perform with the band during the ceremony.

Essential Listening: *Blondie* (1976), *Parallel Lives* (1978), *Plastic Letters* (1978), *Eat to the Beat* (1979), *Autoamerican* (1980)

THE CRAMPS   Formed in 1976 in New York City, the Cramps were part of the early punk scene that hung around CBGBs and pioneers of the psychobilly sound, which fused elements of rockabilly with a strong sense of the macabre. The classic Cramps lineup featured the husband-wife duo of lead singer Lux Interior (Erick Lee Purkhiser) and lead guitarist Poison Ivy (Kristy Mariana Wallace), as well as guitarist Bryan Gregory and drummer Pam Balam.

In 1980, the Cramps released their debut album, *Songs the Lord Taught Us*, which *Rolling Stone* praised for its "psychobilly sound that went way beyond the kitchiest moments of the Ramones or Blondie into a whole new realm of garage-trash novelty." Other notable Cramps albums include *Psychedelic Jungle* (1981), *A Date with Elvis* (1986), and *Stay Sick!* (1990). In 1995, the band appeared on the Halloween episode ("Gypsies, Cramps and Fleas") of the TV drama *Beverly Hills 90210* and performed two songs, "Mean Machine" and "Strange Love."

Trouser Press accurately described the Cramps' eclectic style as "a uniquely weird pastiche of rock 'n' roll, psychedelia, and a monster movie/junk food/swamp-creature aesthetic." Known for their outrageous live shows, the band gained much notoriety when they gave a free concert (supported by San Francisco punk band the Mutants) at the California State Mental Hospital in Napa in June 1978. In an interview, Poison Ivy remarked, "We don't feel like our music is for everybody. It's for those who can identify with being a hoodlum, a misfit. No one else should be expected to like it." Added Lux Interior, "Rock n' roll is a lifestyle. I'm tired of seeing rock 'n' roll being respectable. People when they think of rock 'n' roll don't think of the negative; they have this image of Bruce Springsteen saving starving children somewhere."

Essential Listening: *Songs the Lord Taught Us* (1980), *Psychedelic Jungle* (1981), *A Date with Elvis* (1986)

DEAD BOYS   Originating from Cleveland, Ohio, the Dead Boys were an offshoot of the bands Frankenstein and Rocket from the Tombs. Formed in 1976, the Dead Boys lineup featured lead singer Stiv Bators (Steven Bator), lead guitarist Cheetah Chrome (Eugene O'Connor), rhythm guitarist Jimmy Zero (William Wilden), bassist Jeff Magnum, and drummer Johnny Blitz (John Madansky).

During their short lifespan, the band released two albums: *Young Loud and Snotty* (1977) and *We Have Come for Your Children* (1978). The first album lives up to its title with such raunchy, tasteless, and high-energy tracks as "Sonic Reducer" and "Caught with the Meat in Your Mouth." The album only reached no. 189 on the U.S. charts. A live album, *Night of the Living Dead Boys*, was recorded at CBGBs and released in 1981.

Tragically, Bators died of a traumatic brain injury after getting hit by a car at the age of forty in Paris in 1990. His ashes were reportedly spread over his hero Jim Morrison's grave at Pere Lachaise Cemetery in Paris. In 2017, Blitz and Chrome reunited for the band with a new lineup for a fortieth-anniversary tour that included the recording of an album titled *Still Snotty: Young Loud & Snotty at 40*.

Essential Listening: *Young Loud and Snotty* (1977), *We Have Come for Your Children* (1978)

JOHNNY THUNDERS AND THE HEARTBREAKERS In 1975, Johnny Thunders (real name: John Anthony Genzale) left the New York Dolls and formed the Heartbreakers with Dolls bandmate Jerry Nolan, ex-Television bassist Richard Hell, and ex-Demons guitarist Walter Lure. By this time, both Thunders and Nolan were hardcore heroin addicts. In fact, Hell referred to Thunders as "the rock 'n' roll Dean Martin of heroin." An early flyer for the Heartbreakers exclaimed, "Catch 'em while they're still alive!"

In 1976, Hell soon left to form his own band, Richard Hell and the Voidoids. He was replaced on bass by Billy Rath. The band only released one official album, *L.A.M.F.* (1977), which featured such classics as "Born to Lose" and "Chinese Rocks" (which was written primarily by Dee Dee Ramone). In 1979, the Heartbreakers released *Live at Max's Kansas City*.

Essential Listening: *L.A.M.F.* (1977), *Live at Max's Kansas City* (1979)

RICHARD HELL AND THE VOIDOIDS   In 1976, Richard Hell, formerly of both Television and the Heartbreakers, formed his own group, the Voidoids, with guitarist Robert Quine, Ivan Julien, and Marc Bell (later to join the Ramones as Marky Ramone). The band's name came from an unpublished novella Hell wrote in 1973 (which was finally published by CodeX in 1993). The band's signature song, "Blank Generation," became a punk anthem and featured such lyrics as, "I was sayin' let me out of here before I was even born." The track appeared on the band's debut album, also titled *Blank Generation*, in 1977. Other Voidoid signature tracks included "Love Comes in Spurts," "The Kid with the Replaceable Head," and "Time."

Essential Listening: *Blank Generation* (1977)

PATTI SMITH GROUP   A disciple of symbolist poet Arthur Rimbaud (*A Season in Hell*), Doors lead singer Jim Morrison ("The End"), and Beat Generation author William S. Burroughs (*Naked Lunch*), Patti Smith started out as a poet and playwright (she wrote for *CREEM* magazine and coauthored the play *Cowboy Mouth* with

Sam Shepard in 1971). Smith published two books of poetry, *Witt* and *Seventh Heaven*, before embarking on a singing career.

Known as both the "punk poet laureate" and "punk poetess," Smith formed the Patti Smith Group in 1974 with Lenny Kaye (who had compiled the legendary 1972 *Nuggets* album full of classic garage-rock-band tracks), Ivan Kral, Jay Dee Daugherty, and Richard Sohl. The band released their first single, "Hey Joe," with the B-side being the autobiographical "Piss Factory." In November 1975, the band released their stunning debut album, *Horses*, which was produced by John Cale, formerly of the Velvet Underground. The album includes a cover of the Van Morrison classic "Gloria." Smith's most widely recognized song, "Because the Night," was cowritten with Bruce Springsteen and reached no. 13 on the U.S. charts in 1978. In 2007, Smith was inducted into the Rock and Roll Hall of Fame.

Essential Listening: *Horses* (1975), *Easter* (1978)

SUICIDE   Consisting of vocalist Alan Vega (a former sculptor) and instrumentalist Martin Rev, Suicide was formed in New York City 1970 but did not release their self-titled debut album until 1977. The album features such classics as "Ghost Rider," "Cheree," "Johnny," and "Frankie Teardrop." Although they never received a strong following, the group is today considered influential pioneers of electronic music. They were also known for their confrontational live shows at popular NYC venues such as the Mercer Arts Center, Max's Kansas City, and CBGBs. The band's name came from the title of a Ghost Rider comic book issue: "Satan Suicide." Suicide influenced the likes of Joy Division, New Order, Henry Rollins, the Jesus and Mary Chain, Nick Cave, Pet Shop Boys, Tears for Fears, Dead Kennedys, Sonic Youth, and Soft Cell, among others.

Essential Listening: *Suicide* (1977), *Suicide: Alan Vega and Martin Rev* (1980)

TALKING HEADS   Band members David Byrne, Tina Weymouth, and Chris Frantz first met as students at the Rhode Island School of Design in the early 1970s. Byrne and Frantz formed a band called the Artistics. Although often lumped with other punk bands in the early New York City scene (they performed regularly at CBGBs), Talking Heads evoked an eclectic style that defied easy categorization. The band's name reportedly came from an issue of *TV Guide*. In 1977, the band released their debut album, *Talking Heads 77*, which reached no. 97 on the U.S. charts and featured one of the band's enduring classics, "Psycho Killer." In addition, Talking Heads were known for their bizarre music videos, which received massive amounts of airplay on MTV. The Alternative Reel music video review website describes the band's music video for "Once in a Lifetime" as "Byrne, decked out like a sweaty reject from a *Revenge of the Nerds* audition, 'dancing' around like Lewis Skolnick after he has just hit the crack pipe."

Talking Heads' popularity didn't extend to the United Kingdom. According to Shane MacGowan of the Pogues in his 2001 memoir, "Nobody [in the UK] listened to the Talking Heads. It was all hippy music." According to Byrne,

> Talking Heads were sort of anomalies on [the punk scene]. I don't mean because we were all smarty arty farty—though we had bits of that clinging to us—but so much of the scene was this odd mix of conservatism and rebellion coexisting. The style. The hair. The jackets. The posters. The graphics tended toward a sameness—a lovely handmade angry lunatic sameness.

Director Jonathan Demme (*The Silence of the Lambs*) captured the essence of Talking Heads in concert in his critically acclaimed 1984 film *Stop Making Sense*, which is widely regarded as one of the best concert films of all time. It was filmed over three nights at Pantages Theater in Hollywood, California, in 1983. The set list consisted of such Talking Heads classics as "Psycho Killer," "Heaven," "Burning Down the House," "Life during Wartime," "Once in a Lifetime," and "Take Me to the River." The band broke up quite acrimoniously in 1991. In 2002, Talking Heads were inducted into the Rock and Roll Hall of Fame.

Essential Listening: *Talking Heads 77* (1977), *More Songs about Buildings and Food* (1978), *Remain in Light* (1980), *Fear of Music* (1984)

TELEVISION   Before he joined Johnny Thunders and the Heart-breakers and then started his own group, the Voidoids, Richard Hell teamed with Tom Verlaine, Richard Lloyd, and Billy Ficca to form the band Television, who were early mainstays of the CBGBs scene (they somehow fooled club owner Hilly Kristal into think-ing they played "a little rock, a little country, a little blues, a little bluegrass"). None other than glam rocker David Bowie caught one of their early shows and dubbed them the "most original band I've seen in New York. They have it."

Hell had developed his signature "ripped and torn" look from Jean-Pierre Leaud's rebellious Antoine Doinel character in Fran-cois Truffaut's 1959 New Wave masterpiece, *The 400 Blows*. He even designed a T-shirt that read "Please Kill Me." However, he was "too much of a coward" to wear it, so Lloyd ended up wearing it around. According to Hell, "We were these notch-thin, homeless hoodlums, playing really powerful, passionate, aggressive music that was also lyrical." The band released its critically acclaimed debut album, *Marquee Moon*, in 1977. However, it failed to chart in the United States. The title track "Marquee Moon" ranked no. 173 on *Rolling Stone*'s list of the "500 Greatest Songs of All Time."

Essential Listening: *Marquee Moon* (1977)

5

Anarchy in the UK

The Sex Pistols and the London Punk Movement

> The popularity of punk rock was, in effect, due to the fact that it made ugliness beautiful. —Malcolm McLaren

During one of the early Sex Pistols gigs, Johnny Rotten exclaimed to the audience, "Bet you don't hate us as much as we hate you!" Indeed, the London punk scene was much more confrontational and rebellious than its New York City counterpart. This was partly due to the economic malaise that plagued the UK during the 1970s and, in the case of the Sex Pistols, was also spawned by Malcolm McLaren's anarchistic political leanings shaped by his early studies of the radical Situationist International.

Ironically, it was a July 4, 1976, concert by the Ramones at the Roundhouse in London that sparked the UK punk-rock scene. By the end of that year, many of the most prominent punk bands had been established—including the Clash, X-Ray Spex, Siouxsie and the Banshees, the Adverts, Generation X, the Damned, and the Slits. In addition, the Sex Pistols embarked on their notorious Anarchy Tour.

MALCOLM MCLAREN   Whether you consider him to be one of punk rock's true visionaries or a charlatan (Johnny Thunders called him "the greatest con-man that I've ever met"), Malcolm McLaren was instrumental in crafting both the look and sound of punk rock. Born on January 22, 1946, Malcolm Robert Andrew McLaren was a true renaissance man—visual artist, clothes designer, fashion boutique owner, promoter and manager of bands, musician, and performer. Influenced by the Situationist International, a loose-knit international organization of social revolutionaries, McLaren and his friend, the renowned artist Jamie Reid, forged innovative ideas to combat the so-called "politics of boredom."

McLaren's brief stint as manager of the New York Dolls in early 1975 proved to be a total disaster. He gave them a new, more radical political image that included wearing matching red leather outfits. The band broke up soon thereafter. However, McLaren headed back to London determined to take the look and feel of New York City punk (especially the "ripped and torn" style of Richard Hell) and form a new band from all the lessons he had learned. Equally influential and controversial, the Sex Pistols (along with the Ramones, of course) sparked the punk revolution in the mid-1970s. After the short, amazing roller-coaster ride that became the Sex Pistols, McLaren took on Adam and the Ants as his new project. His vision involved poaching the entire band (sans Adam Ant) and creating an entirely new band, Bow Wow Wow.

In the 1980 British mockumentary *The Great Rock & Roll Swindle*, McLaren exclaimed, "Forget about music and concentrate on generating generation gaps. Terrorize, threaten, and insult your own useless generation." McLaren released his own hit single, "Buffalo Gals," in 1982. He died of peritoneal mesothelioma on April 8, 2010, at the age of sixty-four. McLaren is buried in Highgate Cemetery, and his epitaph reads, "Better a spectacular failure, than a benign success."

SEX Malcom McLaren and fashion designer Vivienne Westwood opened this legendary punk fashion boutique (formerly known as Let It Rock in 1972 and then Too Fast to Live Too Young to Die in 1973) at 430 Kings Road in London in 1974. McLaren appropriated Richard Hell's "ripped and torn" style from his short, disastrous stint in New York City managing the New York Dolls. The boutique was renamed Seditionaries in 1976. According to McLaren, SEX "had a definite ideology—it wasn't about selling anything—it was about creating attitude."

Among the customers at SEX were the four original members of the Sex Pistols—Johnny Rotten, Glen Matlock, Steve Jones, and Paul Cook—as well as Sid Vicious, Chrissie Hynde (later of the Pretenders), Adam Ant, Siouxsie Sioux, and other assorted members of what would later be known as the Bromley Contingent. Matlock, Hynde, and Vicious even worked as clerks at the store at various times.

SEX PISTOLS   Formed in 1975, the Sex Pistols (an early incarnation of the band was known as the Swankers) originally featured the lineup of lead singer Johnny Rotten (John Lydon), guitarist Steve Jones, bassist Glen Matlock (replaced by Sid Vicious in February 1977), and drummer Paul Cook. A frequent customer of SEX, Rotten wore a Pink Floyd T-shirt with the words "I Hate" scrawled above the logo. Rotten reportedly got his band name after Jones

Formed by Malcolm McLaren in 1975, the Sex Pistols only released one studio album, *Never Mind the Bollocks, Here's the Sex Pistols*, which became a staple of punk rock. PHOTOFEST

commented on his "fucking rotten" teeth. In a *Spin* magazine interview, the band's manager, Malcolm McLaren, stated that the band's name "came about by the idea of a pistol, a pin-up, a young thing, a better-looking assassin, a Sex Pistol."

The Pistols only released four singles—"Anarchy in the UK," "God Save the Queen," "Pretty Vacant," and "Holidays in the Sun"— and one classic album, *Never Mind the Bollocks, Here's the Sex Pistols*. However, the impact of the album on the punk subculture can never be understated. According to Mick Jones of the Clash, "Everyone had been waiting for a band like the Pistols to happen."

When Vicious replaced Matlock as bassist in early 1977, he had no idea how to play the instrument. In fact, he was so untalented on bass that his amplifier was kept unplugged during many shows. However, his iconic image soon made him the poster boy for the punk rock movement. According to Rotten, Vicious (whose real name was John Simon Ritchie) received his new moniker from a combination of Syd Barrett of Pink Floyd and a pet hamster. Rotten later remarked that Vicious "believed his own publicity. . . . He was called Vicious because he was such a wanker. He couldn't fight his way out of a crisp bag." Vicious eventually hooked up with perennial American groupie Nancy Spungen, who was dubbed "Nauseating Nancy" by the British press. The two quickly became inseparable hardcore junkies.

On October 28, 1977, the Pistols released their highly influential debut and only album, *Never Mind the Bollocks, Here's the Sex Pistols*, which *Rolling Stone* later dubbed "the Sermon on the Mount of UK punk." Although the album reached no. 1 in Britain, it stalled at no. 106 on the U.S. charts. The brilliant cut-and-paste style of both the album cover and other band artwork came courtesy of the brilliant artist Jamie Reid, who helped forge their unique look and style. By the way, it was Matlock's bass playing featured on the album, not Vicious. Matlock later commented, "When Sid was in the band it became a cartoon strip."

The Sex Pistols embarked on an ill-fated U.S. tour in January 1978 that took them to various redneck dive bars in Atlanta (Great Southeast Music Hall), Memphis (Taliesyn Ballroom), San Antonio (Randy's Rodeo), Baton Rouge (Kingfish Club), Dallas (Dewey Groom's Longhorn Ballroom), Tulsa (Cain's Ballroom), and finally,

San Francisco (Winterland Ballroom). According to Legs McNeil of *Punk* magazine in the punk oral history *Please Kill Me*, "As the Pistols made their way across America, and the hysteria was broadcast on the news every night, kids in Los Angeles, and I imagine the rest of the country, were suddenly transforming themselves with safety pins, spiked haircuts, and ugliness." The entire U.S. tour was a spectacular disaster, and the band broke up after the final show with Johnny Rotten asking the audience, "Ever get the feeling you've been cheated?"

Quoted in the *Punk Diary*, Rotten exclaimed, "I won't work again with any of them and that's no great pity. Steve can go off and be Peter Frampton, Sid can go off and kill himself and nobody will care, Paul can go back to being an electrician, and Malcolm will always be a Wally." Rotten quickly reverted to his real name, John Lydon, and formed a new band, Public Image Ltd. On October 12, 1978, Vicious was arrested for the murder of Spungen. While awaiting trial, Vicious died of a heroin overdose on February 2, 1979, at the age of twenty-one. In his memoir, *I Was a Teenage Sex Pistol*, Matlock stated, "The Sex Pistols were a total failure. . . . It was like a case of premature ejaculation; over in a flash and deeply unsatisfactory."

According to Shane MacGowan of the Pogues in his 2001 memoir, *A Drink with Shane MacGowan,*

> Like, there was a time before the Sex Pistols, when everything was mundane and boring. And then the Sex Pistols came along, and nobody even knew they wanted the Sex Pistols, until they heard the Sex Pistols, you know. They had to hear the Sex Pistols before they realized that that's what they wanted to really listen to, y'know. And everybody rushed out and bought the Sex Pistols.

In addition, Izzy Stradlin of Guns N' Roses once remarked, "Rock 'n' roll in general has just sucked a big fucking dick since the Pistols." In 2006, the Sex Pistols were inducted into the Rock and Roll Hall of Fame but refused to attend the ceremony (with Lydon calling the museum a "piss stain"). They were inducted anyway.

Essential Listening: *Never Mind the Bollocks, Here's the Sex Pistols* (1977)

BROMLEY CONTINGENT   Instrumental in spreading the word about the Sex Pistols, the Bromley Contingent—which included Billy Idol (William Broad, later of Generation X) and Siouxsie Sioux (later of Siouxie and the Banshees)—were hardcore fans of the band. Several members of the Bromley Contingent, including Siouxsie Sioux, stood behind the Sex Pistols during their infamous profanity-laced interview on the *Today* show with host Bill Grundy on December 1, 1976.

The Bromley Contingent helped popularize the fashion style of the early punk movement in the United Kingdom, and many adherents were fans of the glam-rock look of David Bowie and Roxy Music. Other members of the Bromley Contingent included Steven Severin (the bassist of Siouxsie and the Banshees), Soo Catwoman, Simon "Boy" Barker (of punk band Heavy Load), Debbie Juvenile (later a film set designer), Philip Sallon (later a club promoter and fashion designer), Bertie "Berlin" Marshall (later of new wave band Behaviour Red), and Tracie O'Keefe (who tragically died of bone marrow cancer in 1978 at the age of eighteen), among others. Sid Vicious later claimed in interviews that he "despised" members of the Bromley Contingent.

BUZZCOCKS   After catching a typically raucous Sex Pistols concert in London, Pete Shelley (real name: Peter McNeish) and Howard Devoto (real name: Howard Trafford) headed back to their hometown of Manchester and promptly formed Buzzcocks in 1976. The band allegedly got its name from the headline of a *Time Out* magazine article that read "It's the Buzz, Cock!" Buzzcocks' trademark was performing songs at breakneck speed. The following year, the band released their heavily influential *Spiral Scratch* EP on their own New Hormones label that was recorded by legendary producer Martin Hannett and featured the tracks "Boredom," "Friends of Mine," "Breakdown," and "Time's Up." Devoto soon left the band to form post-punk band Magazine with guitarist John McGeogh, keyboardist Bob Dickinson, bassist Barry Adamson, and drummer Martin Jackson.

Buzzcocks' 1978 album *Love Bites* featured the catchy pop-punk hit "Ever Fallen in Love (With Someone You Shouldn't've),"

Highly influential English punk band Buzzcocks exemplified the DIY spirit by releasing their first EP, *Spiral Scratch*, with no record label support. CAROLINE RECORDS/ PHOTOFEST

which later ranked no. 276 on *Rolling Stone*'s list of the "500 Greatest Songs of All Time." The following year, the band released a compilation album titled *Singles Going Steady*, which the music critic of *Pitchfork* called a "punk masterpiece." According to Shelley, "Punk for me was: 'There are no rules.' It was fun. Just a good laugh, really. There was no future in it. No money at all. It was the most uncommercial music you imagine."

Essential Listening: *Another Music in a Different Kitchen* (1978), *Love Bites* (1978)

THE CLASH   When the Sex Pistols crapped out spectacularly in 1978, "the rock press and fans alike looked to the Clash as the [punk] movement's central symbol and hope," according to rock critic Mikal Gilmore in *Night Beat*. Fortunately, the Clash delivered in a big way. Formed in London in 1976, the Clash consisted of singer/lead guitarist Mick Jones, singer/rhythm guitarist Joe Strummer, bass player Paul Simonon, and drummer Nicky "Topper" Headon. Jones wrote nearly all the band's music, while Strummer wrote nearly all of its lyrics. The band's manager, Bernard Rhodes, a protégé of Malcolm McLaren, served as the creative force behind the Clash.

The band released its stunning self-titled debut album in 1977. It peaked at no. 12 on the UK charts and featured such classic tracks as "White Riot," "Janie Jones," "Remote Control," "I'm So Bored with the USA," "London's Burning," "Career Opportunities," "Garageland," and even a cover of the Junior Murvin reggae standard, "Police and Thieves." The Clash song "1977," which appeared on the B-side of "White Riot," declared, "No Elvis, Beatles or the Rolling Stones in 1977." With their rapid success and popularity on both sides of the Atlantic, the Clash were soon dubbed as "The Only Band That Matters." However, some critics were not so impressed. For example, according to Shane MacGowan of the

Billed as "The Only Band That Matters," the Clash was formed in 1976 and consisted of Mick Jones, Joe Strummer, Paul Simonon, and Nicky "Topper" Headon. By John Coffey/Wikimedia Commons

Pogues in his 2001 memoir, "To early punks, the Clash were just a bunch of bandwagon jumpers, y'know? They were too political."

The Clash followed up their debut album with *Give 'Em Enough Rope* (1978), which reached no. 2 on the UK charts; *London Calling* (1979), which is now widely considered one of the greatest rock albums of time; *Sandinista!* (1980), which was later ranked no. 323 on *Rolling Stone*'s list of the "500 Greatest Albums of All Time"; and *Combat Rock* (1982), which charted at no. 7 in the United States and featured the hit singles "Rock the Casbah" and "Should I Stay or Should I Go."

In 1982, the Clash took the stage at the U.S. Festival at Glen Helen Regional Park in San Bernandino, California. Headon left the band in 1982 (he had become addicted to heroin), and Jones was ousted from the band in 1983. Jones went on to form the band Big Audio Dynamite (B.A.D.) with film director Don Letts (*The Punk Rock Movie*). Following the release of their sixth album, *Cut the Crap* (1985), generally acknowledged as their worst effort, the band called it quits in 1986. According to *Trouser Press*, "*Crap* is just that, a painfully tired and hopelessly inept attempt to catch up with an elusive, fading legend."

Essential Listening: *The Clash* (1977), *Give 'Em Enough Rope* (1978), *London Calling* (1979), *Sandinista!* (1980), *Combat Rock* (1982)

THE DAMNED True punk pioneers, the Damned were the first UK punk band to release a single ("New Rose," October 1976), the first UK punk band to release an album (*Damned Damned Damned*, February 1977, which was produced by pub-rock veteran Nick Lowe), and the first UK punk band to tour the United States. The Damned's classic lineup consisted of lead singer Dave Vanian (Dave Lett), guitarist Brian James, red-beret-wearing bassist Captain Sensible (Raymond Burns, a former toilet cleaner!), and drummer Rat Scabies (Christopher Millar). The band reportedly got its name from a combination of the 1969 Luchino Visconti drama, *The Damned*, and *Village of the Damned* (1960) and its sequel, *Children of the Damned* (1964). The Damned supported the Sex Pistols on the infamous Anarchy Tour of 1976 along with the Clash and

Johnny Thunders & the Heartbreakers until they got kicked off the tour by Malcolm McLaren and replaced by Buzzcocks.

The Damned have released eleven albums over the years, the latest being *Evil Spirits* in 2018. They have influenced various bands such as Guns N' Roses (who covered "New Rose" on their 1993 album, *The Spaghetti Incident?*), the Offspring, and AFI, among many others. Directed by Wes Orshoski, the 2015 documentary *The Damned: Don't You Wish That We Were Dead* premiered at the SXSW Film Festival.

Essential Listening: *Damned Damned Damned* (1977), *Machine Gun Etiquette* (1979), *The Black Album* (1980), *Strawberries* (1982)

GENERATION X   Formed in London in 1976, Generation X are today best known as the band that launched the career of their charismatic lead singer Billy Idol (William Broad), who started out as one of the so-called "Bromley Contingent" of hardcore Sex Pistols fans. The band took its name from the 1964 book *Generation X* about the British Mod subculture, by Jane Deverson and Charles Hamblett. The classic Generation X lineup featured Idol on vocals, guitarist Bob Andrews, bassist Tony James, and drummer Mark Laff. In 1978, Generation X released their self-titled debut album, which reached no. 29 on the UK charts and contained the band's signature track, "Your Generation," which featured the line, "Your generation don't mean a thing to me."

Generation X called it quits in 1983, while Idol's solo career took off with a strong boost from his immensely popular MTV music videos for such hits as "Dancing with Myself," "White Wedding," "Rebel Yell," and "Eyes Without a Face." The music video for "Rebel Yell" was directed by none other than Tobe Hooper of *The Texas Chainsaw Massacre* fame. Idol once claimed that "Christ was a punk rocker." In 1991, he was involved in a near-fatal motorcycle accident, followed by a near-fatal drug overdose in 1994. Idol appeared as "Cat" in the 1991 Oliver Stone biopic *The Doors* and as himself in the 1998 comedy *The Wedding Singer* opposite Adam Sandler.

Essential Listening: *Generation X* (1978), *Valley of the Dolls* (1979)

THE JAM   Known for such catchy hit songs as "In the City," "Going Underground," and "That's Entertainment," the Jam were a British mod revival/punk band active between 1972 and 1982 but didn't release their debut album, *In the City*, until 1977. The band's classic lineup featured vocalist/guitarist/keyboardist Paul Weller, vocalist/bassist Bruce Foxton, and drummer Rick Buckler. The Jam scored an astounding four no. 1 hits in the UK: "Start," "Going Underground," "Beat Surrender," and "A Town Called Malice." In addition, their sixth and final album, *The Gift*, reached no. 1 on the UK charts.

Essential Listening: *In the City* (1977), *All Mod Cons* (1978), *Setting Sons* (1979), *Sound Affects* (1980)

SIOUXSIE AND THE BANSHEES   Formed in London in 1976 by two members of the Bromley Contingent—lead singer Siouxsie Sioux and bassist Steven Severin—Siouxsie and the Banshees are today considered pioneers of gothic rock. The band made their rather inauspicious debut at the 100 Club Punk Festival in 1976 with none other than Sid Vicious filling in on drums. After the gig, they recruited guitarist Peter Fenton (soon replaced by John McKay) and drummer Kenny Morris.

In 1978, the band released their debut album, *The Scream*, which has subsequently been cited as an influence on such bands as Joy Division, Killing Joke, the Cure, Sonic Youth, the Jesus and Mary Chain, Faith No More, Massive Attack, and Big Black. However, *Rolling Stone* dismissed the album as "uniformly ghoulish, self-indulgent, and monotonous." In 1980, they changed direction with their third album, *Kaleidoscope*, which climbed to no. 5 on the UK charts. It incorporated the use of drum machines and synthesizers.

Essential Listening: *The Scream* (1978), *Kaleidoscope* (1980), *Juju* (1981), *A Kiss in the Dreamhouse* (1982)

THE VIBRATORS   Founded in 1976 by lead singer Ian "Knox" Carnochan, guitarist John Ellis, bassist Pat Collier, and drummer John "Eddie" Edwards, the Vibrators were one of the pioneering punk-rock bands that played at London hot spots like 100 Club and the Roxy. In 1977, they supported Iggy Pop during his British tour. After signing to Epic Records, the band released their debut album, *Pure Mania* (1977), which reached no. 50 on the UK charts and was later named one of the "50 Best Punk Albums of All Time" by the *Guinness Encyclopedia of Popular Music*. In addition, the Belfast punk band Stiff Little Fingers got their name from one of the album's tracks. Their next album, *V2* (1978), spawned a UK top 40 hit, "Automatic Lover."

Essential Listening: *Pure Mania* (1977), *V2* (1978)

X-RAY SPEX   Formed in 1976, X-Ray Spex highlighted the amazing talents of lead singer Poly Styrene (Marianne Elliott). The band also featured guitarist Jak Airport, bassist Paul Dean, saxophonist Lora Logic, and drummer B. P. Hurding. In 1978, X-Ray Spex released their debut album, *Germfree Adolescents*, which reached no. 30 on the UK charts, and spawned five singles: "Oh Bondage! Up Yours!" "The Day the World Turned Day-Glo," "Identity," "Germfree Adolescents," and "Highly Inflammable."

The single "Oh Bondage! Up Yours!" did not chart but has since been widely acknowledged as one of the greatest punk-rock songs of all time. It later ranked no. 120 on *Rolling Stone*'s list of the "500 Greatest Songs of All Time."

Essential Listening: *Germfree Adolescents* (1978)

6

New Noise
Other Punk Hot Spots
around the World

> At the heart of anything good there should be a kernel of
> something undefinable, and if you can define it, or claim
> to be able to define, it, then, in a sense, you've missed
> the point. —John Peel

Although punk has its roots in New York City and London, the
movement served as an agent of change that affected all corners of
the globe. From Australia to South Africa to Tokyo and Northern
Ireland, punk captured the imagination of a generation and still has
the power to smash through the barriers of the power structure with
its rebelliousness, fearlessness, and relentless creativity.

AUSTRALIA   Believe it or not, Australian punk-rock band the Saints
released their debut single, "(I'm) Stranded," in September 1976—
thereby beating such bands as the Damned, the Sex Pistols, the
Clash, and Buzzcocks to the punch. Soon after, they released their
debut album, also titled *(I'm) Stranded*. The Saints led the way,
and soon the punk scene in Sydney and Melbourne erupted with
such bands as the Young Charlatans, Radio Birdman, Boys Next
Door (formed by Nick Cave and Mick Harvey), the Last Words,
the Hellcats, the Psychosurgeons, Johnny Dole and the Scabs, the
Thought Criminals, the Reals, and the Babeez. Punk also flourished in Brisbane and Perth with the likes of the Quick and the

Dead, Cheap Nasties, the Geeks, and the Victims (who had a hit single, "Television Addict").

BELFAST, NORTHERN IRELAND   Amid the sectarian violence of "The Troubles," the punk rock scene in Belfast somehow managed to thrive and diffuse some of the tensions among the younger generation, who found common ground in the music. Instrumental to the Belfast punk scene was Terri Hooley, who founded the Good Vibrations record store/label and released early works by the Undertones ("Teenage Kicks"), Outcasts ("Justa Nother Teenage Rebel"), Protex ("I Can't Cope"), and Rudi ("Big Time"). In addition, the Belfast quartet Stiff Little Fingers (named after a Vibrators B-side) released cutting-edge and controversial songs dealing directly with the Troubles, such as "Suspect Device," "State of Emergency," "Alternative Ulster," and "Wasted Life," from their 1979 debut album *Inflammable Material*.

Many of the Belfast punk bands, especially the Undertones, found a champion in legendary British DJ John Peel. In addition,

A fixture of the Belfast, Northern Ireland, punk scene in the late 1970s, Stiff Little Fingers released their critically acclaimed debut album, *Inflammable Material*, in 1979. BY SHIRLEY SEXTON/WIKIMEDIA COMMONS

the bands found a welcome venue in the Harp Bar, which quickly became the center of the punk scene in Belfast in the late 1970s. Many local punk bands took the stage here, such as the Outcasts, Stiff Little Fingers, the Defects, and Rudi. According to one Harp Bar regular interviewed on the 2012 BBC Radio 4 show, *The Godfather of Ulster Punk*, "It stank. It smelled of armpit and stale beer. The toilets were dreadful." The Good Vibrations record store closed its doors in 2011. A well-received biopic on Hooley and the Belfast punk-rock scene called *Good Vibrations* was released in 2013.

BOSTON, MASSACHUSETTS   Strongly influenced by the Velvet Underground, Massachusetts native Jonathan Richman formed the Modern Lovers, the first significant proto-punk band in Boston during the early 1970s. The band became best known for its catchy song "Roadrunner," which evolved into a punk standard and was even covered by the Sex Pistols. Much of Boston's punk scene centered around the legendary Rathskeller club (aka "The Rat"). Bands such as the Ramones, Talking Heads, the Cars, Nervous Eaters, Mission of Burma, the Neighborhoods, the Dropkick Murphys, and many others took the stage at the Rat, which has been variously described as "dingy," "dark," and "beer soaked." Other popular Boston clubs and dive bars that hosted punk acts included the Underground, Gallery East, the Paradise, Spit Club (which the *Boston Herald* described as "a decadent den of iniquity"), and Mavericks.

CLEVELAND, OHIO   By the mid-1970s, Cleveland was an industrial wasteland straight out of *Eraserhead*. However, somehow the local punk scene thrived in this dilapidated atmosphere. Many up-and-coming Cleveland punk bands took the stage at the legendary Pirate's Cove at 1059 Old River Road (now the site of Dante's Inferno Flats restaurant). Other popular punk clubs included Clockwork Orange and Viking Saloon. The welcome atmosphere in Cleveland and nearby Akron spawned a slew of legendary proto-punk and punk bands such as Rocket from the Tombs, Toxic Reasons, Dead Boys, Devo, Electric Eels, Pere Ubu, and the Mirrors, which featured drummer Michael Weldon, who later authored the *Psychotronic Encyclopedia of Film* (1983). In addition, the Pagans formed in Cleveland in 1977. Formerly known as the Mad Staggers and Venus in Furs, the band featured lead singer/bassist Mike Hudson, guitarist Mike "Tommy Gunn" Metoff, bassist Tim Allee, and drummer Brian Hudson. One of the band's most notable songs, "What's This Shit Called Love?" was covered by Michigan punk band the Meatmen on their 1985 album *War of the Superbikes*.

GAINESVILLE, FLORIDA A sleepy college town (home to the University of Florida), Gainesville surprisingly spawned a thriving punk-rock scene starting in the early 1980s with the likes of Roach Motel (which organized the city's first punk festival, Florida Slamfest, in 1982), Spoke, Doldrums, Riff Raff, the Mutley Chix, Less Than Jake, and Hot Water Music. The Hardback club served as the place to hear Gainesville punk bands. The most successful of all the Gainesville punk bands—Against Me!—formed in 2000 and released their critically acclaimed debut album, *Reinventing Axl Rose*, in 2002. However, the band's controversial signing to major label Sire Records for their 2007 album *New Wave* alienated some of their hardcore fans and resulted in their tour van being vandalized. Started in 2002, the Fest, a three-day indie and punk-rock music festival in Gainesville, has evolved into one of the longest-running and largest punk music festivals in the United States. Matt Walker's 2016 book, *Gainesville Punk: A History of Bands & Music*, provides a definitive guide to the Gainesville punk scene.

Gainesville punk band Against Me! released their breakthrough album, *Reinventing Axl Rose*, in 2002. By GOROTH (JAN BRAUER), OWN WORK/ WIKIMEDIA COMMONS

LOS ANGELES, CALIFORNIA The City of Angels developed a strong glam-rock scene in the early 1970s centered around Rodney Bingenheimer's English Disco on Sunset Boulevard. Several popular proto-punk bands also emerged, such as Atomic Kid and the Flyboys. In addition, all-female teenage band the Runaways, featuring Joan Jett, formed in 1975 and scored a hit single, "Cherry Bomb." The first wave of Los Angeles punk bands soon followed with the likes of the Dils, the Weirdos, the Screamers, the Germs, the Dickies, the Bags, X, and the Go-Go's. By the late 1970s, the hardcore scene emerged out of the Los Angeles suburbs in the form of Black Flag, Fear, Vicious Circle, Middle Class, the Circle Jerks, Adolescents, Agent Orange, T.S.O.L., China White, Wasted Youth, Social Distortion, D.I., and others. The classic 1981 Penelope Spheeris documentary *The Decline of Western Civilization* expertly captured the early hardcore-punk scene in Los Angeles.

MANCHESTER, ENGLAND The Sex Pistols sparked the Manchester punk scene when they first performed at the city's Lesser Free Trade Hall at the invitation of Pete Shelley and Howard Devoto of Buzzcocks on June 4, 1976. The audience for the show included Tony Wilson (founder of Factory Records), Bernard Sumner (later of Joy Division and New Order), Morrissey (later of the Smiths), Mark E. Smith (later of the Fall), and Mick Hucknall (later of Simply Red). The Pistols returned to Manchester for two gigs during their infamous Anarchy Tour in December 1976. Another pivotal event in the history of Manchester punk was the release of the influential EP *Spiral Scratch* by Buzzcocks on January 29, 1977. *Spiral Scratch* served as the first independent-label punk record. Other lesser-known punk bands from Manchester included the Nosebleeds, the Drones, and the Membranes.

SAN FRANCISCO, CALIFORNIA The early punk scene in San Francisco and surrounding Bay Area featured such bands as the Avengers and the Nuns (both of which opened for the Sex Pistols during their final concert at Winterland Ballroom on January 14, 1978), as well as the Dead Kennedys, Crime, the Mutants, Negative Trend, Flipper, the Groovie Ghoulies, and the Offs. The second wave of punk bands in the mid- to late 1980s and early 1990s in San Francisco included No Use for a Name, the Swingin' Utters, the Lookouts, and Jawbreaker. Green Day also emerged out of the Bay Area and released their phenomenally successful album *Dookie* (1994), which eventually sold over twenty million copies worldwide.

SOUTH AFRICA   The influence of the British punk scene made its way to South Africa, where an antiestablishment, hands-on, DIY attitude pervaded among the likes of Wild Youth, National Wake, Powerage, Dog Detachment, the Radio Rats, and Young Dumb & Violent. More recently, bands such as thrash punks TCIYF (the cum in your face) in Soweto and garage punk psychedelic innovators Runaway Nuns from Cape Town have continued the punk tradition in South Africa. The 2012 documentary *Punk in Africa* explores the history of the multiracial punk movement within South Africa, Mozambique, and Zimbabwe.

TOKYO, JAPAN   The Tokyo punk scene was shaped in the 1970s by such pioneer bands as Friction and the Stalin, both of which took direct inspiration from bands like the New York Dolls and the Ramones. Directed by Sogo Ishii, the outrageous Japanese dystopian punk-rock musical/action film *Burst City* (1982) showcases such bands as the Roosters, the Stalin, and the Rockers. Other highly influential Tokyo punk bands included GISM (one of the first Japanese hardcore bands) and the Blue Hearts.

WASHINGTON, DC   Emerging in the late 1970s, the Washington, DC, hardcore punk scene thrived with the likes of Bad Brains (who eventually made their way to NYC after getting banned from every DC club!), Dag Nasty, Minor Threat (which popularized the straight-edge movement), Government Issue, Jawbox, Youth Brigade, and Fugazi. Ian MacKaye and Jeff Nelson of Minor Threat formed the record label Dischord Records, which released albums by Youth Brigade, Iron Cross, the Faith, Scream, Void, Government Issue, and State of Alert. DC native Henry Rollins (Garfield) started out as a roadie for MacKaye's first band, the Teen Idles. A documentary about the DC hardcore scene, *Punk the Capital: Building a Sound Movement*, was released in 2019 and features interviews with Rollins, MacKaye, H. R. from Bad Brains, Jello Biafra from the Dead Kennedys, and others.

7

Danger Zone
Essential Punk-Rock Labels

I will always believe in punk-rock, because it's about creating something for yourself. —Joe Strummer

Independent record labels exemplified the DIY spirit of punk-rock culture. Basically, since none of the major record labels were interested in anything that wasn't commercially viable, many punk-rock bands simply found a way to release the album on their own and get it in the hands of their most diehard fans. It all started when Buzzcocks released their debut EP, *Spiral Scratch*, on January 29, 1977, and raised £500 from friends and families to pay for the production and manufacture of the record. Pioneering independent record labels like Stiff Records, Alternative Tentacles, Dischord Records, SST Records, and others quickly grabbed the reins and revolutionized the music industry in the process.

ALTERNATIVE TENTACLES Established in 1979 in San Francisco, California, by Dead Kennedys guitarist East Bay Ray and lead singer Jello Biafra, Alternative Tentacles served as a DIY effort to self-produce the band's debut single, "California Uber Alles." They later released their highly influential debut album, *Fresh Fruit for Rotting Vegetables*, through the label in 1980. Biafra became solo owner of the record label in the mid-1980s but lost the rights to all Dead Kennedys recordings after a 2000 lawsuit. Other bands to

release albums under the Alternative Tentacles label include Butthole Surfers, NoMeansNo, D.O.A., T.S.O.L., Leftover Crack, and
even schizophrenic street singer-songwriter Wesley Willis.

DISCHORD RECORDS   Founded in Washington, DC, in 1980 by Ian
MacKaye and Jeff Nelson to release the debut EP *Minor Distur-
bance* for their hardcore punk band the Teen Idles (which morphed
into Minor Threat), Dischord Records also released records from
the likes of Jawbox, Rites of Spring, Dag Nasty, and MacKaye's
later project, Fugazi, among others.

EPITAPH RECORDS   Originally formed by Bad Religion guitarist Brett
Gurewitz in Los Angeles in 1980 to self-produce the band's music,
Epitaph ended up releasing the Offspring's third studio album,
Smash (1994), which eventually sold six million copies worldwide.
Epitaph also released albums from the likes of Rancid, Pennywise,
L7, Bad Religion, and NOFX.

Founded by Bad Religion guitarist Brett Gurewitz in 1980,
Epitaph Records also released albums by the Offspring,
Rancid, Pennywise, L7, and NOFX. ATLANTIC RECORDS/
PHOTOFEST

The critically acclaimed 2002 British comedy/drama, *24 Hour Party People*, depicts the rise and fall of Manchester-based Factory Records, which produced notable bands such as Joy Division, New Order, and Happy Mondays. MGM/PHOTOFEST

FACTORY RECORDS   Founded in 1978 by Tony Wilson and Alan Erasmus, this iconic Manchester, England, label released albums by Joy Division, New Order, Northside, Happy Mondays, the Durutti Column, A Certain Ratio, James, the Hacienda, and others. Directed by Michael Winterbottom, the 2002 comedy-drama *24 Hour Party People* details the rise and fall of Factory Records.

FAT WRECK CHORDS   Started in San Francisco in 1990 by NOFX lead singer Fat Mike (Michael Burkett), Fat Wreck Chords has released over 150 studio albums (as of 2022) from the likes of NOFX, Descendents, Leftover Crack, Anti-Flag, Screeching Weasel, the Loved Ones, Strung Out, Lagwagon, Rise Against, Strike Anywhere, Propagandhi, Against Me!, Sick of It All, and the Gimme Gimmes.

GOOD VIBRATIONS   Started rather inauspiciously in 1976 as a Belfast, Northern Ireland, record store in a rundown building on Great Victoria Street by the legendary Terri Hooley, the Good Vibrations label eventually signed such influential local punk bands as the Undertones (best known for the hit single "Teenage Kicks"), the Outcasts ("Justa Nother Teenage Rebel"), Victim ("Strange Thing by Night"), the Moondogs ("She's Nineteen"), the Shapes ("Blast Off"), and the Tearjerkers ("Love Affair"). The first band to sign with Good Vibrations, Rudi ("Big Time"), one of the most popular Belfast punk bands during the late 1970s, never hit the big time and has been dubbed "the band that time forgot." Reflecting on the Belfast punk scene in his 2010 memoir, *Hooleygan*, Hooley remarked, "I loved the energy and I loved the fact that these kids didn't give a shit about the cops and were prepared to take them on. Punk was anarchy, and I had been waiting for it all my life." A critically acclaimed comedy-drama about Hooley titled *Good Vibrations* was released in 2013.

KILL ROCK STARS   Launched in Oregon in 1991 by Slim Moon and Tinuviel Sampson, Kill Rock Stars was instrumental in releasing key albums from the feminist punk Riot Grrrl movement from the likes of Bikini Kill (*Pussy Whipped*), Heavens to Betsy (*Calculated*), and Sleater-Kinney (*Dig Me Out*).

LOOKOUT! RECORDS   Founded in 1987 by Larry Livermore and David Hayes, Lookout! Records is best known for releasing Green Day's first two studio albums, *39/Smooth* (1990) and *Kerplunk* (1991), as well as *Energy* (1989), the only album of Operation Ivy (which morphed into Rancid). Lookout! also released records by the likes of Alkaline Trio, the Queers, Avengers, Screeching Weasel, the Frumpies, Boris the Sprinkler, Auntie Christ, the Donnas, the Zero Boys, the Groovie Ghoulies, Sewer Trout, the Lookouts, the Mr. T Experience, the Winona Riders, and many others.

SLASH RECORDS   Formed in 1978 by Bob Biggs, Slash Records released the first and only studio album, *GI*, of Los Angeles–based hardcore punk band the Germs in 1979, followed by X's debut album, *Los Angeles*, in 1980. Other bands that released albums through Slash Records (who teamed up with Warner Bros in the early 1980s to gain wider distribution) include Violent Femmes, the Del Fuegos, Fear, the Blasters, Failure, L7, the Plugz, Faith No More, Burning Spear, the Flesh Eaters, Dream Syndicate, and Los Lobos.

SST RECORDS Formed in 1978 by Greg Ginn of Black Flag, SST Records (SST = Solid State Tuners) released not only Black Flag albums but also those of hardcore punk and alternative rock bands such as Bad Brains, Minutemen, Husker Du, the Meat Puppets, Soundgarden, Sonic Youth, and Dinosaur Jr. The label's first release was Black Flag's legendary 1979 debut EP, *Nervous Breakdown*.

STIFF RECORDS Formed in London in 1976 by Dave Robinson and Jake Riviera, Stiff Records signed a slew of influential punk and new wave bands, including the Damned (which released their first UK punk single, "New Rose," on Stiff), Richard Hell and the Voidoids, Elvis Costello, Ian Dury and the Blockheads, the Adverts, Devo, Nick Lowe, Lene Lovich, Wreckless Eric, the Feelies, Madness, the Pogues, and Dr. Feelgood, among many others. Stiff was known for their outrageous promotional slogans, such as "If It Ain't Stiff, It Ain't Worth a Fuck."

8

One Way or Another

The Women Who Defined Punk Rock

> Some people think little girls should be seen and not
> heard/But I think "oh bondage, up yours!" —X-Ray Spex

The story of women in punk rock starts with such pioneering musi-
cal artists in the 1970s and early 1980s as "punk poetess" Patti
Smith, Debbie Harry of Blondie, Exene Cervenka of X, Joan Jett,
Poly Styrene of X-Ray Spex, Lydia Lunch of Teenage Jesus and the
Jerks, Gaye Advert of the Adverts, Viv Albertine and Ari Up of the
Slits, Poison Ivy of the Cramps, Kim Gordon of Sonic Youth, and
Chrissie Hynde of the Pretenders.

In the early 1990s, the underground feminist hardcore punk
Riot Grrrl movement exploded across the Pacific Northwest with
such highly influential bands as Bikini Kill, Bratmobile, Heavens
to Betsy, Sleater-Kinney, and others. Quoted in *The Lost Women
of Rock Music*, writer Caroline Coon comments, "It would be possible to write the whole history of punk music without mentioning
any male bands at all—and I think a lot of [people] would find that
very surprising."

GAYE ADVERT—THE ADVERTS   One of the first female stars of the
punk-rock movement, Gaye Advert, who was born in England on
August 25, 1956, served as the bassist for the Adverts, which she
cofounded with T. V. Smith (whom she later married) in 1976.

Advert has cited the Stooges, the Sex Pistols, the New York Dolls, the Stranglers, and the Damned among bands that influenced her musical style. After the band broke up in 1979, Advert pursued careers as a social services worker and stained-glass artist.

VIV ALBERTINE—THE SLITS   Born in Australia on December 1, 1954, Viviane Katrina Louise Albertine served as guitarist for London-based punk band the Slits from 1977 until 1982. She had earlier been in a punk band called the Flowers of Romance with Sid Vicious as one of her bandmates. After her stint with the Slits, Albertine turned to filmmaking and became a freelance director for the British Film Institute and BBC. She returned to music in 2012, releasing her first and only solo album, *The Vermilion Border*. In 2014, Albertine published a critically acclaimed autobiography, *Clothes, Clothes, Clothes, Music, Music, Music, Boys, Boys, Boys*, followed by a sequel of sorts in 2018 titled *To Throw Away Unopened*.

ALICE BAG—THE BAGS   Cofounder and singer-songwriter of Los Angeles punk band the Bags, Alice Bag (Alicia Armendariz) was born on November 7, 1958, the daughter of Mexican immigrants. The Bags were featured in the landmark documentary *The Decline of Western Civilization* (1981). A tireless educator, activist, musician, and author, Bag published her autobiography, *Violence Girl: From East LA Rage to Hollywood Stage, A Chicana Punk Story*, in 2011. In addition, she has released three solo albums: *Alice Bag* (2016), *Blueprint* (2018), and *Sister Dynamite* (2020).

BELINDA CARLISLE—THE GO-GO'S   Best known as the lead singer of the Go-Go's, Belinda Jo Carlisle was born on August 17, 1958, and raised in southern California. She was reportedly named after her mother's favorite film, *Johnny Belinda* (1948). Believe it or not, Carlisle started her musical career as a drummer for the Germs very briefly under the moniker "Dottie Danger" before joining the Go-Go's (originally known as the Misfits). Formed in 1978, the immensely popular all-female band also featured guitarist Jane Wiedlin, guitarist Charlotte Caffey, bassist Kathy Valentine, and drummer Gina Schock.

In 1981, the Go-Go's released their phenomenally successful debut album, *Beauty and the Beat*, which spawned such hits as "Our Lips Are Sealed" and "We Got the Beat." The album held the no. 1 spot on the U.S. charts for six weeks. As a solo artist, Carlisle scored a no. 1 hit with "Heaven Is a Place on Earth" in 1987. In 2010, Carlisle published her autobiography, *Lips Unsealed*. She was inducted into the Rock and Roll Hall of Fame as a member of the Go-Go's in 2021.

EXENE CERVENKA—X   Singer-songwriter, artist, and poet, Exene Cervenka (born Christene Lee Cervenka on February 1, 1956) is best known as cofounder of Los Angeles punk pioneers X. The band's debut album, *Los Angeles*, which was produced by former Doors keyboardist Ray Manzarek, was hailed as the best album of 1980 by the *Los Angeles Times*. X was featured in the documentary *The Decline of Western Civilization* the following year.

Cervenka coauthored a 1982 book of poetry with Lydia Lunch (of Teenage Jesus and the Jerks fame) titled *Adulterers Anonymous*, released a spoken-word album called *Perfection* in 1984, and collaborated with poet Wanda Coleman ("The Unofficial Poet Laureate of Los Angeles") on a poetry album, *Twin Sisters*, in 1985. Cervenka has released six solo albums, the latest being *The Excitement of Maybe* in 2011. In addition, X continues to tour and released their eighth studio album, *Alphabetland*, in 2020. Cervenka has been married three times to X bandmate John Doe (1980–1985), *The Lord of the Rings* actor Viggo Mortensen (1987–1998), and musician Jason Edge (2002–2014).

KIM GORDON—SONIC YOUTH   Cofounder, bassist, guitarist, and vocalist for alternative rock band Sonic Youth, Kim Althea Gordon was born on April 28, 1953, in Rochester, New York, and raised in Los Angeles, where her father served as a professor at UCLA. After graduating from the Otis College of Art and Design, Gordon headed to New York City to embark on an art career. Instead, she ended up forming Sonic Youth with her future husband, Thurston Moore, in 1981. Over the next thirty years, the band released sixteen studio albums, the last being *The Eternal* in 2009. After

Gordon and Moore divorced, the band broke up 2011. Since then, she has formed the experimental duos Body/Head with Bill Nace and Glitterbust with Alex Knost. She also released her first solo album, *No Home Record*, in 2019.

A record producer, visual artist, actor, fashion designer, and human rights activist, Gordon produced Hole's debut album, *Pretty on the Inside*, in 1993 and founded the Los Angeles–based clothing line X-Girl the same year. She also has appeared in several films, including *Last Days* (2005), *I'm Not There* (2007), and *Don't Worry, He Won't Get Far on Foot* (2018). In 2015, Gordon published an autobiography called *Girl in the Band*. In an October 4, 2019, interview with the *Guardian*, Gordon remarked, "Trump is the ultimate capitalist, destroying everything."

NINA HAGEN   Born in East Germany on March 11, 1955, Catharina "Nina" Hagen is known for her theatrical vocals and has been nicknamed the "Godmother of Punk." She formed the Nina Hagen Band and released a critically acclaimed self-titled debut album in 1978 that sold over 250,000 copies. In 1982, Hagen released her first English-language album, *NunSexMonkRock*, which peaked at no. 184 on the U.S. charts, followed by *Fearless* in 1983 and *Exstasy* in 1985. Known for her human and animal rights activism, Hagen has published three autobiographies: *Ich Bin ein Berliner* (1988), *Nina Hagen: That's Why the Lady Is a Punk* (2003), and *Bekenntnisse* (2010).

KATHLEEN HANNA—BIKINI KILL   A true pioneer of the feminist-punk Riot Grrrl movement, Hanna was born on November 12, 1968, studied photography at Evergreen College in Olympia, Washington, and ran an art gallery before becoming the lead singer of Bikini Kill (best known for their feminist punk anthem, "Rebel Girl"). After the band broke up in 1997, Hanna fronted the electronic rock band Le Tigre. Since 2010, she has performed and recorded with the Julie Ruin. In 2013, a documentary was released about Hanna titled *The Punk Singer*, which detailed her musical career, years-long battle with Lyme disease, and marriage to Adam "Ad-Rock" Horovitz of the Beastie Boys. Last but certainly not least, according to legend, Kurt Cobain got the idea for the title of "Smells Like Teen Spirit" from Hanna, who had spray-painted the phrase on a wall in his apartment.

DEBBIE HARRY—BLONDIE Born Angela Trimble on July 1, 1945, in Miami, Florida, Harry was adopted as a baby and raised in Hawthorne, New Jersey. In the late 1960s, she held several odd jobs, including Playboy Bunny, before embarking on her singing career in 1968 as a member of the folk band the Wind in the Willows. Harry cofounded Blondie with Chris Stein in 1974. The group's breakthrough album, *Parallel Lines* (1978), featured the hit single "Heart of Glass" and sold twenty million copies worldwide. Harry released her solo debut album, *KooKoo*, in 1981, one year before Blondie broke up. In the 1980s, Harry pursued an acting career with memorable roles in such films as *Union Blues* (1980), *Videodrome* (1983), and *Hairspray* (1988). Blondie reunited in the 1990s and released an album, *No Exit* (1999), followed by *The Curse of Blondie* (2003). In 2006, Harry was inducted into the Rock and Roll Hall of Fame as a member of Blondie. VH1 has ranked Harry no. 12 on its list of the "100 Greatest Women in Rock 'n' Roll."

PJ HARVEY Celebrated English singer-songwriter PJ Harvey was born Polly Jean Harvey on October 9, 1969. She started her musical career in 1988 by joining a local band called Automatic Dlamini. In 1991, Harvey formed the eponymous trio PJ Harvey with Stephen Vaughan and Robert Ellis. The band released two albums: *Dry* (1992) and *Rid of Me* (1993). After the group disbanded, Harvey continued as a solo artist and has released nine studio albums since 1995, the latest being *The Hope Six Demolition Project* in 2016. Her 2000 album, *Stories from the City, Stories from the Sea*, was ranked no. 313 on *Rolling Stone*'s list of the "500 Greatest Albums of All Time." In 2003, Harvey was named a Member of the Order of the British Empire (MBE).

CHRISSIE HYNDE—THE PRETENDERS A founding member, lead vocalist, guitarist, and primary songwriter for the Pretenders, Christine Ellen Hynde was born in Akron, Ohio, on September 7, 1951. After

A founding member of the Pretenders, which formed in 1978, Chrissie Hynde was inducted into the Rock and Roll Hall of Fame with her fellow band members in 2005. BY RAPH_PH/WIKIMEDIA COMMMONS

attending Kent State University for three years, she headed to London in her mid-twenties and worked briefly at the SEX boutique for Vivienne Westwood and Malcolm McLaren, as well as writing reviews for *NME*. At one point she asked either Johnny Rotten or Sid Vicious to marry her so she could score a work permit and stay in London.

Instead, Hynde returned to Ohio and formed the Pretenders in 1978 with Pete Farndon, James Honeyman-Scott, and Martin Chambers. The band scored their first no. 1 hit on the UK charts with "Brass in Pocket" in 1979. The Pretenders performed a riveting set at Live Aid in 1985 that featured "Time the Avenger," "Message of Love," "Stop Your Sobbing," "Back on the Chain Gang," and "Middle of the Road." Over the years, the band has released eleven studio albums, the latest being *Hate for Sale* in 2020.

Hynde was inducted into the Rock and Roll Hall of Fame in 2005 as a member of the Pretenders. Today, she is the band's only original member. Besides her work with the Pretenders, Hynde has collaborated with the likes of Frank Sinatra, Cher, UB40, and others. She also released a solo album, *Stockholm*, in 2014. VH1 has ranked Hynde no. 7 on its list of the "100 Greatest Women of Rock

N' Roll." An animal rights and environmental activist, she published an autobiography, *Reckless: My Life as a Pretender*, in 2015. Hynde has a daughter, Natalie, from her relationship with the Kinks' Ray Davies. In addition, she was married to Simple Minds lead singer Jim Kerr between 1984 and 1990.

POISON IVY—THE CRAMPS In 1976, Poison Ivy Rorschach (born Kristy Marlana Wallace on February 20, 1953) and her husband Lux Interior (Erick Purkhiser) moved to New York City and formed the psychobilly band the Cramps along with guitarist Bryan Gregory and drummer Pam Ballan. She had met Interior while attending Sacramento State College. In 1980, the Cramps released their debut studio album, *Songs the Lord Taught Us*. The Cramps disbanded in 2009 after the death of Interior, and Ivy has kept a relatively low profile ever since.

JOAN JETT—JOAN JETT AND THE BLACKHEARTS As a teenager, Joan Jett (born Joan Marie Larkin on September 22, 1958) got her start fronting the all-female rock band the Runaways, which was managed by

Known as the "Queen of Rock 'n Roll," Joan Jett was an original member of the Runaways ("Cherry Bomb") before launching an incredibly successful solo career. By JMABEL/WIKIMEDIA COMMONS

Los Angeles rock icon Kim Fowley. The band, which also featured Lita Ford, Cherie Currie, Jackie Fox, and Sandy West, scored a hit single with "Cherry Bomb" off their self-titled debut album in 1976.

After the Runaways fizzled out in 1979, Jett produced the Germs' first and only studio album, *GI*, in 1979 and then formed Joan Jett and the Blackhearts, which landed a no. 1 hit on the U.S. charts in 1981—"I Love Rock 'n' Roll" (previously recorded by British group the Arrows in 1975). Other hits from the band included "Bad Reputation," "Crimson and Clover," "Do You Wanna Touch Me (Oh Yeah)," "Light of Day," "I Hate Myself for Loving You," and "Dirty Deeds." Known as the "Queen of Rock 'n' Roll," Jett was inducted into the Rock and Roll Hall of Fame as a member of Joan Jett and the Blackhearts in 2015.

COURTNEY LOVE—HOLE   Known as much for her turbulent relationship with Nirvana's Kurt Cobain as for her musical career with Hole (as well as some memorable acting roles), Love was born Courtney Michelle Harrison in San Francisco on July 9, 1964, the daughter of psychotherapist Linda Carroll and the Grateful Dead's first manager, Hank Harrison. During the 1980s, Love worked as a stripper at Jumbo's Clown Room in Los Angeles (director David Lynch supposedly wrote the script for *Blue Velvet* while hanging out here). She formed Hole in 1989 with bassist Kristen M. Pfaff, drummer Patty Schemel, and guitarist Eric Erlandson. The band released their first studio album, *Pretty on the Inside*, in 1991. It was produced by Kim Gordon of Sonic Youth.

Love and Cobain got married in 1992 and had a daughter, Frances Bean Cobain. On April 5, 1994, Cobain committed suicide from a self-inflicted gunshot wound to the head. Just nine days later, Hole released its second studio album, *Live Through This*. Two months later, on June 16, 1994, Pfaff was found dead of a heroin overdose.

In addition to scoring a bit role in *Sid and Nancy* (1986), Love achieved her breakthrough role as porn mogul Larry Flynt's long-suffering wife Althea in *The People vs. Larry Flynt* (1996), which earned her a Golden Globe Award nomination. Her filmography also includes *200 Cigarettes* (1998), *Man on the Moon* (1999), *Julie*

Johnson (2001), and *Trapped* (2002), among others. She released her first solo album, *America's Sweetheart,* in 2004.

Love is also well known for her confrontational stage antics such as hurling her microphone stand into the crowd and striking a fan in the head during a surprise performance at Manhattan nightclub Plaid in 2004 and once screaming at an audience, "I'm going to abuse you, because you fuckin' deserve it, you shits!"

LYDIA LUNCH—TEENAGE JESUS AND THE JERKS   The lead singer and guitarist of Teenage Jesus and the Jerks, multimedia artist Lydia Lunch (who was born Lydia Anne Koch on June 2, 1959, in Rochester, New York) became the figurehead of the "no wave" scene in New York City. Known for her lively spoken word performances and confrontational style, Lunch wrote a novel, *Paradoxia: A Predator's Diary,* in 1997. She also has collaborated with the likes of Kim Gordon and Thurston Moore of Sonic Youth, Nick Cave, Henry Rollins, author Hubert Selby Jr. (*Last Exit to Brooklyn*), and many others. In addition to acting in underground films, Lunch has released nine solo albums, the latest being *Urge to Kill* in 2015. She is also the subject of the career-spanning documentary *Lydia Lunch: The War Is Never Over* (2019).

PATTI SMITH   A disciple of Arthur Rimbaud, Jim Morrison, and William S. Burroughs, Patricia Lee Smith was born on December 30, 1946, the daughter of a New Jersey factory worker. A former writer for *CREEM* magazine, Smith published two books of poetry, *Witt* and *Seventh Heaven,* before embarking on a singing career. She also cowrote (with Sam Shepard) and starred in a 1971 play, *Cowboy Mouth,* which lasted for one performance.

Known as both the "Punk Poet Laureate" and "Punk Priestess," Smith formed the Patti Smith Group in 1974 with Lenny Kaye, Ivan Kral, Jay Dee Daugherty, and Richard Sohl. That same year, the band released their debut single, "Hey Joe," which featured the memorable B-side track "Piss Factory" (detailing the drudgery of her experience working on a factory assembly line). The Patti Smith Group soon became a fixture on the early punk scene at CBGBs in New York City. In November 1975, Smith released her stunning debut album, *Horses*, which includes a rendition of Them's "Gloria." Smith could whip herself into a total frenzy onstage and once confessed, "All I know is that in some moment every night, I'm so committed that I piss myself or come on stage." Her biggest hit, "Because the Night," was cowritten with Bruce Springsteen. It reached no. 13 on the U.S. charts.

Smith married Fred "Sonic" Smith of the MC5 in 1980, and the couple settled in Detroit with their two children. She was inducted into the Rock and Roll Hall of Fame in 2007. In 2010, Smith won the National Book Award in the nonfiction category for her memoir *Just Kids*, which details her life in New York City in the 1960s and 1970s, as well as her relationship with controversial artist Robert Mapplethorpe. The *Outlaw Bible of America Literature* called Smith "the emblematic avant-garde figure of our time, moving easily between the worlds of literature, performance art, and rock."

SIOUXSIE SIOUX—SIOUXSIE AND THE BANSHEES Known as both the "High Priestess of Punk" and the "Godmother of Goth," the lead singer of Siouxsie and the Banshees, Siouxsie Sioux (born Susan Janet Ballion on May 27, 1957) first gained notice in punk rock circles as a member of the Bromley Contingent of Sex Pistols admirers. In fact, she was with the band during their infamous *Today* show interview with Bill Grundy on December 1, 1976. One of the sensational headlines from the *Daily Mirror* following the event read "Siouxsie's a Punk Shocker."

Between 1976 and 1996, Siouxsie and the Banshees recorded eleven studio albums and scored several UK top 20 singles such as "Hong Kong Garden," "Happy House," and "Peek-a-Boo," as well as a U.S. top 25 hit, "Kiss Them for Me." The band was also featured on the soundtracks for *Batman Returns* (1992) and *Showgirls* (1995). Siouxsie Sioux also formed a second group, the Creature, which was active between 1981 and 2005 and scored a hit with "Right Now." As a solo artist, Siouxsie Sioux released the critically acclaimed 2007 album *Mantaray*.

POLY STYRENE—X-RAY SPEX Known as the "Judy Garland of Punk" for her colorful and flamboyant style, X-Ray Spex lead singer Poly

The lead singer of English punk band X-Ray Spex, Poly Styrene was dubbed the "Judy Garland of Punk" for her flamboyant style. EMI/PHOTOFEST

Styrene was born Marianne Joan Elliott-Said on July 3, 1957. She formed X-Ray Spex in 1976, and the band's 1977 debut single "Oh Bondage! Up Yours!" became a rallying cry for the punk movement. An early fan of the Sex Pistols, Styrene favored outrageous costumes featuring Day-Glo colors. She left the band in 1979 and released her first solo album, *Translucence*, in 1981.

During the 1980s, Styrene briefly became a Hare Krishna adherent. As an unabashed feminist, she also paved the way for the Riot Grrrl movement. According to Kathleen Hanna of Bikini Kill, "If her work wasn't there, I'm not positive Riot Grrrl would exist." Styrene died of breast cancer on April 25, 2011, at the age of fifty-three. In 2019, Styrene's daughter Celeste Bell cowrote with Zoe Howe the biography *Dayglo: The Poly Styrene Story*. The 2021 documentary *Poly Styrene: I Am a Cliché* details her fascinating life and musical career, along with her struggles with mental illness.

ARI UP—THE SLITS   Best known as the lead singer of English all-female punk band the Slits, Ari Up (Arianna Forster) was born on January 17, 1962, in Munich, West Germany. The Slits released their debut album, *Cut*, in 1979, the same year that her mother, Nora Forster, married John Lydon (Rotten) of the Sex Pistols. The Slits broke up in 1981. Up and Slits bassist Tessa Pollitt reformed the band in 2001 and released an album, *Trapped Animal*, in 2009. On October 20, 2010, Up died of breast cancer at the age of forty-eight.

WENDY O. WILLIAMS—PLASMATICS   Born on May 28, 1949, in Webster, New York, the mohawk-sporting Williams is best known for her outrageous onstage antics as lead singer of the notorious Plasmatics between 1978 and 1983. These included chain-sawing guitars, smashing TVs with a sledgehammer, and blowing up cars. In 1980, Stiff Records released the Plasmatics' debut album, *New Hope for the Wretched*, which spawned the single "Butcher Baby," which peaked at no. 55 on the UK charts.

Prior to her stint in the Plasmatics, Williams held a variety of jobs such as working behind the counter at Dunkin' Donuts and at a strip club before appearing in the 1978 XXX film *Candy Goes to Hollywood*, which starred Carol Connors. After departing the Plasmatics, Williams embarked on a solo career and released her debut album *WOW* in 1984. The following year, Williams was nominated for a Grammy Award for "Best Female Rock Vocal Performance" but lost out to Tina Turner. Frequently suffering from depression, Williams committed suicide at the age of forty-eight on April 6, 1998.

9

New Dawn Fades
The Best and Worst Punk Subgenres

> Rock 'n' roll is the greatest way for weirdos like us to find
> a purpose in life. —Lux Interior, the Cramps

After the first bands were labeled "punk" in the mid-1970s, the movement morphed into a plethora of diverse subgenres, ranging from the sublime (Celtic punk) to the ridiculous (Christian punk). Regardless, each of these various subgenres have made their own unique contributions to the punk movement in terms of both sound and influences.

AFRO-PUNK   The term *afro-punk* originated from the award-winning 2003 documentary *Afro-Punk*, which was directed by James Spooner and explores the contributions made by African Americans in the history of punk. The movie featured live performances by the likes of Bad Brains, Cipher, Ten Grand, and Tamar-kali. Spooner, along with Matthew Morgan, founded the Afropunk Music Festival in 2005.

ANARCHO-PUNK   Quite simply put, anarcho-punk is punk rock that promotes anarchism. The anarcho-punk movement was spawned in the UK among such bands as Crass, Icons of Filth, and Conflict in the late 1970s and early 1980s. *Trouser Press* called Crass the "lords of English punk's extreme left" who "didn't just sing about anarchy in the UK—they *did* something about it." In addition, Malcolm McLaren and Jamie Reid collaborated to bring a spirit of anarchism to the Sex Pistols (whose first single, of course, was "Anarchy in the UK"). The hardcore-punk scene in the United States also featured anarchistic sensibilities among bands such as Dead Kennedys, Black Flag, and Reagan Youth, among others.

CELTIC PUNK   Best exemplified by the English band Pogues (which was fronted by the legendary Shane MacGowan) in the 1980s, Celtic punk at its best successfully blended traditional Celtic music and punk rock with some fascinating results. In his 2020 book, *Music's Cult Artists*, John Riordan writes, "The Pogues combined the energy, DIY ethos, and confrontational attitude of punk with traditional Irish music." In the United States, Celtic punk bands the Dropkick Murphys ("I'm Shipping Up to Boston") and Flogging Molly ("Drunken Lullabies") both became known for their highly energetic live performances. In addition, Australian Celtic punk band the Rumjacks scored a hit single with "An Irish Pub Song" in 2010.

COWPUNK   Also known as country punk, cowpunk combines punk rock with folk, country, blues, and rockabilly influences. A wide range of punk bands have evinced cowpunk tendencies, such as the Blasters, Meat Puppets, Violent Femmes, Social Distortion, the Beat Farmers, Dash Rip Rock, the Gun Club, Jason and the Scorchers, Dead Milkmen, the Long Ryders, Goober & the Peas, and others.

CRUST PUNK   By far the most nihilistic offshoot of punk, crust punk (aka stenchcore) was spawned in the UK during the early 1980s. Adherents of crust punk are referred to as crusties or gutter punks. Notable crust-punk bands include Nausea, Disfear, Doom, Amebix, Tragedy, His Hero Is Gone, Wolfbrigade, Driller Killer, Discharge, Antisect, and Hellbastard. Directed by Penelope Spheeris, *The Decline of Western Civilization III* (1998) documents the Los Angeles crust-punk scene in the late 1990s.

DEATH ROCK One of the more bizarre punk offshoots, death rock typically incorporates campy horror elements into its look and sound. Notable death-rock bands include Super Heroines, Zombina and the Skeletones, 45 Grave (fronted by Dinah Cancer, "the High Priestess of Death Rock"), Christian Death, Voodoo Church, and Kommunity FK. Death rock sometimes overlaps with horror punk, which is typically more melodic and aggressive (example: Misfits).

Formed in New Jersey in 1977, the Misfits have been widely recognized as progenitors of the horror punk subgenre. BY JONAS ROGOWSKI/WIKIMEDIA COMMONS

EMO Defined by its heavy emotional expression through confessional lyrics, emo (aka emotional hardcore or emocore) first emerged out of the mid- to late-1980s hardcore-punk scene in Washington, DC, with pioneering bands such as Embrace and Rites of Spring. Notable emo bands include My Chemical Romance, Panic! at the Disco, Fall Out Boy, Death Cab for Cutie, Brand New, Jimmy Eat World, Paramore, Jawbreaker, Mineral, Texas is the Reason, Weezer, Pierce the Veil, Falling in Reverse, Escape the Fate, American Football, and Sunny Day Real Estate.

HARDCORE Notable hardcore bands include Black Flag, Bad Brains, Dead Kennedys, the Circle Jerks, Fear, Minor Threat, Fugazi, the Germs, Cro-Mags, and Agnostic Front. For more information about hardcore, see chapter 10—"Life of Pain: The Rise of American Hardcore Punk."

NO WAVE Originating in New York City, the avant-garde No Wave movement offered an extreme reaction against commercialized new-wave music. Influential artists in the No Wave movement

A pioneer of the New York City No Wave movement in the 1970s, Lydia Lunch served as singer and guitarist for Teenage Jesus and the Jerks. By Schorle, Own work / Wikimedia Commons

included Teenage Jesus and the Jerks (Lydia Lunch), James Chance and the Contortions, DNA, Mars, Theoretical Girls, and Rhys Chatham. The 1978 compilation album *No New York* served to document the No Wave movement.

OI! (STREET PUNK) A British slang term for *hey* or *hey there*, the Oi! movement arose in the UK in the late 1970s and was applied to such working-class bands as Sham 69, Cockney Rejects, the 4-Skins, the Business, Anti-Establishment, Combat 84, Blitz, the Blood, and Angelic Upstarts. Oi! was later appropriated by skin-heads and neo-Nazi elements associated with the National Front (typified by explicitly White-supremacist punk band Skrewdriver). However, none of the earliest Oi! bands promoted racism or far-right politics.

QUEERCORE   Began in the mid-1980s, queercore expressed itself through issues related to sexual and gender identity. Notable queercore bands included Pansy Division, Limp Wrist, and Queer Mutiny. San Francisco–based Outpunk Records specialized in queercore bands and released two influential queercore compilations: *There's a Faggot in the Pit* and *There's a Dyke in the Pit*, both released in 1992. An annual international queercore festival and gathering, Queeruption, was held annually between 1998 and 2017.

RIOT GRRRL   Notable Riot Grrrl bands include Bikini Kill, Bratmobile, and Sleater-Kinney, among others. For more information about the Riot Grrrl movement, see chapter 25: "Surface Envy: The Riot Grrrl Movement and Punk Rock Feminism."

SKA PUNK   Blending Jamaican and Caribbean rhythms with horn sections and punk-rock energy, the ska punk sound was exemplified by such bands as Operation Ivy, the Mighty Mighty Bosstones, Fishbone, Dance Hall Crashers, Sublime, the Porkers, Mad Caddies, English Beat, Citizen Fish, Less Than Jake, the Specials, Reel Big Fish, the Ernies, Culture Shock, the Interrupters, Goldfinger, Mustard Plug, and the Aquabats.

SKATE PUNK   Quoted in *More Fun in the New World*, skateboarding legend Tony Hawk declared, "Like skating, punk was raw. It was real. It was energetic. And it was pretty much all we listened to." Notable skate-punk bands include NOFX, Suicidal Tendencies, Bad Religion, Pennywise, Millencolin, JFA, Face to Face, Lagwagon, Rich Kids on LSD, Descendents, Aggression, Drunk Injuns, the Big Boys, Gang Green, Strung Out, Rancid, No Use for a Name, Blink-182, and the Offspring.

STRAIGHT EDGE   Coined by Ian MacKaye of Washington, DC, hardcore-punk band Minor Threat, the straight-edge movement advocated abstinence from recreational drug use, alcohol, tobacco, caffeine, and/or promiscuous sex as a reaction against the self-destructive excesses of the punk-rock scene. Some straight-edge

advocates also adopted a vegetarian or vegan lifestyle. The movement was named after the Minor Threat track "Straight Edge" off
the band's 1984 self-titled debut album, which featured the lyrics
"I've got better things to do/Than sit around and fuck my head."
Other bands that adopted the straight-edge ethic at one time or
another include Youth of Today, SSD, 7 Seconds, Bold, Uniform
Choice, Gorilla Biscuits, and Straight Ahead, among others.

10

Life of Pain

The Rise of American Hardcore Punk

One person's roar is another's whine, just as one person's music is another's unendurable noise. —Henry Rollins

In a 1981 article titled "L.A. Punk" for *New Music Express*, rock critic Mick Farren captured the essence of hardcore punk: "Something nasty is lurking on the fringes of Reaganland. The children of this polluted capitalist utopia are being dragged by a grim, black anger into the nihilist world of Darby Crash. They are being infected with an inarticulate rage against everything that has been sold to them as good and desirable since the time they could crawl."

In contrast to the early days of the punk scene in New York City and London, hardcore arose in unlikely places, like the affluent suburbs of Orange County, California, with bands such as Black Flag, the Germs, T.S.O.L., the Circle Jerks, Red Kross, Adolescents, and Fear. The Washington, DC, hardcore scene also thrived with such classic bands as Bad Brains and Minor Threat.

Hardcore isn't for everyone. In *A Cultural Dictionary of Punk*, Nicholas Rombes commented, "Here is a criticism of hardcore: Basically, it all sounds the same. Screamed lyrics, short songs, fast tempos."

ADOLESCENTS Formed in Fullerton, California, in 1980, this highly energetic hardcore punk band exemplified teenage angst and featured the original lineup of lead singer Tony Cadena, guitarists (and brothers) Rikk Agnew and Frank Agnew Jr., bassist Steve Soto, and drummer Casey Royer. The Adolescents were one of the major Orange County bands to emerge in the early 1980s, along with Social Distortion and Agent Orange. The band released their self-titled debut album (aka the "Blue Album") in 1981 on the Frontier label to critical acclaim, featuring memorable tracks such as "Kids of the Black Hole" ("Kids in the fast lane living for today/No rules to abide by and no rules to obey"), "Amoeba," "L.A. Girl" (a response to the Doors' classic track "L.A. Woman"), and "Self Destruct." In "Wrecking Crew," they declared themselves "just a wrecking crew/ Bored boys with nothing to do."

Essential Listening: *Adolescents* (1981), *Balboa Fun*Zone* (1988)

AGNOSTIC FRONT   Formed in New York City in 1982, Agnostic Front has been dubbed the "Godfathers of Modern Hardcore." The band was a staple of CBGB's hardcore matinee shows in the early 1980s and released the album *Live at CBGB* in 1989. The original Agnostic Front lineup featured lead singer Roger Miret, guitarist Vinnie Stigma, bassist Adam Moochie, and drummer Ray Beez.

Essential Listening: *Victim in Pain* (1984)

BAD BRAINS   Formed in Washington, DC, in 1977 (as a jazz fusion band called Mind Power!), Bad Brains are widely regarded as pioneers of hardcore punk, although their blistering speed and distinctive sound also incorporated elements of reggae (all the band members became dedicated Rastafarians), as well as funk, hip hop, soul, and heavy metal. The band's name came from the Ramones song "Bad Brain," off their fourth studio album, *Road to Ruin* (1978). The classic Bad Brains lineup consisted of highly talented but often erratic and aloof lead singer H.R. (aka Human Rights, aka Paul Hudson), lead guitarist Gary "Dr. Know" Miller, bassist Darryl Jenifer, and H.R.'s brother Earl Hudson on drums. The band released their first single, "Pay to Cum," in 1980. The track lasted just one minute and twenty-four seconds. Bad Brains has broken up and re-formed several times over the years (after 1998 briefly under

Originally a jazz fusion band called Mind Power!, pioneering hardcore punk band Bad Brains was called "the mother of all black hard-rock bands" by *Rolling Stone*. Sony Pictures Classics/Photofest

the name Soul Brains). The fascinating 2016 film *Finding Joseph I: The HR from Bad Brains Documentary* details H.R.'s life, career, and struggles with schizophrenia.

Essential Listening: *Bad Brains* (1982), *Rock for Light* (1983), *I Against I* (1986)

BAD RELIGION   Formed in Los Angeles in 1980, Bad Religion was started by high school buddies Greg Graffin and Brett Gurewitz, along with Jay Bentley. In the true spirit of DIY, the band formed their own label, Epitaph Records. In 1982, Bad Religion released their debut studio album, *How Could Hell Be Any Worse*, which featured one of the band's most enduring tracks, "We're Only Gonna Die." The band, which has experienced multiple lineup changes over the years, has influenced the likes of the Offspring,

Green Day, and Blink 182. Bad Religion released its seventeenth album, *Age of Reason*, in 2019.

Essential Listening: *How Could Hell Be Any Worse?* (1983), *Suffer* (1988), *No Control* (1989), *Against the Grain* (1990), *Stranger Than Fiction* (1994)

BLACK FLAG   Formed by Greg Ginn and Chuck Dukowski (Gary McDaniel, who changed his name as a tribute to writer Charles Bukowski) in Hermosa Beach, California, in 1977, Black Flag (originally known as Panic) are true pioneers of hardcore punk. The band had inauspicious beginnings, however, scoring one of their first gigs by claiming they were a Fleetwood Mac cover band. The band's first lead singer, Keith Morris, later went on to form the Circle Jerks. According to Morris in his 2016 memoir, *My Damage*, "The first time I heard Greg [Ginn] play I was absolutely floored. I didn't expect what I heard blasting out of the speakers to be coming from *him*. The energy, the tempo, and most of all, the *anger* were completely unexpected. . . . Here was this tall, goofy-looking guy just wailing away on his guitar in a way I'd never seen before."

Ginn formed the independent record label SST in 1978 (which would go on to release the work of such bands as Husker Du, the Meat Puppets, Sonic Youth, and the Minutemen) and released the first Black Flag EP, *Nervous Breakdown*, which featured "Nervous Breakdown," "Fix Me," "I've Had It," and "Wasted"—which comprised "five minutes of unvarnished punk rock fury," according to Morris. Cultural historian Nicholas Rombes, in *A Cultural*

Artist Raymond Pettibon of SST Records became renowned for his flyer art for bands such as Black Flag (the band's founder and guitarist Greg Ginn was his brother).

Dictionary of Punk, characterizes the sound of *Nervous Breakdown* as "punk boiled down to a level of frightening purity. There is no fat on these songs, no excess."

In 1980, Henry Rollins (born Henry Garfield) joined Black Flag, which released their first full-length album, *Damaged*, the following year. Before he became the band's lead singer, Rollins had been the manager of a Washington, DC, Haagen-Daz ice cream shop and roadie for the Teen Idles (which later morphed into hardcore punk band Minor Threat). *Damaged* is full of such straight-to-the-chase classics as "Spray Paint," "Police Story," "TV Party," and "Six Pack." In an early interview, Rollins described his intense performance style: "I feel pain every day of my life. When you see me perform, it's that pain you're seeing coming out. I put all my emotions, all my feelings, and my body on the line."

Known for their serious disposition (one critic wrote that the band had "all the humor of a muscular dystrophy telethon") and relentless touring across the United States, Black Flag broke up in 1986, but has reunited in various incarnations over the years. By the way, the first punk rock show Kurt Cobain attended was Black Flag at Mountaineer Club in Seattle, Washington, in 1984.

Essential Listening: *Damaged* (1981), *The First Four Years* (1983), *My War* (1984), *Slip It In* (1984)

CIRCLE JERKS   Formed in 1979 by Black Flag's first lead singer, Keith Morris, and former Red Kross guitarist Greg Hetson, the Circle Jerks released their debut album, *Group Sex*, in 1980. The album features fourteen songs in fifteen minutes—including four songs that Morris had performed with Black Flag: "Wasted," "Don't Care," "Behind the Door," and "Red Tape." In 1984, the band appeared in the cult film *Repo Man*, performing an acoustic lounge version of "When the Shit Hits the Fan." The Circle Jerks have influenced such bands as the Offspring, Pennywise, Anti-Flag, and Dropkick Murphys. In 2016, Morris published his critically acclaimed autobiography, *My Damage: The Story of a Punk Survivor*, in which he remarks, "The whole idea behind the Circle Jerks was to have fun: No pressure. No rules. Let's party and have a good time. . . . We wanted to be the band who was playing the party, pumping the keg, and pouring drinks for everybody."

Essential Listening: *Group Sex* (1980), *Wild in the Streets* (1982), *Golden Shower of Hits* (1983)

DEAD KENNEDYS   Formed in San Francisco in 1978 and arguably the most political of American hardcore bands, the Dead Kennedys featured lead singer Jello Biafra (Eric Boucher), guitarist East Bay Ray (Raymond John Pepperell), bassist Klaus Flouride (Geoffrey Lyall), and Ted (Bruce Slesinger), who was later replaced by D. H. Peligro (Darren Henley). Although the band's name was criticized for sheer tastelessness, Biafra remarked that it symbolized "the end of the American Dream and the beginning of the decline and fall of the American empire." In 1979, the band released its debut single, "California Uber Alles," which served as a satirical attack directed toward then California governor Jerry Brown.

Biafra and East Bay Ray formed the independent record label Alternative Tentacles in 1979 (the same year that Biafra ran for mayor of San Francisco and finished fourth out of ten candidates!). In addition to Dead Kennedys albums, Alternative Tentacles released records by Neurosis, Butthole Surfers, Leftover Crack, and Zolar X, among others. Released by IRS Records in 1980, the Dead Kennedys' debut album, *Fresh Fruit for Rotting Vegetables*, featured such enduring punk classics as "Kill the Poor," "California Uber Alles," and "Holiday in Cambodia." Other classic Dead Kennedys songs include "Too Drunk to Fuck," "Police Truck," "MTV Get Off the Air," "Bleed for Me," "Let's Lynch the Landlord," "Riot," "We Got a Bigger Problem Now," and "Nazi Punks Fuck Off." In a 1985 *Maximum RocknRoll* interview, Biafra remarked, "Our whole reason for starting a band was to annoy the living fuck out of everyone we could." The Dead Kennedys called it quits in 1986.

Essential Recordings: *Fresh Fruit for Rotting Vegetables* (1980), *Plastic Surgery Disasters* (1982)

DEAD MILKMEN   Formed in Philadelphia in 1983, the Dead Milkmen are best known for two catchy hits: "Bitchin' Camaro," from the band's 1985 debut album, *Big Lizard in My Backyard*; and the MTV staple "Punk Rock Girl," from their 1988 *Beelzebubba* album. According to legend, the band took its name from the character Milkman Dead in Toni Morrison's 1977 novel, *Song of Solomon*. The original Dead Milkmen lineup consisted of vocalist/keyboardist Rodney Anonymous (Rodney Linderman), guitarist/vocalist Joe Jack Talcum (Joe Genaro), bassist Dave Blood (Dave Schulthise), and drummer Dean Clean (Dean Sabatino). The band split up in 1995 but regrouped in 2008 and released two more albums: *The King in Yellow* (2011) and *Pretty Music for Pretty People* (2014). Schulthise died of an intentional drug overdose at the age of forty-seven on March 10, 2004.

Essential Listening: *Big Lizard in My Backyard* (1985)

DESCENDENTS   One of the first things everyone remembers about the Descendents is that they have a mascot: a cartoon caricature of singer Milo Aukerman that first appeared on the band's critically acclaimed 1982 debut album, *Milo Goes to College* (Milo actually did go to college and received his PhD in biology from UC San Diego). The Descendents were formed in 1977 in Manhattan Beach, California, by guitarist Frank Navetta, bassist Tony Lombardo, and drummer Bill Stevenson, who soon enlisted his high school friend, Aukerman, into the band.

The Descendents have released only eight albums over the years, the latest being *9th & Walnut* in 2021. However, they have influenced many pop-punk and skate-punk bands, such as NOFX, the Offspring, the Ataris, Green Day, Pennywise, Blink-182, and the Bouncing Souls, among others. Blink-182 vocalist/guitarist Tom DeLonge stated, "Everything about how I sing and play guitar came from this band." A documentary about the band, *Filmage: The Story of Descendents/All*, premiered in 2014. It features interviews with the likes of Fat Mike of NOFX, Chuck Dukowski of Black Flag, Dave Grohl of Nirvana and Foo Fighters, Keith Morris of Black Flag and Circle Jerks, Kim Shattuck of the Muffs, and Mike Watt of Minutemen.

Essential Listening: *Milo Goes to College* (1982), *I Don't Want to Grow Up* (1985), *Cool to Be You* (2004)

FEAR Formed in Los Angeles in 1977, Fear was known for its relentless verbal abuse of its audience, as well as a notorious appearance on *Saturday Night Live* on Halloween 1981, when stage divers and slam dancers (including *SNL* legend John Belushi) created total havoc. The classic Fear lineup featured lead singer Lee Ving, guitarist Philo Cramer, bassist Derf Scratch, and drummer Spit Stix. The band performed some of their classic material in the 1981 documentary *The Decline of Western Civilization*, such as "Beef Bologna," "I Don't Care about You" (a great punk anthem with a simple message: "I don't care about you/Fuck you"), "I Love Livin' in the City," and "Let's Have a War." Ving simultaneously pursued an extremely low-key acting career that included bit roles as a sleazy strip club owner in *Flashdance* (1983), an obnoxious cable guy in *The Wild Life* (1984), and a sadistic gang leader in *Dudes* (1987). In addition, Fear's "Let's Have a War" was included on the punk-inspired soundtrack of the 1984 cult film *Repo Man*.

Essential Listening: *The Record* (1982)

FLIPPER With their signature slowed-down, bass-driven style, Flipper later influenced such grunge bands as the Melvins and Nirvana (Krist Novoselic played with the band in the 2000s). Formed in San Francisco in 1979, the band featured vocalist Ricky Williams (formerly of the Sleepers), guitarist Ted Falconi (formerly of Rad Command), bassist Will Shatter (formerly of Negative Trend), and drummer Steve DePace (formerly of Negative Trend). Williams was soon fired from the band and replaced by Bruce "Loose" Calderwood. The band released only four studio albums over the years: *Album: Generic Flipper* (1982), *Gone Fishin'* (1984), *American Grafishy* (1993), and *Love* (2009), which features Novoselic. Flipper appears in the 2006 documentary *American Hardcore: The History of American Punk Rock 1980–1986* performing "Ha Ha Ha."

Essential Listening: *Album—Generic Flipper* (1982), *Gone Fishin'* (1984)

THE GERMS The Germs hit the Los Angeles punk scene in 1976, briefly calling themselves Sophistifuck and the Revlon Spam Queens. The band was the brainchild of Darby Crash (aka Bobby Pyn; real name: Jan Paul Beahm) and Pat Smear (Georg Ruthenberg). Believe it or not, Belinda Carlisle of the Go-Go's was the band's original drummer. She was known as Dottie Danger at the time! However, the classic Germs lineup featured Crash on vocals, Smear on guitar, bassist Lorna Doom (Teresa Marie Ryan), and drummer Dan Bolles. The band drew early inspiration from the New York Dolls, Iggy Pop, the Ramones, David Bowie, and the Sex Pistols (although Crash was also a big fan of Queen!). They

Led by highly eccentric frontman, Darby Crash, the Germs helped pioneer the Los Angeles punk scene in the late 1970s and appeared in the 1981 documentary, *The Decline of Western Civilization.*

recorded the first real L.A. punk single, "Forming." Music critic Barney Hoskyns in *Waiting for the Sun* referred to Crash as "LA's own Sid Vicious, a dysfunctional Hollywood hooligan chasing a fantasy of Iggy-style self-destruction." The lyrics to "Manimal" pretty much capture Crash's deranged mind-set: "I came into this world like a puzzled panther/Waiting to be caged/But something stood in the way/I was never quite tamed."

The essence of the Germs live in concert was perfectly captured in the classic 1981 documentary *The Decline of Western Civilization*, in which the band performs "Manimal" and "Shutdown." According to Angry Samoans guitarist Gregg Turner, "I always hated the Germs, yet at the same time it was a perfect commentary on LA. Here was some guy who was just regurgitating Bowie and every single rock-star move, and yet it was grotesque and funny." The Germs managed to release only one album, *GI* (1979), which was produced by Joan Jett and received critical accolades. On December 7, 1980, Crash died of an intentional heroin overdose at the age of twenty-two. His life story was depicted in the 2005 film *What We Do Is Secret*. Smear went on to perform with both Nirvana and Foo Fighters, among other bands.

Essential Listening: *GI* (1979)

HUSKER DU Named after a board game in the early 1950s that means "Do you remember?" in Danish, this eclectic St. Paul, Minnesota, trio formed in 1979 and featured guitarist/vocalist Bob Mould, bassist/vocalist Greg Norton, and drummer/vocalist Grant Hart. The band created their own label, Reflex Records, and released their debut album, *Everything Falls Apart*, in 1983, followed by the critically acclaimed double album *Zen Arcade* in 1984. They disbanded in 1988. Nirvana's Krist Novoselic once exclaimed that Nirvana's musical style was nothing new since "Husker Du did it before us." Novoselic's Nirvana bandmate Dave Grohl described *Zen Arcade* as "the Byrds meet Black Flag."

Essential Listening: *Everything Falls Apart* (1983), *Zen Arcade* (1984), *New Day Rising* (1985), *Flip Your Wig* (1985), *Warehouse: Songs and Stories* (1987)

MINOR THREAT Lead singer Ian MacKaye (a teenage skateboard fanatic) and drummer Jeff Nelson formed Washington, DC–based hardcore band Minor Threat in 1980 and quickly recruited guitarist Lyle Preslar and bassist Brian Baker to complete the original lineup (the band was originally known as the Teen Idles). Influenced by both Bad Brains and the Cramps, MacKaye and Nelson also formed their own label, Dischord Records, which later released works by such notable bands as Jawbox, Soulside, Dag Nasty, and Fugazi (another of MacKaye's bands). None other than a young Henry Garfield (Rollins) served as the band's roadie for a time.

According to *Trouser Press*, Minor Threat "played fast, impassioned music that defined the [hardcore punk] genre while never succumbing to its shortcomings." The band's 1982 song "Straight Edge" served to define the straight-edge movement characterized by abstinence from drugs, alcohol, and promiscuous sex. "Out of Step (with the World)" also summed up the straight-edge movement with its lyrics "I don't smoke/Don't drink/Don't fuck/At least I can fucking think." The band released a single highly influential album, *Out of Step*, in 1983. It is considered to be a landmark album of the hardcore-punk genre. After Minor Threat broke up in 1983, MacKaye founded the post-hardcore band Fugazi. The band's name was taken from the 1986 book *Nam*, a critically acclaimed collection of Vietnam veteran war stories edited by Mark Baker (*fugazi* being military slang for a "fucked-up situation"). According to Joe Strummer of the Clash, "Ian's the only one who ever did the punk thing right from day one and followed through on it all the way."

Essential Listening: *Out of Step* (1983), *Minor Threat* (1984)

MINUTEMEN   Formed in San Pedro, California, in 1980, Minutemen were known for pioneering post-hardcore and alternative rock. The band featured guitarist/vocalist D. Boon (Dennis Dale Boon), bassist/vocalist Mike Watt, and drummer Georg Hurley. Minutemen cited such influences as Captain Beefheart, Richard Hell & the Voidoids, Wire, Gang of Four, and the Urinals. According to Watt, "I think punk rock, especially for me, was a big middle finger to this whole talent thing." The band released their debut album, *The Punch Line*, in 1981 via SST Records, followed by *What Makes a Man Start Fires?* (1983), *Double Nickels on the Dime* (1984), and *3-Way Tie (for Last)* (1985). Tragically, Boon died at the age of twenty-seven in a van accident on Interstate 10 in the Arizona desert on December 22, 1985, and the rest of the band decided to call it quits.

Essential Listening: *The Punch Line* (1981), *What Makes a Man Start Fires?* (1983), *Double Nickles on the Dime* (1984)

MISFITS   These days it seems like those iconic Misfits T-shirts are practically everywhere, but it's a good bet that a solid majority of those people wearing the shirts have never heard a single song from the band. Pioneers of the so-called "horror-punk" subgenre and known for their gothic schlock horror look and campy theatrics, the band was founded in Lodi, New Jersey, in 1977, by singer/songwriter/keyboardist Glenn Danzig and drummer Manny Martinez. They soon recruited bassist Jerry Only. The band's name came from Marilyn Monroe's last film, *The Misfits* (1962), which was directed by John Huston and also starred Clark Gable and Montgomery Clift.

In 1982, the Misfits released their debut album, *Walk among Us*, which features such classics as "Night of the Living Dead," "Skulls," and "Mommy, Can I Go Out and Kill Tonight?" According to *Trouser Press*, the album "practically wallows in psychotronic shock imagery." The Misfits have influenced the likes of Metallica, Guns N' Roses, Green Day, the Offspring, NOFX, My Chemical Romance, AFI, and Marilyn Manson.

Essential Listening: *Walk among Us* (1978)

NOFX   Formed in Los Angeles in 1983, NOFX featured the original lineup of vocalist/bassist Fat Mike (Michael John Burkett), guitarist Eric Melvin, and drummer Erik Sandin. El Hefe (Aaron Abeyta) joined the band in 1991. The band has released fourteen albums over the years, the first being *Liberal Animation* (1988) and the latest being *Single Album* (2021). Their fifth album, *Punk in Drublic* (1994), was arguably their best effort. The band has influenced the likes of the Melvins, Nirvana, the Offspring, Blink-182, Sum 41, and Green Day.

Essential Listening: *Punk in Drublic* (1994), *So Long and Thanks for All the Shoes* (1997), *Pump Up the Valuum* (2000), *The War on Errorism* (2003)

SOCIAL DISTORTION   Known as the "Godfathers of SoCal punk," Social Distortion was formed in Fullerton, California, in 1978. Current band members include lead singer/guitarist Mike Ness (who has been the band's only constant member over the years), rhythm guitarist Jonny Wickersham, bassist Brent Harding, keyboardist David Kalish, and drummer David Hidalgo Jr. The band released their debut album, *Mommy's Little Monster*, in 1983, followed by

Prison Bound in 1988. However, their popularity skyrocketed with the release of their self-titled third album in 1990, which featured the hit singles "Story of My Life" and "Ball and Chain," as well as a cover of the Johnny Cash classic "Ring of Fire." Social Distortion's influence has extended to the likes of Bad Religion, Rancid, the Offspring, Guns N' Roses, and Backyard Babies.

Essential Listening: *Mommy's Little Monster* (1983), *Prison Bound* (1988), *Social Distortion* (1990)

SUICIDAL TENDENCIES Founded by lead singer Mike "Cyco Miko" Muir in Venice, California, in 1980, Suicidal Tendencies is known as one of the "Fathers of Crossover Thrash," a blend of thrash metal and hardcore punk rock. The band's classic lineup also featured guitarist Rocky George, guitarist Mike Clark, bassist Robert Trujillio, and drummer R. J. Herrera. In 1983, the band released their self-titled debut album, which spawned the popular single and MTV staple "Institutionalized." In 1990, Suicidal Tendencies released their fifth album, *Lights . . . Camera . . . Revolution!* which spawned two more tracks that got heavy rotation on MTV's *Headbangers Ball*: "You Can't Bring Me Down" and "Send Me Your Money." With an ever-changing lineup, Suicidal Tendencies has released thirteen studio albums over the years, their latest being *Still Cyco Punk after All These Years* in 2018.

Essential Listening: *Suicidal Tendencies* (1983), *Lights . . . Camera . . . Revolution!* (1990)

T.S.O.L. Formed in Long Beach, California, in 1978, T.S.O.L. (True Sounds of Liberty) were regulars on the Orange County punk circuit and performed regularly at the legendary Cuckoo's Nest in Costa Mesa (as depicted in the 2012 documentary *Clockwork Orange County*). The original T.S.O.L. lineup featured vocalist Jack Grisham, guitarist Ron Emory, bassist Mike Roche, and drummer Todd Barnes. According to legend, the band acquired their instruments by breaking into a music store in the middle of the night. They released their debut album, *Dance with Me*, in 1981. T.S.O.L. has been featured on the soundtracks for the films *Suburbia*

(1984), *The Return of the Living Dead* (1985), and *Dangerously Close* (1986).

Essential Listening: *Dance with Me* (1981), *Beneath the Shadows* (1983), *Change Today?* (1984)

11

Burning Down
the House

Legendary Punk-Rock Clubs

Where there is young people and vitality, you're going to
find punk rock. —Henry Rollins

When it comes to infamous punk-rock venues, just about everyone
has their personal favorite shithole dive bar, such as the original
9:30 Club in Washington, DC; the Rat in Boston; City Gardens in
Trenton, New Jersey; or the Anthrax in Stamford, Connecticut. Of
course, during the golden age of punk rock in NYC in the mid- to
late 1970s, legendary clubs like CBGBs and Max's Kansas City
ruled the roost, while across the pond, punk simultaneously took
off at renowned venues such as 100 Club, the Marquee, and Roxy.
On the West Coast, the hardcore punk scene arrived and thrived
at such popular dives as the Masque, Cuckoo's Nest, and Cathay
de Grande.

9:30 CLUB—WASHINGTON, DC   An infamous dive bar, the 9:30 Club
first opened its doors in 1980 at 930 F Street NW in a decrepit section of Washington, DC, that still had boarded-up buildings resulting from the 1968 riots, which took place between April 4 and 8
of that year following the assassination of civil rights leader Martin
Luther King Jr. Notable bands that took the stage at the 9:30 Club
over the years included Black Flag, Red Hot Chili Peppers, Public
Enemy, Fugazi, Bad Brains, R.E.M., Nirvana, and Green Day, as

well as the occasional outlier such as veteran crooner Tony Bennett. In 1996, the 9:30 Club moved to a new location at the old
gospel radio station WUST's building at 815 V Street, where Duke
Ellington's Club had been in the late 1940s. The Smashing Pumpkins launched the new venue with two sold-out shows. Decades
later, the 9:30 Club continues to thrive.

100 CLUB—LONDON, ENGLAND   Starting out as a bustling jazz and
swing club in the 1940s known as the Feldman Jazz Club, the 100
Club at 100 Oxford Street in the West End of London evolved into
the UK's answer to New York City's CBGBs as a punk venue during the mid-1970s. In fact, the 100 Club today proudly boasts itself
as the "Oldest Independent Venue Worldwide" and the "spiritual
home" of the punk-rock movement. In fact, the Sex Pistols played
their first gig at the 100 Club on March 30, 1976.

In addition, the first annual 100 Club Punk Festival (aka Club
Punk Special) took place here in 1976. The festival's lineup featured the essence of the early London punk scene with bands such
as the Sex Pistols, Subway Sect, the Clash, the Vibrators, Siouxsie
and the Banshees, Stinky Toys, the Damned, and Buzzcocks taking
the stage. The opening line of *Melody Maker*'s review of the 100
Club Punk Festival read, "The 600 strong line that stretched across
two blocks was indisputable evidence that a new decade in rock is
about to begin."

THE ANTHRAX—STAMFORD, CONNECTICUT   An all-ages music venue
that hosted a great mix of punk and hardcore concerts during the
early to mid-1980s, the Anthrax was situated in the rundown basement of a makeshift art gallery. Among the many bands that took
the stage at the Anthrax included Black Flag, NOFX, Descendents,
Die Kreuzen, Dag Nasty, Fugazi, and Government Issue. In 1986,
the Anthrax closed its doors and reopened in a larger venue in
nearby Norwalk that eventually closed in 1990. Chris Daly's 2009
book *Everybody's Scene: The Story of Connecticut's Anthrax Club*
offers the definitive account of this fabled punk club.

CATHAY DE GRANDE—HOLLYWOOD, CALIFORNIA   A lively nightclub located at 1600 Argyle Avenue on the corner of Argyle and Selma in Hollywood, Cathay de Grande catered to the punk and alternative-rock crowd with a steady diet of raw and edgy performances by the likes of Bad Religion, Minutemen, Tex and the Horseheads, Dr. Know, Entropy, Social Distortion, the Vandals, Love Canal, T.S.O.L., Agent Orange, the Knitters, and others. One local publication even deemed the Cathay "the most dangerous club in America."

The Red Hot Chili Peppers performed for the first time here under their new band name (believe it or not, they were briefly performing under the name Tony Flow and the Miraculously Majestic Masters of Mayhem). In addition, local legends Top Jimmy & the Rhythm Pigs took the stage here every Monday night for three years. The Cathay closed its doors for good in 1985 with a farewell concert that featured the Circle Jerks, Violent Psychosis, and the Mentors with El Duce. In the NOFX song "The Desperation's Gone," Fat Mike sings, "Cathay de I miss your smell." Today, the Cathay site is occupied by the Argyle, an "elegant" dance and night-club that features craft cocktails.

CBGBS—NEW YORK CITY, NEW YORK   Widely regarded as the "Birth-place of Punk Rock," CBGB & OMFUG (Country, Bluegrass, Blues and Other Music for Uplifting Gormandizers) was opened by Hillel "Hilly" Kristal in 1973 in a former nineteenth-century saloon at 315 Bowery in the rundown Bowery district of Manhattan's East Village. A slew of up-and-coming bands took the tiny stage at this legendary dark and dingy club in the 1970s such as New York Dolls, Television, the Ramones, Johnny Thunders & the Heart-breakers, Patti Smith Group, Blondie, the Damned, the Cramps, the Police, Elvis Costello, Talking Heads, Lydia Lunch, and Dead Boys, among many others. Debbie Harry referred to Kristal as "the punk patron of music and art."

According to John Holmstrom, founder of *Punk* magazine, "Without CBGBs, there would've never been any punk rock, no Mudd Club, no Talking Heads, Television, Patti Smith, and therefore no hardcore scene, no grunge—just disco, hair metal,

Known as the "Birthplace of Punk," CBGBs in New York City closed its doors for good in 2006, but the club's original awning is on display at the Rock and Roll Hall of Fame in Cleveland, Ohio. By SAM HOWZIT/WIKIMEDIA COMMONS

Madonna, and MTV." In addition, many other immensely popular local and regional acts that failed to gain much national recognition also performed at CBGBs like the Dictators ("Teengenerate"), Mink Deville ("Spanish Stroll"), Sic Fucks ("Insects Rule My World"), Tuff Darts ("Your Love Is Like Nuclear Waste"), the Shirts ("Laugh and Walk Away"), Pere Ubu ("Life Stinks"), Wayne County and the Electric Chairs ("If You Don't Wanna Fuck Me, Fuck Off"), and Steel Tips ("Crazy Baby").

CBGBs also had the notorious reputation of having the most disgusting, graffiti-infested restroom of any New York City club (or throughout the United States for that matter!). In his foreword to *The Official Punk Book of Lists*, Danny Fields, the Ramones' first manager, called the toilet at CBGBs, "the epicenter of 'punk' culture in New York, the icon of our tight little universe." According to "Handsome" Dick Manitoba of the Dictators, "[CBGBs] was a shithole, but it was our shithole." Following a rent dispute, CBGBs closed its doors for good on October 15, 2006, with a final performance by none other than "punk poetess" Patti Smith. In 2013, the former site of CBGBs was added to the National Register of Historic Places as part of the Bowery Historic District. Published in 2005, *CBGB & OMFUG: Thirty Years from the Home of Underground Rock* serves as the definitive guide to CBGBs.

CITY GARDENS—TRENTON, NEW JERSEY   Described as an "odd-shaped concrete bunker" located in a burned-out section of Trenton, City Gardens (1979–2001) hosted the likes of the Ramones, the Circle Jerks, Danzig, R.E.M., Descendents, Fugazi, Butthole Surfers, Agnostic Front, Sonic Youth, the Bouncing Souls, A Flock of Seagulls, Thompson Twins, and Sinead O'Connor. Comedian Jon Stewart served as a bartender here in the mid-1980s. City Garden was profiled in both a 2014 documentary, *Riot on the Dance Floor*, and a 2014 book titled *No Slam Dancing, No Stage Diving, No Spikes: An Oral History of New Jersey's Legendary City Gardens*, by Amy Yates Wuelfing and Steven DiLodovico.

THE CROCODILE—SEATTLE, WASHINGTON   Known as the "Unofficial Capital of Grunge," the Crocodile (aka Crocodile Café or the Croc)

Opened in Seattle in 1991, the Crocodile Café soon earned a reputation as the "Unofficial Capital of Grunge." BY JOE MABEL/WIKIMEDIA COMMONS

opened in 1991 and hosted the likes of Nirvana, Pearl Jam, the Melvins, Mudhoney, Soundgarden, Social Distortion, Green Day, Cheap Trick, Dinosaur Jr., the Beastie Boys, and the Strokes.

CUCKOO'S NEST—COSTA MESA, CALIFORNIA   Immortalized in the off-beat 2012 documentary *Clockwork Orange County*, the Cuckoo's Nest was opened by Jerry Roach in 1976, at 1714 Placentia Avenue in Costa Mesa, and named after the 1975 film *One Flew Over the Cuckoo's Nest*. Orange County–area punk bands that performed at the Cuckoo's Nest included Black Flag, the Circle Jerks, T.S.O.L., Social Distortion, the Bags, the Controllers, Steamin' Freeman, the Slashers, the Vandals, and Vicious Circle.

During its entire existence between 1976 and 1981, the Cuck-oo's Nest was the site of frequent conflicts between the punks and local police, as well as between the punks and the rednecks who patronized Zubie's Bar & Grill, an "urban cowboy" joint next door. On the night of January 30, 1981, a Cuckoo's Nest regular named Pat Brown tried to run over two police officers in his car. The inci-dent was captured for posterity by the Vandals in their song "The Legend of Pat Brown." The complete insanity that surrounded the Cuckoo's Nest was documented in the 1981 black-and-white and grainy film, *Urban Struggle: The Battle of the Cuckoo's Nest*.

HONG KONG CAFÉ—LOS ANGELES, CALIFORNIA   Opened at 425 Gin Ling Way in the Chinatown district of Los Angeles in 1979, the Hong Kong Café competed for music acts with nearby Madame Wong's. However, the Hong Kong Café often hosted edgier punk-rock acts such as the Alley Cats, the Weirdos, the Plugz, Catholic Discipline, the Mau-Mau's, the Smart Pills, the Weasels, X, Bates Motel, Suburban Lawns, the Germs, and the Bags. A flyer promoting a show featuring the Germs and Middle Class at the Hong Kong Café exclaimed, "In celebration of the crippled, the psychotic, the battered, the dying." Concert footage shot at the Hong Kong Café appears in the 1981 documentary *The Decline of Western Civilization*.

THE LOFT—BALTIMORE, MARYLAND   Also known as the Eutaw Street Clubhouse and Jules' Loft, the Loft served as the gathering place for Baltimore's hardcore punk scene during the 1980s. Bands such as Descendents, the Crucifucks, Government Issue, and Youth Brigade took the stage here, as well as local groups such as Bollocks, Fear of God, OTR, and Law & Order.

MABUHAY GARDENS—SAN FRANCISCO, CALIFORNIA   Sometimes referred to as the "CBGBs of San Francisco," Mabuhay Gardens (aka "The Mab" and "The Fab Mab") served as one of the best of the West Coast punk clubs. A diverse array of bands took the stage here, such as the Dead Kennedys, Avengers, Black Flag, Blondie, the Nuns, the Dills, Pearl Harbor and the Explosions, the Mortals, Devo, the Go-Go's, Toy Dolls, Jim Carroll Band, the Runaways, and many more. Known as the "Pope of Punk" and "Poor Man's Bill Graham," the somewhat abrasive and always entertaining local personality Dirk Dirksen served as music promotor and emcee for the Mab, which was located among several strip clubs at 443 Broadway in North Beach, just down the street from the legendary Beat Generation hangout, City Lights Bookstore. The Mab closed its doors for good in 1987 and today is home to an event showplace called Fame Venue.

MARQUEE CLUB—LONDON, ENGLAND   The famous Marquee Club originally opened as a jazz joint in 1958 at its first location on Oxford Street. In 1964, the Marquee moved to a new location at 90 Wardour Street and soon hosted performances from the likes of the Rolling Stones, the Who, and Jimi Hendrix. In the late 1970s, pub-rock, punk, and new-wave bands such as Eddie and the Hot Rods, the Stranglers, the Sex Pistols, X-Ray Spex, the Cure, Generation X, Adam and the Ants, Joy Division, the Police, and the Jam took the stage here.

THE MASQUE—HOLLYWOOD, CALIFORNIA   Billed as "an alternative rock and roll cabaret" and tucked in the basement of the Pussycat Theater at 1655 North Cherokee Avenue on Hollywood Boulevard, the Masque was only open for about a year from 1977 to 1978.

However, in that short period, the club showcased the early Los Angeles punk scene by hosting such up-and-coming bands as the Germs, Avengers, Black Flag, the Weirdos, the Mau-Mau's, X, the Flesh Eaters, the Dickies, the Bags, the Alley Cats, the Screamers, Rhino 39, the Controllers, the Nerves, the Skulls, the Plugz, the Dils, and the Zeros, among many others.

The Masque was the brainchild of Scottish-born entrepreneur Brendan Mullen, who cowrote (with Marc Spitz) the 2001 book *We Got the Neutron Bomb: The Untold Story of LA Punk* and authored *Live at the Masque: Nightmare in Punk Alley*. According to Keith Morris in his 2016 memoir *My Damage*, the Masque "was *the* place to go see punk rock music in LA. In many ways it was LA's version of CBGB, only it was way more under the radar—it was literally underground—and it lasted only for a short time. You can't tell the story of LA punk rock without the Masque."

MAX'S KANSAS CITY—NEW YORK CITY   Known as the place where pop art, glam rock, and punk intersected, Max's Kansas City was located at 213 Park Avenue South in Lower Manhattan and often frequented by the likes of Andy Warhol, Iggy Pop, Lou Reed, and David Bowie. Debbie Harry of Blondie was a server here briefly in the early 1970s. In their first-ever New York City performance, Bob Marley and the Wailers opened for Bruce Springsteen at Max's in 1973. In the mid-1970s, bands such as the Heartbreakers, the Fast, Suicide, the Cramps, the Senders, Devo, Patti Smith, Wayne County, the Blessed, and Cherry Vanilla performed at Max's. In their song "New York," the Sex Pistols referenced Max's: "Think it is well playing Max's Kansas/You're looking bored/And you're acting flash/With nothing in your gut." In November 1981, Max's closed for good, with Bad Brains and the Beastie Boys performing the final show.

MUDD CLUB—NEW YORK CITY   One of the major hot spots to showcase New York City's underground music scene, Mudd Club first opened its doors at 77 White Street in Lower Manhattan on Halloween night 1978. Believe it or not, the club's name referenced Dr. Samuel Mudd, the doctor who treated John Wilkes Booth after he assassinated President Abraham Lincoln in 1865. Performers such as Lou Reed, Johnny Thunders, the Cramps, X, the Bongos, Debbie Harry, and Lydia Lunch took the stage here. The B52's played their first New York City show at the Mudd Club. The Talking Heads' song "Life during Wartime" features the lyrics "This ain't no Mudd Club or CBGB/I ain't got time for that now."

The Mudd Club has also been immortalized in other songs such as "The Return of Jackie and Judy" by the Ramones ("Jackie is a punk/Judy is a runt/They went down to the Mudd Club/And they both got drunk") and "Mudd Club" by Frank Zappa. In addition, Beat Generation legends Allen Ginsberg ("Howl") and William S. Burroughs (*Naked Lunch*) gave literary readings here. The Mudd Club closed its doors for good in 1983.

THE RAT—BOSTON, MASSACHUSETTS   First opened in 1974, the cavernous Rathskeller (aka "The Rat") at 528 Commonwealth Avenue was known as the "granddaddy" of Boston rock clubs and catered to the college crowd. Known as both a "slam dancer's paradise" and as "CBGB's little brother" (both venues had disgusting toilets), the Rat was basically a cramped and smelly basement club with a beer-soaked floor.

Over the years, the Rat hosted such performers as Blondie, the Ramones, the Jam, the Pixies, Dead Kennedys, Talking Heads, R.E.M., the Motels, Dinosaur Jr., Sonic Youth, the Police, Soundgarden, the Young Snakes (featuring lead singer Aimee Mann), the Cars (who got their start here), and the Dropkick Murphys, among many others. The Rat closed its doors in 1997. The California rock band Camper Van Beethoven took a shot at the Rat in their 1988 song "Never Go Back," which features the lyrics "Never going to go back to the Rat/And play another mafia show again." Today the former site of the Rat is home to the luxurious Hotel Commonwealth.

THE ROXY—LONDON, ENGLAND   First opened at 41-43 Neal Street in London's Covent Garden on January 1, 1977, with a performance by the Clash, the Roxy quickly evolved into "the most happening place in the punk scene," according to T. V. Smith of the Adverts. Bands that took the stage here included the Damned, Eater, the

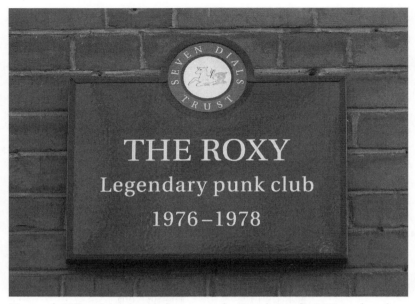

Many early UK punk bands took the stage at the Roxy during the 1970s such as the Damned, Siouxsie and the Banshees, Sham 69, and many more. BY SPUDGUN67/WIKI-MEDIA COMMONS

Jam, Wire, Slaughter and the Dogs, the Stranglers, Siouxsie and the Banshees, Sham 69, the Heartbreakers, GBH, and the Slits. The 1978 Crass song "Banned from the Roxy" features the line "I never much liked playing there anyway."

THE VIPER ROOM, WEST HOLLYWOOD, CALIFORNIA   Opened on August 14, 1993, the Viper Room at 8852 Sunset Boulevard in West Hollywood is "the most consistently hip club in town," according to the *Los Angeles Times*. Tragedy struck just a little over three months after the Viper Room opened in the early morning hours of Halloween night 1993 when actor River Phoenix collapsed outside the club and died of a drug overdose at the age of twenty-three. Actor Johnny Depp served as part owner of the Viper Room until 2004.

Musicians who have performed here over the years include Green Day, Iggy Pop, the Go-Go's, Billy Idol, the Black Crowes, Stone Temple Pilots, Counting Crows (lead singer Adam Duritz also served as a bartender here for a time), Oasis, Everclear, Concrete Blonde, Lenny Kravitz, Run-D.M.C., Bruce Springsteen, Pussycat Dolls, Matchbox 20, Tom Petty and the Heartbreakers, Neurotic Outsiders, Red Hot Chili Peppers, and even the "Man in Black" himself, Johnny Cash. The Viper Room also makes an appearance in the offbeat 2004 documentary *Dig!* which highlights the contentious relationship between two bands, the Brian Jonestown Massacre (BJM) and the Dandy Warhols. In *Dig!* raging megalomaniac Anton Newcombe, the outrageous lead singer of BJM, suffers a total meltdown and begins fighting with other members of the band during a notorious Viper Room performance.

WHISKY A GO GO—HOLLYWOOD, CALIFORNIA   An anchor of the Sunset Strip in Los Angeles, the Whisky a Go Go (aka The Whisky) at 8901 Sunset Boulevard has been around since 1964. Some of rock's biggest names have graced its stage, such as the Doors, Van Halen, Led Zeppelin, Kiss, Guns N' Roses, AC/DC, Metallica, and Mötley Crüe. In addition, the Whisky hosted early punk and new-wave performances by the likes of the Ramones, the Dictators, Misfits, Blondie, Talking Heads, XTC, the Jam, and Elvis Costello. In addition, local punk band the Germs recorded their first album here: *Germicide: Live at the Whisky, 1977.*

12

Smash It Up
The Most Notorious Punk-Rock Concerts and Tours

> A real theatrical experience shakes the calm of the senses, liberates the compressed unconscious and drives towards a kind of potential revolt. —Antonin Artaud

The essence of punk rock at its best is its sheer unpredictability. That's why a classic punk performance could take place literally anywhere, such as the Sex Pistols performing on a river cruise during the Silver Jubilee to ruffle the feathers of the royal family itself, Fear performing "Let's Start a War" in front of a mostly disgusted national audience of viewers on *Saturday Night Live*, or even psychobilly pioneers the Cramps playing a show at a California mental hospital! Sometimes the utter incongruity of a punk show can make it one for the ages, as when Black Flag filled in for none other than the Air Force Big Band at an outdoor concert in front of an audience of mostly affluent families at Polliwog Park in Manhattan Beach, California. The bottom line is that the very nature of punk is messy, iconoclastic, and always morphing into something else. That's why the spirit of punk will never die.

SEX PISTOLS—ANARCHY TOUR, ENGLAND (1976)   One of the most infamous tours in rock history, the Sex Pistols' Anarchy Tour was supposed to take place between December 3 and 26, 1976, to promote the band's debut single, "Anarchy in the UK," which Sex Pistols manager Malcolm McLaren had declared to be "a call to arms for the kids who believe that rock and roll was taken away from them. It's a statement of self-rule, of ultimate independence." In support of the Anarchy Tour were the Clash, the Damned, and Johnny Thunders and the Heartbreakers. However, most of the tour dates were cancelled by terrified local councils and student unions fearful of any incident that would cause negative publicity. Out of twenty or so gigs lined up for the band, only seven live shows didn't face the chopping block. Johnny Rotten later referred to the Anarchy Tour as the "go-nowhere-and-do-nothing tour."

Two days before the scheduled launch of the Anarchy Tour, on December 1, 1976, the Sex Pistols appeared as guests on the *Today* show for an infamous, profane-laden interview broadcast live and uncensored with British talk show host Bill Grundy after Queen dropped out at the last minute (lead singer Freddie Mercury needed emergency dental surgery). During the contentious exchange, Steve Jones called Grundy a "dirty fucker" and "fucking rotter" after the host subtly attempted to flirt with Siouxsie Sioux, who was part of the Bromley Contingent entourage present during the interview. Surprisingly, Johnny Rotten was rather restrained during the interview and only uttered the word *shit*. In fact, the whole interview seems quite tame by today's standards when loud and obnoxious talk shows like *The Jerry Springer Show* have dominated daytime television for decades.

Following the Grundy debacle, concert promoters pulled the plug on most of the gigs lined up for the upcoming Anarchy Tour. Grundy received a two-week suspension, but the interview did long-term damage to his career. The famous headline "The Filth and the Fury" appeared in the British tabloid *The Daily Mirror* a day after the interview, with the article's opening line exclaiming, "A pop group shocked millions of viewers last night with the filthiest language ever heard on British television." The *Daily Mirror* also reported that a truck driver allegedly became so upset after watching the show that he kicked in his TV screen.

On December 3, 1976, the Sex Pistols embarked on their bus tour with the goal of taking the stage at the University of East Anglia Student Union in Norwich for the first show of the Anarchy

Tour. However, the school's vice chancellor banned the show "on the grounds of protecting the safety and security of persons and property." The unpopular decision led to a sit-in by approximately fifty students. On December 6, the Pistols arrived at Leeds Polytechnic in Leeds, and an interviewer caught up with band, asking, "It's said that you're sick on stage, you spit at the audience and so on. I mean how could this be a good example to children?" Malcolm McLaren replied, "Well people are sick everywhere. People are sick and tired of this country telling them what to do." Later that

The Sex Pistols first gained widespread notoriety after appearing in a profanity-laden interview with Bill Grundy on the *Today* show on December 1, 1976. PHOTOFEST

night during the show, Rotten sarcastically addressed the rather lackluster crowd, "You're not wrecking the place. The *News of the World* will really be disappointed!"

On December 9, the Pistols performed at Electric Circus in Manchester, and Buzzcocks were hired to replace the Damned, whom McLaren had thrown off the tour "because they were no fucking good," according to the manager. On December 14, the band took the stage at Castle Cinema in Caerphilly, Wales. They were picketed by a group of carol-singing Christian protesters, whom Glen Matlock referred to as "religious maniacs" in his 1990 memoir. On December 19, the Pistols performed a second show at Electric Circus, followed by a gig at Cleethorpes' Winter Garden on December 20 and two shows at Woods Centre, Plymouth, on December 21 and 22. According to Jon Savage in *England's Dreaming*, the band then "returned to London exhausted, broke, homeless, and with an uncertain future."

Following the publicity storm generated by the *Today* appearance with Bill Grundy and the disastrous Anarchy Tour, British record label EMI terminated the Sex Pistols' contract on January 6, 1977, after only three months and a single song released, "Anarchy in the UK." In a hastily written press release, the record label stated, "EMI feels it is unable to promote this group's records internationally in view of the adverse publicity which has been generated over the last two months, although recent press reports of the behavior of the Sex Pistols appear to have been exaggerated." In response to the termination, the band fired off the so-called diss track "E.M.I.," which eventually appeared on *Never Mind the Bollocks, Here's the Sex Pistols*. *Paste* magazine referred to the song as "the group's middle finger salute aimed at the record industry."

PATTI SMITH—CURTIS-HIXON HALL, TAMPA, FLORIDA (1977)   In one of the stranger rock-concert lineups of all time, the iconoclastic Patti Smith Group opened for far more traditional rockers Bob Seger & the Silver Bullet Band at the now-defunct Curtis-Hixon Hall in Tampa, Florida, on January 23, 1977. During a highly energetic rendition of "Ain't It Strange," Smith nearly died for her art by tripping and plunging fifteen feet into the orchestra pit. The fall left her with a fractured spine and broken vertebrae in her neck, as well as a head wound that required twenty-two stitches, and she had to undergo months of intensive physical therapy. During her extended break from touring, Smith worked on material for her third studio album, *Easter*, which was released on March 3, 1978, and spawned her highest-charting single, "Because the Night" (cowritten with Bruce Springsteen), which reached no. 13 on the U.S. charts.

The "punk poet laureate" later blamed Seger's road crew for leaving her too little space on stage for her performance. Recalling the unfortunate incident in a July 2012 *Uncut* magazine interview, Smith remarked, "There've been many rumors. . . . 'Oh, she was stoned.' It wasn't like that. I was being careful on the stage because there wasn't as much room or light. I didn't whirl around as much as usual, but when I hit the monitor with my foot, it was half hanging over the lip of the stage."

SEX PISTOLS—RIVER THAMES JUBILEE BOAT CRUISE, LONDON, ENGLAND

(1977) Not everyone was thrilled by the prospect of Queen Elizabeth II celebrating the twenty-fifth anniversary of her accession to the throne on February 6, 1977, which set off a year of festivities known as the Silver Jubilee. In response to the Silver Jubilee and as a promotional stunt for the release of their second single, "God Save the Queen," the band's manager, Malcolm McLaren, rented a river boat to sail the performing Sex Pistols and a select group of partying passengers along the Thames River on June 7. The band—which by this point consisted of Johnny Rotten, Steve Jones, Paul Cook, and Sid Vicious—launched into "Anarchy in the UK" just as the boat passed by the Houses of Parliament.

After a frantic set that also included "God Save the Queen," "No Feeling," and "Pretty Vacant," police boats soon encircled the Sex Pistols party boat. Once the boat arrived back at Charing Cross pier, McLaren and several other members of the entourage were arrested, but not before the "P. T. Barnum of Punk Rock" screamed, "You fucking fascist bastards," at the police. According to Johnny Rotten in *The Bollocks Diaries*, "I didn't even know it was Jubilee. All I knew was we had a gig on a barge, that was it. All that police attention on the River Thames, wow. OK, we're annoying someone here, big time, which is great."

THE STRANGLERS—BATTERSEA PARK, LONDON, ENGLAND (1978)

During a legendary gig supported by Peter Gabriel and Scottish punk band the Skids at Battersea Park in London on September 16, 1978, pub rock/proto-punk band the Stranglers invited several strippers to join them onstage and disrobe during the band's rendition of their latest single, "Nice 'n' Sleazy," which had reached no. 18 on the UK charts. Some overzealous fans (and band members!) joined in the action and started stripping completely naked as well. Eventually the police showed up and put an end to the spectacle. The next day's headlines screamed, "Stranglers in Nude Woman Horror Shock." The Stranglers' first live album, *Live (X Cert)*, which was released in 1979, contains tracks recorded at the Battersea Park concert along with a performance at the Roundhouse in 1977.

THE CRAMPS—NAPA STATE MENTAL HOSPITAL, NAPA, CALIFORNIA

(1978)   One of the most bizarre and downright disturbing concerts in rock history took place when the Cramps (along with San Francisco punk band the Mutants) performed live at Napa State Mental Hospital in Napa, California, on June 13, 1978. The audience consisted of about one hundred patients, a scattering of hospital staff, and a dozen punkers who somehow got access to the gig.

For better or worse, about twenty minutes of the Cramps' set was captured for posterity by Target Video in grainy black-and-white images via a Sony Portapak camera. For unknown reasons, no video footage of the Mutants' set exists. The Cramps opened their set with "Mystery Plane," which features the opening lyrics: "My Daddy drives a UFO/Drops me off then he goes." Then lead singer Lux Interior announced to the crowd, "We're the Cramps and we're from New York City and we drove three thousand miles to play for you." Someone in the audience can be heard screaming, "Fuck you!" Interior continued his introduction, "And somebody told me you people are crazy, but I'm not so sure about that. You seem to be all right to me." In a January 14, 2015, interview with *Vice*, Brendan Early of the Mutants recalled of the concert, "It was like going to Mars, in terms of the interaction with the audience."

SEX PISTOLS—WINTERLAND BALLROOM, SAN FRANCISCO, CALIFORNIA

(1978)   The Sex Pistols' disastrous U.S. tour culminated with an infamous performance at Winterland Ballroom in San Francisco in front of a crowd of 4,500 onlookers on January 14, 1978. By this time, Johnny Rotten was barely speaking with his bandmates, and Sid Vicious had developed a serious heroin addiction (his bass was either unplugged or turned down for most of the band's live performances, including this one).

Local punk bands the Nuns and the Avengers opened for the Pistols, who embarked on a rather chaotic and lackluster set that included "God Save the Queen," "I Wanna Be Me," "Seventeen," "New York," "E.M.I.," "Belsen Was a Gas," "Bodies," "Holidays in the Sun," "Liar," "No Feelings," "Problems," and "Pretty Vacant." The band finished with a cover of the Stooges' classic "No Fun," after which Rotten famously asked the crowd, "Ever get the feeling you've been cheated?" He then dropped the microphone and quickly departed backstage.

According to rock critic Mikal Gilmore, an eyewitness to the debacle, in *Night Beat,*

> That night, Rotten danced—waded, actually—through a mounting pile of debris: everything from shoes, coins, books, and umbrellas, all heaved his way by a tense, adulatory crowd. Draped in a veil of smoke and sweat, the scene resembled nothing so much as a rehearsal for Armageddon, and Rotten rummaged through it all like some misplaced jester.

Winterland served as the last Sex Pistols performance until the band's "Filthy Lucre" reunion tour in 1996. A little over a year after the Winterland show, Sid Vicious, who was facing trial for the murder of his girlfriend, Nancy Spungen, died of a heroin overdose on February 2, 1979. The Sex Pistols' *Live at Winterland 1978* album was released in 2001.

The Sex Pistols' final show wasn't the only historic event that took place at Winterland. It was also the site of the Band's farewell concert on Thanksgiving Day 1976 that featured guest performances by Bob Dylan, Eric Clapton, Neil Young, Joni Mitchell, Ringo Starr, Muddy Waters, Ronnie Wood, Neil Diamond, and others. The event was memorialized by Martin Scorsese in the critically acclaimed documentary *The Last Waltz* (1978). The Winterland closed its doors for good after a New Year's Eve concert in 1978 that featured performances by the Grateful Dead, New Riders of the Purple Sage, and the Blues Brothers. The venue was demolished in 1985 and replaced by an apartment complex.

"ELKS LODGE RIOT"—ELKS LODGE HALL, LOS ANGELES, CALIFORNIA (1979) During the so-called "Elks Lodge Riot," "Elks Lodge Massacre, or "Punk Massacre" (take your pick) on March 17, 1979, the Los Angeles Police Department showed up in overwhelming numbers to break up a punk show at the Elks Lodge Hall in downtown Los Angeles featuring the Wipers, the Plugz, the Zeros, the Go-Go's, the Alley Cats, and X (the latter two bands never even got the opportunity to take the stage). Organized by legendary

With their debut album, *Beauty and the Beat* (1981), the Go-Go's became the first and only all-female rock band to reach No.1 on the Billboard album chart. PHOTOFEST

music promoter Brendan Mullen, the St. Patrick's Day event was supposed to serve as a benefit for the Masque, his groundbreaking Hollywood punk club.

The Wipers, Zeros, and Go-Go's all performed without a hitch. However, during the Plugz's set, the LAPD in full riot gear stormed the venue without explanation and herded the crowd of about six-hundred punks to the exits. According to various reports, seven fans were jailed and several others were hospitalized after being clubbed by police officers. The incident was later immortalized in the song "Elks Lodge Blues" by Los Angeles punk band the Gears.

BLACK FLAG—POLLIWOG PARK, MANHATTAN BEACH, CALIFORNIA (1979)   One of the most surreal performances in punk history took place when Black Flag took the stage during a free outdoor concert at Polliwog Park in laid-back and affluent Manhattan Beach, California, on July 22, 1979. Believe it or not, the legendary Los Angeles punk band was tapped to fill in for the Air Force Big Band and only got the gig because Black Flag's cofounder and guitarist Greg Ginn convinced concert promoters that they were a Fleetwood Mac cover band.

The Polliwog Park audience was primarily composed of families looking forward to spending a relaxing afternoon in the park, along with a handful of raucous, beer-swilling Black Flag fans. According to then lead singer Keith Morris (as related in his 2016 memoir *My Damage*), "As soon as we hit the first note the heavens opened up and it started raining down beer cans and banana peels, half-eaten cantaloupes and watermelon rinds. KFC bones and soggy sandwiches. All sorts of stuff. Whatever the crowd could find they threw at us." Bassist Chuck Dukowski reportedly picked up a sandwich off the stage, casually ate it, and continued playing his guitar. At one point, Morris yelled to the audience, "You can either be here with us or you can go home and watch Walt fuckin' Disney!" The Black Flag gig lasted a total of twenty-five minutes before concert promoters wisely pulled a plug on the performance. By that point, many parents had already collected their children and fled the park in disgust.

FEAR—SATURDAY NIGHT LIVE, STUDIO 8H, NBC STUDIOS, NEW YORK CITY

(1981) Legendary comedian and punk rock fan John Belushi somehow managed to convince the producers of *Saturday Night Live* to book abrasive Los Angeles punk band Fear as musical guests for a live performance on the 1981 Halloween episode of the late-night comedy show. Veteran film actor Donald Pleasence (Dr. Loomis from *Halloween*), who was that week's SNL host, introduced the band: "Ladies and gentlemen, Fear!" In front of an enthusiastic slam-dancing and stage-diving crowd (that included Belushi as well as Ian MacKaye of Minor Threat, Harley Flanagan of Cro-Mags, Tesco Vee of the Meatmen,

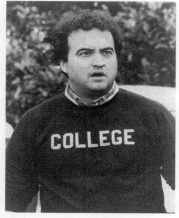

Punk fan John Belushi was instrumental in securing the notorious guest appearance of Fear on *Saturday Night Live* on October 31, 1981, that led to the band being permanently banned from the show. UNIVERSAL PICTURES/PHOTOFEST

and John Brannon of Negative Approach), Fear performed "I Don't Care about You," "Beef Bologna," "New York's Alright if You Like Saxophones," and a portion of "Let's Have a War" before *SNL* producers pulled the plug on the chaotic scene and took the live show straight to a commercial break.

As might be expected, Fear was banned for life from appearing on *Saturday Night Live*. The headline of the next day's *New York Post* read, "Fear riot leaves 'Saturday Night' glad to be alive." The newspaper falsely claimed that the punks had caused $200,000 in damages to the NBC studio. Tragically, Belushi died of a drug overdose just a little over four months after the Halloween debacle on March 5, 1982, at the age of thirty-three. He is buried at Abel's Hill Cemetery on Martha's Vineyard, and his epitaph reads, "I may be gone but Rock and Roll lives on."

G. G. ALLIN—CAVITY CLUB, AUSTIN, TEXAS (1992)   Let's face it—just about any "performance" by demented punk rocker G. G. Allin would have made this list. Even by the edgy standards of punk, the notorious Allin stood out for pushing the envelope into uncharted territory with his vile, stomach-churning stage antics. Such was the case on a legendary night in Austin, Texas, when Allin and his band, the Murder Junkies, took the stage at a sleazy dive bar called the Cavity Club (appropriately known as Austin's "scuzziest punk venue" at the time) on February 18, 1992. The Murder Junkies featured Allin's brother Merle on bass, guitarist Bill Weber, and drummer Donald "Dino Sex" Sachs.

A menacing Allin—complete with shaved head and goatee—opened the set with "Bite It You Scum," which set the appropriate tone for the events to follow. By the fourth number, the maniacal lead singer was completely nude, sweating and bleeding, while defecating onstage, and heaving his feces into the (mostly) stunned audience. Police were immediately called to the chaotic scene. To make matters worse, someone sprayed mace into the crowd for no apparent reason. The Austin police report noted that when police officers arrived at the club, they saw attendees "running away from the stage gasping and covering their faces." The entire "performance" had lasted just under twenty-five minutes.

According to the police report, one of the police officers "noted a white male on the band stand was nude and staggering around the stage bleeding from the forehead. . . . Allin stated that throwing feces was part of his act and that the club manager was aware of this when he booked the band." Allin was transported to a nearby hospital to be treated for his self-inflicted head wound, and then arrested and deported to Michigan, where he was wanted for violating parole on an assault charge.

The Cavity Club incident was later immortalized somewhat inaccurately in the 1999 song "The Night G.G. Allin Came to Town" by Drive-By Truckers: "It says he took a shit on the stage and started throwing it into the crowd/But he was gone before the cops could come and shut him down." As for Allin, he never fulfilled his long-standing goal of committing suicide onstage. A little over a year after the Cavity Club fiasco, on June 28, 1993, the so-called "toughest rockstar in the world" died of an accidental heroin overdose at the age of thirty-six. His epitaph reads, "For my mission ends in termination, vicinity of death. LIVE FAST DIE."

13

Rise Above

The Most Influential
Punk-Rock Songs

Embrace the honesty of imperfection and you will be unstoppable. —Alice Bag

The New York–based publication, *Consequence* has defined the essence of a great punk song as "fast-paced music, lyrics rooted in anti-establishment, and a welcome sense of danger." Just about all of the great punk-rock songs listed below meet that criteria in one way or another. Note that I'm a purist, so no proto-punk bands like the Stooges made the list (even though they are most deserving, to say the least). A list of the best proto-punk bands can be found in chapter 3. The list is also in alphabetical order so as not to play any favorites!

"ANARCHY IN THE UK" (1976)—SEX PISTOLS "I am an antichrist/And I am an anarchist." Released as the Sex Pistols' debut single (with the B-side "I Wanna Be Me") on November 26, 1976, "Anarchy in the UK" was later featured on their debut album, *Never Mind the Bollocks, Here's the Sex Pistols*. Malcolm McLaren declared that the song was "a call to arms to the kids who believe that rock and roll was taken away from them. It's a statement of self-rule, of ultimate independence." "Anarchy in the UK" later ranked no. 125 on *Rolling Stone's* list of the "500 Greatest Songs of All Time."

"BLANK GENERATION" (1976)—RICHARD HELL AND THE VOIDOIDS   "I was sayin' let me out of here before I was/Even born." In 1975, Richard Hell departed Television to join Johnny Thunders and the Heartbreakers but soon left that band to form Richard Hell and the Voidoids. "Blank Generation" served as the title track of the band's 1977 debut album. The nihilistic lyrics of this punk anthem include "I belong to the blank generation but/I can take it or leave it each time." According to legend, the song inspired Sex Pistols manager Malcolm McLaren to challenge the band to write their own version of "Blank Generation," and the result was "Pretty Vacant."

"BLITZKRIEG BOP" (1976)—THE RAMONES   "Hey ho, let's go!" The Ramones' debut single was released in February 1976. A timeless anthem written by Tommy Ramone and Dee Dee Ramone, "Blitzkrieg Bop" (original title: "Animal Hop") also appeared as the opening track on the Ramones' self-titled debut album, which was

Believe it or not, the Ramones never had a top-40 hit, although the band's signature song, "Blitzkrieg Bop," later ranked no. 64 on *Rolling Stone*'s list of the "500 Greatest Songs of All Time." PHOTOFEST

released on April 23 of that year. Joey Ramone later confessed that the song's signature chant was influenced by "Saturday Night" by the Bay City Rollers. Tragically, "Blitzkrieg Bop" was used in a 1991 Bud Light commercial. "Blitzkrieg Bop" later ranked no. 64 on *Rolling Stone*'s list of the "500 Greatest Songs of All Time." In addition, *Q* magazine placed it no. 31 on its list of the "100 Greatest Guitar Tracks."

"EVER FALL IN LOVE" (1978)—BUZZCOCKS   "You disturb my natural emotions/You make me feel like dirt and I'm hurt." Written by Buzzcocks singer-songwriter/guitarist Pete Shelley (who was inspired to write the song from a line in the 1955 movie *Guys and Dolls*), "Ever Fallen in Love (With Someone You Shouldn't've)" was a no. 12 hit on the UK charts and later appeared on the band's second album, *Love Bites*.

"HOLIDAY IN CAMBODIA" (1980)—DEAD KENNEDYS   "And you know you've seen it all/In daddy's car, thinking you'll go far." One of the signature songs of the Dead Kennedys, "Holiday in Cambodia" was released by Optional Music in May 1980 with "Police Truck" as the B-side. In addition, the track appears on the band's first album, *Fresh Fruit for Rotting Vegetables*, which was released on September 2, 1980. The single contrasts the cozy life of a privileged American college student with the atrocities of the Cambodian genocide by the Khmer Rouge. If the subject matter wasn't controversial enough, the cover of the single features a disturbing image from the Thammasat University massacre in Thailand on October 6, 1976.

"I LOVE LIVIN' IN THE CITY" (1978)—FEAR   "My house smells just like zoo/It's chock full of shit and puke." Notorious for audience baiting, obnoxious banter, and lyrics dripping with sarcasm, Los Angeles punk band Fear left an enduring mark on both the 1981 documentary *The Decline of Western Civilization* and their chaotic appearance on *Saturday Night Live* that same year. Fear's debut single, "I Love Livin' in the City," captures the essence of the band with lyrics such as "Cockroaches on the walls/Crabs are crawling on my balls." Indeed, the stark and uncompromising imagery of "I Love

Livin' in the City" recalls the gritty poetry of Los Angeles writer Charles Bukowski, the so-called "Poet Laureate of Skid Row." *Village Voice* music critic Kim Kelly characterized the song as "a shit-stained love letter to the filthy beating heart of the city itself." The single was released in 1978 via Criminal Records with "Now You're Dead" as the B-side and rerecorded for the band's 1982 debut album, *The Record*. "I Love Livin' in the City" also appears on the *SLC Punk!* (1998) soundtrack.

"(I'M) STRANDED" (1976)—THE SAINTS   "Livin' in a world insane/They cut out some heart and some brain." The powerful debut single of Australian punk band the Saints was released in September 1976 (with "No Time" as the B-side) on the band's own Fatal Records label, thereby beating the Damned, Sex Pistols, Buzzcocks, and the Clash to the punch. The Saints formed in 1974 with a lineup that featured lead singer Chris Bailey, guitarist Ed Kuepper, and drummer Ivor Hay. They released their debut album, also titled *(I'm) Stranded*, in 1977. Legendary music critic Kris Needs of *Zigzag* exclaimed that the album would "sear great holes in the turntable with shards of screaming feedback and guitar walls a hundred miles high . . . like having your hair burned off with a flame thrower." Kuepper left the band in 1978 to form the experimental post-punk band Laughing Clowns.

In 2001, "(I'm) Stranded" ranked no. 15 on the Australasian Performing Right Association (APRA) list of the "Top 30 Australian Songs of All Time." None other than the Boomtown Rats' Bob Geldof once remarked, "Rock music in the '70s was changed by three bands—the Sex Pistols, the Ramones, and the Saints."

"KIDS OF THE BLACK HOLE" (1981)—ADOLESCENTS   "Sex, drugs and fun is their only thought and care/Another swig of brew, another overnight affair." Perfectly capturing the alienation of suburban American teenagers in the early 1980s, the Adolescents' signature song, "Kids of the Black Hole," features such nihilistic lyrics as "Kids in a fast lane living for today/No rules to abide by and no one to obey." The song appears on the band's self-titled debut album (aka "The Blue Album"), which featured the talents of lead vocalist Tony

Cadena, lead guitarist Frank Agnew, rhythm guitarist Rikk Agnew, bassist Steve Soto, and drummer Casey Royer. "Kids of the Black Hole" depicts the Fullerton, California, apartment of Social Distortion lead singer Mike Ness—a "graffiti-covered drug den that was a hangout for punks," according to one report.

"LOVE WILL TEAR US APART" (1980)—JOY DIVISION   "When routine bites hard/And ambitions are low." A haunting ballad that depicts a dying relationship, "Love Will Tear Us Apart" is sung to perfection by lead singer Ian Curtis of Manchester-based rock band Joy Division. Sadly, the single was released in June 1980 (with the B-side "These Days") just one month after the twenty-three-year-old Curtis committed suicide by hanging himself on May 18, 1980. The single reached no. 13 on the UK charts. *NME* named "Love Will Tear Us Apart" as the "greatest single of all time" in 2002. *Rolling Stone* later ranked the song no. 41 on its list of the "500 Greatest Songs of All Time." Curtis is buried in Macclesfield Cemetery, and his epitaph reads, "LOVE WILL TEAR US APART."

"NEW ROSE" (1976)—THE DAMNED   "I got a feeling inside of me/It's kind of strange like a stormy sea." Released by Stiff Records in October 1976, "New Rose" is considered the first pure punk single from a UK punk group. The B-side featured a sped-up cover of the Beatles' "Help!" Written by guitarist Brian James, "New Rose" also appeared on the band's debut album, *Damned Damned Damned* (1977), which is considered the first punk album released by a UK punk band. In a February 2013 *MOJO* interview, James commented, "Everyone thinks 'New Rose' is about a girl or a new relationship but it's not. It was about the emerging scene, this lovely buzz that you'd never dreamed could possibly happen. It was like, 'I'd got my own Swinging '60s,' that sorta vibe."

Guns N' Roses paid tribute to the Damned by recording a cover of "New Rose" on the band's 1993 album of covers, *The Spaghetti Incident?* When asked about the Guns N' Roses cover in a 2015 *NME* interview, the Damned's guitarist Captain Sensible remarked, "The truth is, I haven't heard it, because I don't listen to any music made after 1980." *The Spaghetti Incident?* also features inspired

Released by Stiff Records, The Damned's 1976 single, "New Rose," is considered the first pure punk single from a UK punk group. PHOTOFEST

covers of "Down on the Farm" by UK Subs, "Human Being" by the New York Dolls, "Raw Power" by Iggy and the Stooges, "Ain't It Fun" by the Dead Boys, "Attitude" by Misfits, "You Can't Put Your Arms around a Memory" by Johnny Thunders, and "I Don't Care about You" by Fear, among others. The album's liner notes read, "A great song can be found anywhere. Do yourself a favor and go find the originals."

"ONE CHORD WONDERS" (1977)—THE ADVERTS "When we're halfway through our favorite song/We look up and the audience has gone." One of the very first punk singles, "One Chord Wonders" was released by Stiff Records in 1977 with "Quickstep" as the B-side. The track, which directly addresses the amateurism inherent in punk bands, also appeared on the Adverts' 1978 debut album, *Crossing the Red Sea with the Adverts*, which was recorded at Abbey Road Studios. The Adverts' equally impressive second single, "Gary Gilmore's Eyes" (about the double murderer who was executed by firing squad in Utah in 1977 and had requested that his corneas be used for transplants) reached the top 20 on the UK charts. The band's lineup featured lead singer T. V. Smith, Gaye Advert, guitarist Howard Pickup, and drummer Laurie Driver.

"PAY TO CUM" (1980)—BAD BRAINS   "And so it's now we choose to fight/To stick up for our bloody right." The debut single of pioneering Washington, DC–based hardcore punk band Bad Brains, "Pay to Cum" was released in June 1980 by Bad Brain Records (with "Stay Close to Me" as its B-side). It has since become widely considered one of the best hardcore-punk singles of all time. *Filter* magazine described it as "one of the fastest, most furious songs ever recorded." The song appeared on the soundtrack of the 1985 black comedy, *After Hours*, which was directed by Martin Scorsese. It also appears during the opening credits of the 2006 documentary *American Hardcore: The History of American Punk Rock 1980–1986*.

"RISE ABOVE" (1981)—BLACK FLAG   "Jealous cowards try to control/ Rise above! We're gonna rise above!" A powerful hardcore-punk anthem, "Rise Above" appears as the opening track on Black Flag's 1981 debut album, *Damaged*, and features the refrain "We are tired of your abuse/Try to stop us; it's no use!" The *Damaged* album features vocalist Henry Rollins, lead guitarist Greg Ginn, rhythm guitarist Dez Cadena, bassist Chuck Dukowski, and drummer Robo. While the album gained little attention upon release, it has since been acknowledged as a hardcore-punk classic.

Black Flag's powerful hardcore punk anthem, "Rise Above," appeared on the band's 1981 debut album, *Damaged*. PHOTOFEST

"TEENAGE KICKS" (1979)—THE UNDERTONES   "I wanna hold her, wanna hold her tight/Get teenage kicks right through the night." Upbeat and catchy, "Teenage Kicks" served as the Undertones' debut single (with the B-side "True Confessions") and appeared on the Northern Ireland band's 1979 self-titled debut album, which was released by Sire Records. Initially released in June 1978 by Belfast record label Good Vibrations (founded by the legendary Terri Hooley), the single was rereleased by Sire Records in October of that year and reached no. 31 on the UK charts. The song was famously championed by legendary BBC Radio 1 DJ John Peel, who remarked, "Maybe once a fortnight, after a few days of listening to sizzling new releases and worrying that the music is merging into angst but otherwise characterless soup, I play 'Teenage Kicks' to remind myself exactly how a great record should sound." Peel even requested that "Teenage Kicks" be played at his funeral. The epitaph on Peel's grave reads, "Teenage dreams so hard to beat."

"WHITE RIOT" (1977)—THE CLASH   "And everybody's doing/Just what they're told to." A raw and powerful debut single from the Clash, "White Riot" was released on March 18, 1977, by CBS Records with the B-side "1977." It reached no. 38 on the UK charts and featured the talents of lead vocalist/rhythm guitarist Joe Strummer, lead guitarist Mick Jones, bass guitarist Paul Simonon, and drummer Terry Chimes. The message of "White Riot" was that downtrodden White youth lacked the willingness of inner-city Black youth to take direct action to fight back against institutional poverty and police brutality. According to rock historian Jon Savage in *England's Dreaming*, "With its wailing chorus, 'White Riot' expressed a desperate longing that a voice and face should be given to the white dispossessed."

14

Complete Control

The Greatest Punk-Rock
Albums of All Time

Chaos is a great factor in making art happen. —Debbie
Harry

According to Henry Rollins in the foreword to *Punk Rock: An
Oral History*, "Punk came at the right time and did the right thing.
The better albums from the genre hold up without failure no mat-
ter what has happened in the world of music since their release."
Every self-respecting punk-rock vinyl collection must start with the
basics: *Ramones* (1976) and *Never Mind the Bollocks, Here's the Sex
Pistols* (1977). Everything after this is pretty much subjective. For
example, *Rolling Stone*'s top five punk-rock albums include:

1. *Ramones*;
2. *The Clash*;
3. *Never Mind the Bollocks*;
4. The Stooges' *Funhouse*; and
5. Gang of Four's *Entertainment!*

In contrast, *Revolver Magazine* lists the Ramones, Sex Pistols, and
Clash in the top three spots, but adds two hardcore bands to round
out the top five: Bad Brains and Minor Threat. The following list
of "greatest" punk-rock albums offers a personal, eclectic, and very
subjective look at some of my own personal favorites.

HORSES (1975)—PATTI SMITH   Produced by the Velvet Underground's John Cale and released on December 13, 1975, by Arista Records, *Horses* served as the debut album of the Patti Smith Group. Arguably the first punk-rock album, *Horses* also features eclectic covers of rock standards "Gloria" and "Land of a Thousand Dances." The iconic album cover was taken by legendary photographer Robert Mapplethorpe, Smith's soulmate. According to *Trouser Press*, "Too idiosyncratic to be generally influential, *Horses* is a brilliant explosion of talent by a challenging, unique artist pioneering a sound not yet fashionable or, by general standards, even acceptable."

Many musical artists have cited the influence of *Horses*, such as Viv Albertine of the Slits, Siouxsie Sioux of Siouxsie and the Banshees, Morrissey of the Smiths, Courtney Love of Hole, PJ Harvey, and Michael Stipe of R.E.M., among many others. In 2009, *Horses* was selected for preservation by the Library of Congress into the National Recording Registry as being "culturally, historically or aesthetically significant." The album was inducted into the Grammy Hall of Fame in 2021.

Widely considered the first punk rock album, *Horses* by the Patti Smith Group was released to critical acclaim in November 1975. ARISTA RECORDS/PHOTOFEST

Track List: "Gloria," "Redondo Beach," "Birdland," "Free Money," "Kimberly," "Break It Up," "Land," "Elegie"

***DAMNED DAMNED DAMNED* (1977)—THE DAMNED**   Produced by Nick Lowe and issued by Stiff Records on February 18, 1977, *Damned Damned Damned* was the first full-length album released by a British punk group and reached no. 34 on the UK charts. Recorded in just two days, the album featured such punk classics as "New Rose" and "Neat Neat Neat," as well as a cover of "I Feel Alright" by the Stooges. *Trouser Press* called *Damned Damned Damned* "a stripped-down punk album of high-speed songs filled with raunchy guitar rock and equally aggressive sentiments."

Track List: "Neat Neat Neat," "Fan Club," "I Fall," "Born to Kill," "Stab Your Back," "Feel the Pain," "New Rose," "Fish," "See Her Tonite," "1 of the 2," "So Messed Up," "I Feel Alright"

***RAMONES* (1976)—RAMONES**   Let's face it, the Ramones pretty much launched punk rock into orbit with this stunning self-titled debut album, which was recorded at Plaza Sound Studios in Radio City Music Hall for just $6,000 and released by Sire Records on April 23, 1976. The album contained fourteen amazing tracks and clocked in at just over twenty-nine minutes. However, despite receiving critical acclaim, the album stalled at no. 111 on the U.S. charts. With such punk classics as "Blitzkrieg Bop," "I Wanna Be Your Boyfriend," "Now I Wanna Sniff Some Glue," and "Beat on the Brat," it has been widely recognized as one of the most influential punk recordings of all time. Photographed by *Punk* magazine's Roberta Bayley, the iconic album cover for *Ramones* perfectly captures the band's personality in stark black-and-white with their signature leather jackets, T-shirts, and ripped jeans as they lean against a brick wall in New York City. It has since become one of the most imitated album covers in rock history.

   Ramones influenced countless musical acts, including the Clash, the Damned, Black Flag, Misfits, and Green Day, among many others. According to Tony James of Generation X, "When [Ramones] came out, all the English groups tripled speed overnight. Two-minute-long songs, very fast." In 2001, *Spin* magazine ranked *Ramones* no. 1 on its list of the "50 Most Essential Punk Records," and the album landed at no. 47 on *Rolling Stone*'s 2021 list of the "500 Greatest Albums of All Time." In addition, *Ramones* has been preserved by the National Recording Registry, deeming it "culturally, historically, and aesthetically significant."

Track List: "Blitzkrieg Bop," "Beat on the Brat," "Judy Is a Punk," "I Wanna Be Your Boyfriend," "Chain Saw," "Now I Wanna Sniff Some Glue," "I Don't Wanna Go Down to the Basement," "Loudmouth," "Havana Affair," "Listen to My Heart," "53rd & 3rd," "Let's Dance," "I Don't Wanna Walk Around," "Today Your Love, Tomorrow the World"

***BLANK GENERATION* (1977)—RICHARD HELL AND THE VOIDOIDS**   After Richard Hell departed Television and then the Heartbreakers, he formed Richard Hell and the Voidoids (the name was derived from one of Hell's unpublished novels) with Robert Quine, Ivan Julian, and Marc Bell (the future Marky Ramone). They were one of the pioneering bands that defined the early New York City punk-rock scene. Produced by Richard Gottehrer, completed in just three weeks, and released by Sire Records in September 1977, *Blank Generation* served as the band's debut album. Its title track became a true punk anthem: "I belong to the blank generation and/I can take it or leave it each time." According to legend, Malcolm McLaren brought back the lyrics for "Blank Generation" to the Sex Pistols and challenged them to write something similar. The result was "Pretty Vacant."

Released on Sire Records in September 1977, *Blank Generation* by Richard Hell and the Voidoids was recorded and mixed at Electric Lady Studios in NYC in just three weeks. PHOTOFEST/NEW LINE CINEMA

Track List: "Love Comes in Spurts," "Liars Beware," "New Pleasure," "Betrayal Takes Two," "Down at the Rock and Roll Club," "Who Says?" "Blank Generation," "Walking on the Water," "The Plan," "Another World"

NEVER MIND THE BOLLOCKS, HERE'S THE SEX PISTOLS (1977)—SEX PISTOLS

Arguably the most influential punk album of all time, *Never Mind the Bollocks* was released in the UK on October 28, 1977, by Virgin Records (the Sex Pistols had already been dumped previously by both A&M and EMI). The album reached no. 1 on the UK charts. According to Steve Wide in *A Field Guide to Punk*, it "cleared the path for anyone who wanted to form a band but never thought they could." Sid Vicious did not play on the finished album—Glen Matlock did all the bass playing.

Never Mind the Bollocks briefly had the working title of *God Save Sex Pistols*. Steve Jones came up with the eventual title after overhearing two hotdog sellers on the West End who constantly repeated the phrase "Never mind the bollocks" back and forth to each other. The simple fact that the word *bollocks* (slang for *testicles*) was featured on the sleeve resulted in the arrest of Virgin Records owner Richard Branson, as well as a record store owner in Nottingham. They were charged under the "Indecent Advertising Act of 1889." In the end, the judge determined that "we must reluctantly find you not guilty."

Track List: "Holidays in the Sun," "Bodies," "No Feelings," "Liar," "Problems," "God Save the Queen," "Seventeen," "Anarchy in the UK," "Submission," "Pretty Vacant," "New York," "E.M.I."

THE CLASH (1977)—THE CLASH

Released on April 8, 1977, the Clash's self-titled debut album featured a slew of punk classics, including "White Riot," "I'm So Bored with the USA," "Janie Jones," and "Remote Control," as well as a cover of Junior Murvin's reggae standard "Police & Thieves." Recorded in just three weeks for £4,000, *The Clash* reached no. 12 on the UK charts.

According to rock critic Mikal Gilmore in *Night Beat*, the album

was archetypal, resplendent punk. While the Sex Pistols prof-
fered a nihilistic image, the Clash took a militant stance that,
in an eloquent, guttural way, vindicated punk's negativism. Har-
rowed rhythms and coarse vocals propelled a foray of songs aimed
at the bleak political realities and social ennui of English life,
making social realism—and unbridled disgust—key elements in
punk aesthetics.

In his *Sniffin' Glue* punk-rock zine, Mark Perry wrote, "The Clash
album is like a mirror. It reflects all the shit. It shows us the truth.
To me, it is the most important album ever released."

Track List: "Janie Jones," "Remote Control," "I'm So Bored with
the USA," "White Riot," "Hate and War," "What's My Name,"
"Deny," "London's Burning," "Career Opportunities," "Cheat,"
"Protex Blue," "Police & Thieves," "48 Hours," "Garageland"

GERMFREE ADOLESCENTS (1978)—X-RAY SPEX   The debut and one-
and-only album released by quirky British punk band X-Ray Spex,
Germfree Adolescents reached no. 18 on the UK charts and was
declared "a masterpiece" by *Trouser Press*. The album contained
three hit singles: "The Day the World Turned Day-Glo," "Identity,"
and "Germ Free Adolescents." In May 2001, *Spin* magazine ranked
Germfree Adolescents at no. 5 on its list of the "50 Most Essential
Punk Records," behind *Ramones* (Ramones), *Pink Flag* (Wire), *The
Clash* (the Clash), and *Los Angeles* (X).

Track List: "Art-I-Ficial," "Obsessed with You," "Warrior in
Woolworths," "Let's Submerge," "I Can't Do Anything," "Identity,"
"Genetic Engineering," "I Live off You," "I Am a Poseur," "Germ Free
Adolescents," "Plastic Bag," "The Day the World Turned Day-Glo"

GI (1979)—THE GERMS   Produced by Joan Jett, recorded in about
three weeks at a cost of $6,000, and released in 1979, *GI* serves
as the only studio album by the Germs, a pioneering Los Angeles
punk band that truly exemplified the dark side of hardcore punk. In
fact, self-destructive lead singer Darby Crash committed suicide a

little over a year after the album's release at the age of twenty-two on December 7, 1980. *Trouser Press* called the album "a kinetic outburst of brute punk force." Henry Rollins referred to the Germs track "Shut Down (Annihilation Man)" as "the sound of a cold, dark, solitary walk into the abyss."

Track List: "What We Do Is Secret," "Communist Eyes," "Land of Treason," "Richie Dagger's Crime," "Strange Notes," "American Leather," "Lexicon Devil," "Manimal," "Our Way," "We Must Bleed," "Media Blitz," "The Other Newest One," "Let's Pretend," "Dragon Lady," "The Slave," "Shut Down (Annihilation Man)"

***INFLAMMABLE MATERIAL* (1979)—STIFF LITTLE FINGERS**   The debut album of Northern Irish punk band Stiff Little Fingers highlights the so-called "Troubles" (aka Northern Ireland Conflict) with powerful tracks related to the struggles growing up in Belfast, such as their signature song "Alternative Ulster," as well as "Suspect Device," "Wasted Life," and "Here We Are Nowhere." The album also features a cover of "Johnny Was" by Bob Marley and the Wailers. *Inflammable Material* peaked at no. 14 on the UK charts. Stiff Little Fingers featured lead singer/guitarist Jake Burns, guitarist Henry Cluney, bassist Ali McMordie, drummer Brian Faloon, and bassoonist Andy Kelly.

Track List: "Suspect Device," "State of Emergency," "Here We Are Nowhere," "Wasted Life," "No More of That," "Barbed Wire Love," "White Noise," "Breakout," "Law and Order," "Rough Trade," "Johnny Was," "Alternative Ulster," "Closed Groove"

***UNKNOWN PLEASURES* (1979)—JOY DIVISION**   The debut album of Manchester-based band Joy Division took just three weeks to produce and was released on June 15, 1979, by Factory Records. Legendary artist Peter Saville designed the distinctive album cover. According to *Trouser Press*, the album "contrasts the message of decay and bemused acceptance of life's paradoxes with the energy and excitement of a band set loose in a studio for the first time." Although the album did not chart, it has subsequently been named one of the best rock albums of all time by such publications as *Rolling Stone*, *NME*, and *Spin*.

Joy Division featured vocalist Ian Curtis, guitarist/keyboardist Bernard Sumner, bassist Peter Hook, and drummer Stephen Morris. Tragically, Curtis committed suicide on May 18, 1980, at the age of twenty-three, just two months before the band's second and final album, *Closer*, was released. After Curtis's death, his bandmates decided to form New Order.

Track List: "Disorder," "Day of the Lords," "Candidate," "Insight," "New Dawn Fades," "She's Lost Control," "Shadowplay," "Wilderness," "Interzone," "I Remember Nothing"

***GROUP SEX* (1980)—CIRCLE JERKS**   The best aspect about Los Angeles punk band the Circle Jerks is that they never took themselves seriously. Considered to be a landmark hardcore-punk album, the band's debut album, *Group Sex*, was released by Frontier Records on October 1, 1980. Incredibly, it features fourteen tracks in just over fifteen minutes! The band featured lead singer Keith Morris (formerly of Black Flag), guitarist Greg Hetson, bassist Roger Rogerson, and drummer Lucky Lehrer. The same year that *Group Sex* was released, the Circle Jerks appeared in the 1981 documentary *The Decline of Western Civilization* performing five songs that appeared on the album: "Back against the Wall," "Beverly Hills," "I Just Want Some Skank," "Red Tape," and "Wasted." In a 2021 interview with the *Orlando Weekly* to promote the Circle Jerks' North American tour to celebrate the fortieth anniversary of the release of *Group Sex*, Keith Morris remarked that making the record "was the blind leading the blind . . . just being carefree and careless, and not worrying about anything, and just blasting and making a bunch of noise."

Track List: "Deny Everything," "I Just Want Some Skank," "Beverly Hills," "Operation," "Back against the Wall," "Wasted," "Behind the Door," "World Up My Ass," "Paid Vacation," "Don't Care," "Live Fast Die Young," "What's Your Problem," "Group Sex," "Red Tape"

***FRESH FRUIT FOR ROTTING VEGETABLES* (1980)—DEAD KENNEDYS**   Intense, unrelenting, and riotously satiric, the debut album from the Dead Kennedys pulls no punches. The album was initially released through Cherry Red Records in the United Kingdom on September 2, 1980, and later issued by Jello Biafra's own Alternative Tentacles label in the United States. A *Trouser Press* review of the album concluded that *Fresh Fruit for Rotting Vegetables* "may be the only legitimate companion piece to the Sex Pistols' *Never Mind the Bollocks*." The album cover features a photo of several police cars on fire that took place during the so-called White Night riots in San Francisco on May 21, 1979. The riot began as a protest about the light sentence former city supervisor Dan White received for the murder of Mayor George Moscone and supervisor Harvey Milk.

Track List: "Kill the Poor," "Forward to Death," "When Ya Get Drafted," "Let's Lynch the Landlord," "Drug Me," "Your Emotions," "Chemical Warfare," "California uber alles," "I Kill Children," "Stealing People's Mail," "Funland at the Beach," "Ill in the Head," "Holiday in Cambodia," "Viva Las Vegas"

***LOS ANGELES* (1980)—X** Produced by ex-Doors keyboardist Ray Manzarek and released by Slash Records on April 26, 1980, X's debut album, *Los Angeles*, captured the gritty underside of the "City of Night" and helped define the West Coast punk scene. Notable tracks include "Johny Hit and Run Paulene," "Sex and Dying in High Society," and "The World's a Mess; It's in My Kiss." *Los Angeles* also featured a cover of the Doors song "Soul Kitchen," from the band's 1967 self-titled debut album. One of the album's tracks, "Nausea," was performed by X in the 1981 documentary *The Decline of Western Civilization*.

The classic X lineup featured lead singer Exene Cervenka, guitarist Billy Zoom, bassist John Doe, and drummer D. J. Bonebrake. Manzarek also produced both of X's follow-up albums: *Wild Gift* (1981) and *Under the Big Black Sun* (1982). According to Cervenka, "I thought punk was gonna end the corporate takeover of America's rock 'n' roll, our real music, and we would never have to give in to the dumbing-down, mass-minded crap of the now-ruined radio." X released a total of seven studio albums before disbanding in the mid-1990s. They reunited in the early 2000s and still tour periodically.

Track List: "Your Phone's off the Hook, But You're Not," "Johny Hit and Run Paulene," "Soul Kitchen," "Nausea," "Sugarlight," "Los Angeles," "Sex and Dying in High Society," "The Unheard Music," "The World's a Mess; It's in My Kiss"

***RUM, SODOMY & THE LASH* (1985)—THE POGUES**   Produced by Elvis Costello, the second album of Celtic punk band the Pogues was released on August 5, 1985, and reached no. 13 on the UK charts. *Q* magazine later ranked the album no. 93 on its list of the "100 Greatest British Albums Ever." The Pogues' name is derived from *pogue mo chone* (Gaelic for "kiss my arse"). The name of the album

Fronted by legendary hell-raiser Shane MacGowan, Celtic punk band the Pogues scored a no. 13 hit on the UK charts with their second album, *Rum Sodomy & the Lash*, in 1985. Island Records/Photofest

refers to a quote attributed to Winston Churchill: "Don't talk to me about naval tradition. It's nothing but rum, sodomy, and the lash."

According to Pogues legendary lead singer Shane MacGowan in his 2001 memoir, "What I wanted to do was go back beyond rock 'n' roll, before rock and roll, and do Irish music but do it for a pop audience because I think Irish music is very like rock and roll, it's one of the musics that influenced rock and roll, it's one of the musics that makes up rock and roll." Legendary for both his prodigious alcohol consumption and the horrific condition of his teeth, MacGowan inspired the Mojo Nixon tune "Shane's Dentist," which features the lyrics "Shane's dentist don't work too hard/Always at the Pub/Shane says he ain't coming back/'Til they're down to a nub."

Track List: "The Sick Bed of Cuchulainn," "The Old Main Drag," "The Wild Cats of Kilkenny," "I'm a Man You Don't Meet Every Day," "A Pair of Brown Eyes," "Sally MacLennane," "Dirty Old Town," "Jesse James," "Navigator," "Billy Bones," "The Gentleman Soldier," "And the Band Played Waltzing Matilda"

15

Pissing in a River

Top 10 Punk Albums
You've Never Heard

> A lot of punk rock is not going to be in the mainstream.
> It's below the radar. The beauty of it is that you're not
> supposed to always know. It's subterranean. —Billie Joe
> Armstrong

Overlooked. Underrated. Forgotten. Hidden treasures. Some classic
punk-rock albums are just a little ahead of their time. So the bands
fade away as quickly as they emerged, and the albums themselves
ended up in the bargain bin of your local record store alongside
Hootie and the Blowfish's *Cracked Rear View*, Chumbawamba's
Tubthumper, and Spin Doctors' *Pocket Full of Kryptonite*. Granted,
true punk aficionados will know all of these albums. However, if
you've only taken a cursory plunge into punk rock and want to dig
a little deeper beyond the Ramones and the Sex Pistols, there is no
better place to start than with these classic punk albums forgotten
in time.

***THE ALBUM* (1977)—EATER**   Formed in North London in 1975, Eater
featured the youngest band on the English punk scene with lead
singer/guitarist Andy Blade, guitarist Brian Chevette, bassist Ian
Woodcock, and drummer Dee Generate (Roger Bullen, who was
only fourteen when he joined the band!). The band took its name
from a line from "Suneye," a T-Rex song that featured the lyrics

143

"Tyrannosaurus Rex, the eater of cars." With little musical experience whatsoever, Eater learned how to play their instruments on the job at early gigs. The band's debut album, *The Album*, was released by the label The Label (not kidding!) and featured sped-up covers of the Velvet Underground's "Sweet Jane" and "I'm Waiting for the Man," as well as a cover of David Bowie's "Queen Bitch" and an eclectic version of Alice Cooper's "I'm Eighteen" retitled "Fifteen." None other than Henry Rollins of Black Flag listed *The Album* among his twenty all-time favorite punk albums.

Track List: "You," "Public Toys," "Room for One," "Lock It Up," "Sweet Jane," "Fifteen," "I Don't Need It," "Anne," "Get Raped," "Space Dreaming," "Queen Bitch," "My Business," "Waiting for the Man," "No More," "No Brains," "Luv & Piece"

FULHAM FALLOUT (1978)—THE LURKERS Known as "The British Ramones," the Lurkers formed in London in 1976 and released their debut album, *Fulham Fallout*, in June 1978. Released on the Beggar's Banquet label, *Fulham Fallout* reached only no. 51 on the UK charts. The Lurkers consisted of vocalist Pete "Plug" Edwards (replaced by Howard Wall), guitarist Pete Stride, bassist Nigel Moore, and drummer Pete "Manic Esso" Haynes.

Track List: "Ain't Got a Clue," "I Don't Need to Tell Her," "Total War," "Hey You," "Shadow," "Then I Kicked Her," "Go, Go, Go," "Jenny," "Time of Year," "Self Destruct," "It's Quiet Here," "Gerald," "I'm on Heat," "Be My Prisoner"

DO IT DOG STYLE (1978)—SLAUGHTER & THE DOGS The debut album of this underappreciated Manchester punk band was released by Decca Records in 1978. The album features covers of the Velvet Underground's "Waiting for the Man" and the New York Dolls' "Who Are the Mystery Girls." The band consisted of lead singer Wayne Barrett, guitarist Mick Rossi, bassist Howard "Zip" Bates, and drummer Brian "Mad Muffet" Grantham. Slaughter & the Dogs supported the Sex Pistols during their legendary gig at Manchester Lesser Free Trade Hall on July 20, 1976.

Track List: "Where Have All the Boot Boys Gone," "Victims of the Vampire," "Boston Babies," "I'm Waiting for the Man," "I'm Mad," "Quick Joey Small," "You're a Bore," "Keep on Trying," "We Don't Care," "Since You Went Away," "Who Are the Mystery Girls," and "Dame to Blame."

***THE INCREDIBLE SHRINKING DICKIES* (1979)—THE DICKIES** Notable as the first California punk band to sign with a major label (A&M), the Dickies released their debut album, *The Incredible Shrinking Dickies*, in February 1979. Highlights of the album include sped-up covers of both Black Sabbath's "Paranoid" and Barry McGuire's "Eve of Destruction." The album peaked at no. 18 on the UK charts but totally fizzled out in the United States. *Trouser Press* called the album "a burst of late-'70s hyperactive California punk" from "a *Mad* magazine–flavored punk self-parody." Formed in 1977, the Dickies consisted of lead singer Leonard Graves Phillips, guitarist Stan Lee (not the comic book writer!), keyboardist Chuck Wagon (Bob Davis), bassist Billy Club (Bill Remar), and drummer Karlos Kaballero (Carlos Cabellero). In 1978, the band performed "Hideous" on the TV comedy show *C.P.O. Sharkey*, which starred Don Rickles. By the way, Johnny Ramone listed the Dickies in his assessment of the top 10 punk bands of all time.

Track List: "Give It Back," "Poodle Party," "Paranoid," "She," "Shadow Man," "Mental Ward," "Eve of Destruction," "You Drive Me Ape (You Big Gorilla)," "Waterslide," "Walk Like an Egg," "Curb Job," "Shake & Bake," "Rondo (The Midgets Revenge)"

***THE RAINCOATS* (1979)—THE RAINCOATS** The Raincoats were formed in 1977 by Ana da Silver and Gina Birch while they were both students at Hornsey College of Art in London. Released by the independent Rough Trade label on November 21, 1979, the Raincoats' self-titled debut album featured an eclectic cover of the Kinks' "Lola." In addition, the final track—"No Looking"—included lyrics translated and adapted from a poem by French poet and screenwriter Jacques Prevert. None other than Nirvana's Kurt Cobain championed the Raincoats, who opened for the band on their final tour in 1994. In addition, Hole covered "The Void" in 1994.

Track List: "No Side to Fall In," "Adventures Close to Home," "Off Duty Trip," "Black and White," "Lola," "The Void," "Life on the Line," "You're a Million," "In Love," "No Looking"

***BACK FROM SAMOA* (1982)—ANGRY SAMOANS**   Released by Bad Trip Records in 1982, *Back from Samoa* served as the debut album of Los Angeles–based punk band Angry Samoans. The album contains such delightful and vulgar tracks as "My Old Man's a Fatso," "They Saved Hitler's Cock," and "Tuna Taco." Believe it or not, *Back from Samoa* also features a cover of "Time Has Come Today" by the Chambers Brothers. A review in *Alternative Press* commented that the album "rocks like a spastic colon," while *Trouser Press* labeled the band as "junk culture junkies." Known for their hilariously raunchy lyrics, the band was formed in Los Angeles in 1978. The original lineup featured vocalist/guitarist "Metal" Mike Saunders, lead guitarist Bonze Blayk, vocalist/guitarist Gregg Turner, bassist Todd Homer, and drummer Bill Vockeroth.

Track List: "Gas Chamber," "The Todd Killings," "Lights Out," "My Old Man's a Fatso," "Time Has Come Today," "They Saved Hitler's Cock," "Homo-Sexual," "Steak Knife," "Haizman's Brain Is Calling," "Tuna Taco," "Coffin Case," "You Stupid Jerk," "Ballad of Jerry Curlan," "Not of This Earth"

***MEAT PUPPETS* (1982)—MEAT PUPPETS**   The Meat Puppets' self-titled debut album features a much more hardcore sound than their later efforts, which blended punk with psychedelic rock and country. It also contains the unlikeliest of covers: "Walking Boss" by legendary North Carolina flat-picker Doc Watson (1923–2012) and "Tumbling Tumbleweeds" by singer-songwriter Bob Nolan (1908–1980), a founding member of the Sons of the Pioneers. Formed in Phoenix, Arizona, in 1980, the band consisted of Curt Kirkwood (vocals/guitar), Cris Kirkwood (bass/vocals), and Derrick Bostrom (drums). According to Curt Kirkwood, "The first [album] was our LSD record. We were three days in the studio, and we tripped the whole time. And it was really cool, and really trying, too, because we went insane."

The Meat Puppets' 1982 self-titled debut album blended punk rock with psychedelic rock and country, and featured a cover of Doc Watson's "Walking Boss." BY TREEFORT MUSIC FEST/WIKIMEDIA COMMONS

Track List: "Reward," "Love Offering," "Blue-Green God," "Walking Boss," "Melons Rising," "Saturday Morning," "Our Friends," "Tumbling Tumbleweeds," "Milo, Sorghum, and Maize," "Meat Puppets," "Playing Dead," "Litterbox," "Electromud," "The Gold Mine"

***AVENGERS* (1983)—AVENGERS**   During the brief tenure of the Avengers (1977–1979), the band never managed to release a full studio album. That's why this compilation album is the closest way to get a feel for the sound of this San Francisco punk band. Highlights of *Avengers* includes "The American in Me," "No Martyr," "Second to None," "Desperation," a cover of the Rolling Stones' "Paint It Black," and a live version of "Fuck You."

The Avengers (along with the Nuns) secured a cherished place in punk history as the band that opened for the Sex Pistols during their final gig on their ill-fated U.S. tour at the Winterland Ballroom in San Francisco on January 14, 1978. Led by singer Penelope Houston, the band also consisted of drummer Danny "Furious"

O'Brien, guitarist Greg Ingraham, and bassist James Wilsey. The band released an EP titled *We Are the One* in 1977 that included "We Are the One," "I Believe in Me," and "Car Crash." *Punk* magazine called the Avengers "the only West Coast group worth listening to more than once."

Track List: "We Are the One," "Car Crash," "I Believe in Me," "Open Your Eyes," "No Martyr," "Desperation," "Thin White Line," "Paint It Black," "The American in Me," "White Nigger," "Uh Oh," "Second to None"

STAINS (1983)—STAINS   One of the first punk bands from East Los Angeles, the Stains formed in 1976 and released their self-titled debut album in 1983. The album has since been recognized as an important bridge between hardcore punk and heavy metal. The band featured vocalist Rudy Navarro, guitarist Robert Becerra, bassist Ceasar Viscarra, and drummer Gilbert Berumen.

Dead Milkmen's 1985 debut album, *Big Lizard in My Backyard*, featured the quirky hit, "Bitchin' Camaro," which helped the band secure an underground following.
PHOTOFEST

Track List: "Sick and Crazy," "Violent Children," "Gang Related Death," "Get Revenge," "Germany," "Political Scandal," "Pretty Girls," "Nowhere," "Quit the Human Race," "I'm Normal," "Young Nazis"

***BIG LIZARD IN MY BACKYARD* (1985)—DEAD MILKMEN**   Released by Restless Records in 1985, *Big Lizard in My Backyard* served as the debut album of the Dead Milkmen. Even though the album yielded no singles, it garnered widespread acclaim, and the track "Bitchin' Camaro" (which featured a humorous improvised dialogue intro) received a lot of college-radio airplay and helped the band gain an underground following. The band consisted of Rodney Linderman, Joseph Genaro, David Schulthise, and Dean Sabatino.

Track List: "Tiny Town," "Beach Song," "Plum Dumb," "Swordfish," "V.F.W. (Veterans of a Fucked Up World)," "Rastabilly," "Serrated Edge," "Lucky," "Big Lizard in My Backyard," "Gorilla Girl," "Bitchin' Camaro," "Filet of Sole," "Spit Sink," "Violent School," "Takin' Retards to the Zoo," "Junkie," "Right Wing Pigeons," "Dean's Dream," "Laundromat Song," "Nutrition," "Tugena"

16

No Class

The Most Controversial
Punk-Rock Songs

> When you talk like an asshole and look like an asshole,
> you're an asshole. —John Lydon

The most controversial punk-rock songs are divided between such leading-edge politically charged anthems like "God Save the Queen" by the Sex Pistols and "Alternative Ultster" by Stiff Little Fingers, which were banned because of their political content, and the shock-rock type of tracks designed purely to be offensive, such as "Golden Shower" by the Mentors and "Anal Cunt" by G. G. Allin and the Murder Junkies. For better or worse, even the worst of it encompasses the true spirit of punk—the ability to express yourself in every way possible. As Jello Biafra of the Dead Kennedys once remarked, "I've never been a big fan of subtle art. I like art that gets deep into my head and starts my brain spinning with new ideas and inspiration and my whole body is full of energy."

"ALTERNATIVE ULSTER"—STIFF LITTLE FINGERS "Is this the kind of place you wanna live?/Is this where you wanna be?" Unlike some of their contemporary Northern Ireland punk bands such as the Undertones ("Teenage Kicks"), Stiff Little Fingers was known for its politically charged lyrics that directly addressed "The Troubles" period of deadly sectarian violence. Originally released as a single on October 17, 1978, "Alternative Ulster" also appeared on the band's debut studio album, *Inflammable Material*, the following year. However, lead singer Jake Burns later reflected that the song was "written in the classic punk mode of having nothing to do . . . the sheer tedium of having nowhere to go and nothing to do when you got there."

"ANAL CUNT"—GG ALLIN   "Just another dead fuck, it means nothing to me." Believe it or not, a Boston-based band formed in 1988 called Anal Cunt released such highly offensive songs as "You Robbed a Sperm Bank Because You're a Cum Guzzling Fag" and "I Made Your Kid Get AIDS So You Could Watch It Die." However, the band did not name themselves after the G. G. Allin song "Anal Cunt," as is commonly believed. In fact, Allin's song was not released until his eighth and final studio album, *Brutality and Bloodshed for All* (1993). Just about any song by G. G. Allin and the Murder Junkies could make this list. Some of the band's other "classics" include "I Wanna Piss on You," "Stink Finger Clit," "Castration Crucifixion," "Suck My Ass It Smells," and "I Hate People." You get the drift.

"BEAT ON THE BRAT"—RAMONES   "Beat on the brat with a baseball bat." The second track on the Ramones' self-titled debut album from 1976, "Beat on the Brat" was written by Joey Ramone, who claimed it referred to "all the spoiled brats in Queens," where he grew up. Believe it or not, U2 covered "Beat on the Brat" on the 2003 tribute album *A Tribute to the Ramones: We're a Happy Family*. The song was also recorded by Weird Al Yankovic for the 2018 album *Dr. Demento Covered in Punk*.

"BELSEN WAS A GAS"—SEX PISTOLS   "Life is fun and I wish you were here." Interviewed in *Q* magazine in 1996, John Lydon remarked, "[Belsen Was a Gas] was a very nasty, silly little thing . . . that should've ended up on the cutting room floor." Generally credited to Sid Vicious as a song he wrote in the Flowers of Romance prior to joining the Sex Pistols, "Belsen Was a Gas" refers to the Nazi concentration camp Bergen-Belsen, which was liberated by British troops on April 15, 1945. It was also where fifteen-year-old Anne

Frank and her older sister Margot both died of typhus in February or March of that year. The Sex Pistols performed the song during their final concert at Winterland Ballroom in San Francisco on January 14, 1978. "Belsen Was a Gas" also appears in two versions (including the live Winterland recording) on *The Great Rock 'n' Roll Swindle* and Vicious's solo album, both of which were released in 1979. In 2003, the Sex Pistols performed an adapted version of the song retitled "Baghdad Was a Blast" during their reunion tour of the United States, which took place just after the start of the Iraq War.

"THE DWARVES ARE STILL THE BEST BAND EVER"—DWARVES "Let's get high and fuck some sluts." Initially formed in Chicago as a garage-rock band known as Suburban Nightmare, the Dwarves are known for their offensive lyrics (sometimes referred to as "scum punk") and violent early shows. With tracks such as "Let's Fuck," "Skin-Poppin' Slut," and "Insect Whore," the Dwarves' 1990 album *Blood Guts & Pussy* has been called the "most offensive album of all time" by *SPIN* magazine. "The Dwarves Are Still the Best Band Ever" is rather representative of the Dwarves' sound. Listen at your own risk!

"FUCK CHRISTMAS"—FEAR "All the children on the street/Hope they get something good to eat." No strangers to controversy (read about their notorious 1981 *Saturday Night Live* appearance in chapter 12), Los Angeles–based punk band Fear released "Fuck Christmas" as their second single after "I Love Livin' in the City." The B-side contained a censored version, "(Beep) Christmas," designed to promote the single on radio. "Fuck Christmas" later appeared as a bonus track on the CD reissue of Fear's debut studio album, *The Record*. Bad Religion later covered the song at Almost Acoustic Christmas, an annual concert hosted by Los Angeles radio station KROQ, in 1993 and 1994.

"FUCK THE POPE"—ANTI-FLAG "Living in the past/Ruining people's lives." If the title alone weren't enough to cause controversy, "Fuck the Pope" featured such lyrics as "I don't want your fucking bullshit/ You infect everyone you teach." Well-known for their progressive political activism, Anti-Flag was cofounded by lead singer/guitarist Justin Sane and drummer Pat Thetic. The band hailed from Pittsburgh, Pennsylvania. "Fuck the Pope" appeared on the 1993 EP, *Rock'n with Father Mike*, which also included two tracks by the Bad Genes.

"GOD SAVE THE QUEEN"—SEX PISTOLS "We're the flowers in the dustbin/We're the poison in the human machine." Released as the Sex Pistols' second single after "Anarchy in the UK" and later appearing on the band's only album, *Never Mind the Bollocks, Here's the Sex Pistols*, "God Save the Queen" (original title: "No Future") proved especially controversial since it was released to coincide with Queen Elizabeth II's Silver Jubilee in 1977. With anti-monarchy lyrics such as "God save the queen/the fascist regime," the song got banned by both the BBC and Independent Broadcasting Authority. According to John Lydon (Rotten), "I wrote the song 'God Save the Queen' as a laugh. It's a giggle, it's vaudeville, it's burlesque. It's not a rampant anti-royal statement." Although "God Save the Queen" reached no. 1 on the UK charts, it was officially listed as no. 2, behind "I Don't Want to Talk about It" by Rod Stewart.

"GOLDEN SHOWER"—THE MENTORS "Our relationship I don't want to spoil it/You are my personal toilet." Known for their shock-rock lyrics and bizarre stage performances in which they wore executioner hoods, the notorious punk-rock/thrash/heavy metal band led by "El Duce" (Eldon Hoke) even caught the attention of the pro-censorship Parents Music Resource Center founded by Tipper Gore. In fact, some of the offensive lyrics to "Golden Shower" were read on the congressional floor. The Mentors were founded in Seattle, Washington, in 1976 by El Duce, Sickie Wifebeater (Eric Carlson), and Dr. Heathen Scum (Steve Broy). In the 1998 British documentary *Kurt & Courtney*, El Duce made the claim that Courtney Love had offered him $50,000 to "whack" Cobain. Eight days after the interview was filmed, El Duce was killed by a freight train while intoxicated at the age of thirty-nine. The gritty, DIY-style documentary *The Mentors: Kings of Sleaze Rockumentary* was released in 2017.

"JESUS ENTERING FROM THE REAR"—FEEDERZ   "We nailed you to a cross/But you're still a fuckin' pain." Arizona punk band the Feederz first released the song "Jesus" on their debut EP of the same name in 1980. The track, featuring the expanded title "Jesus Entering from the Rear," appeared on the notorious *Let Them Eat Jellybeans!* compilation album that was released by Alternative Tentacles in 1981. *Let Them Eat Jellybeans!* which was subtitled "17 Extracts from America's Darker Side," also features "Nazi Punks Fuck Off" (Dead Kennedys), "Police Story" (Black Flag), "Pay to Cum" (Bad Brains), "The Prisoner" (D.O.A.), "Prostitution" (Really Red), and "Slave to My Dick" (Subhumans), among others.

"LITTLE BIT OF WHORE"—JOHNNY THUNDERS   "Well there's a little bit of whore/In every girl." The self-destructive New York Doll and Heartbreaker Johnny Thunders released the solo album *Que Sera Sera* (1985), which featured this controversial nugget as the fourth track. Thunders even name-drops Jacqueline Kennedy Onassis and sings "how she goes down/Lower than anyone else." Six years later, on April 23, 1991, Thunders died of an apparent drug overdose at the age of thirty-eight.

After stints with the New York Dolls and Heartbreakers, Johnny Thunders embarked on a solo career and released the 1985 album, *Que Sera Sera*, which featured the controversial track, "Little Bit of Whore." BY THOMAS GOOD/ WIKIMEDIA COMMONS

"ORGASM ADDICT"—BUZZCOCKS   "Well you tried it just for once/ Found it all right for kicks." English punk-rock band Buzzcocks released "Orgasm Addict," a song about masturbation and sexual obsession, as their debut single (with "Whatever Happened To . . . ?" as the B-side) on November 4, 1977. Due to its sexual content, the song was banned by the BBC. Buzzcocks lead singer Pete Shelley later said the song "is embarrassing. It's the only one I listen to and . . . shudder."

"PEACHES"—THE STRANGLERS   "Down on the beaches/Just look at all the peaches." Banned by the BBC because of its sexually charged lyrics, "Peaches" appeared in a censored version for radio play with "bikini" replacing "clitoris," "oh no" replacing "oh shit," and "what a summer" replacing "what a bummer." The Stranglers' second single, "Peaches" (with the B-side "Go Buddy Go"), peaked at no. 8 on the UK charts and appeared on the 1977 album *Rattus Norvegicus*. "Peaches" was later featured in Jonathan Glazer's 2000 gangster film *Sexy Beast*.

First appearing on the 1977 album, *Rattus Norvegicus*, the Stranglers' song "Peaches" was banned by the BBC for its sexually charged lyrics. BY EDDY BERTHIER, BRUSSELS, BELGIUM/WIKIMEDIA COMMONS

"SPASTICUS AUTISTICUS"—IAN DURY "So place your hard-earned peanuts in my tin/And thank the Creator you're not in the state I'm in." Appearing as the final track on English singer-songwriter Ian Dury's second solo album, *Lord Upminster*, "Spasticus Autisticus" was reportedly penned as a protest against the International Year of Disabled Persons. Dury, who suffered from polio, which he contracted as a youth, apparently considered the gesture to be patronizing to people with disabilities. He referred to it as an "anti-charity song." Rather predictably, the BBC deemed the lyrics offensive and banned the song outright.

"TAKIN' RETARDS TO THE ZOO"—THE DEAD MILKMEN "Down a winding road, just daydreaming/Down a winding road with the retards screaming." Arguably the shortest offensive punk song ever written, "Takin' Retards to the Zoo" is just forty-eight seconds long. It appeared on the Philadelphia-based band's 1985 debut album, *Big Lizard in My Backyard*.

Honorable Mention: "Fuck You, That's Why" (Smut Peddlers), "Hamburger Lady" (Throbbing Gristle), "Bodies" (Sex Pistols), "So What!" (Anti-Nowhere League), "Hate the Police" (the Dicks), "Holiday in Cambodia" (Dead Kennedys), "Fuck You" (the Stiffs), "The Kids Aren't Alright" (the Offspring), "Last Caress" (Misfits), "I'm Not a Loser" (Descendents), "One Dead Cop" (Leftover Crack), "Let's Get Fucked Up" (the Cramps), "We Were on Heroin" (Wasted Youth), "Punk Prayer" (Pussy Riot), "She Fucks for Drugs" (B-Day Vacation), "Mother" (Danzig), "Public Assistance" (Agnostic Front), "I'm Not a Loser" (Descendents), "So What" (Anti-Nowhere League), "Two Cups of Tea" (Star Fucking Hipsters)

17

Everybody's
Happy Nowadays
Classic Punk-Rock Music Videos

> My job is to help destroy/What's left of your imagination/
> By feeding you endless doses of sugar-coated mindless
> garbage. —Dead Kennedys, "MTV—Get Off the Air"

Jello Biafra got it right. There's something about the rebellious spirit
of punk rock that makes it the antithesis of the so-called MTV revolution, which was all about corporate record labels creating slick
promotional videos to move albums. According to Nicholas Rombes
in *A Cultural Dictionary of Punk*, "MTV launched in August 1981,
just five years after punk broke. And yet, those early MTV years
seem far, far away from punk. The smiling VJs, the looming sense
that what you are seeing is promotion as careful, scripted, and
empty as some five-year plan drafted long after five-year plans have
gone out of fashion." However, a few punk-rock bands somehow
managed to create innovative music videos that stand the test of
time. Here are just a few of the best of the lot.

"I WANNA BE SEDATED"—RAMONES "Nothing to do/Nowhere to
go home." One of the Ramones' best-loved songs, "I Wanna Be
Sedated," was written by Joey Ramone and first appeared on their
fourth studio album, *Road to Ruin* (1978). Directed by Bill Fishman (*Tapeheads*), the music video for "I Wanna Be Sedated" was
not released until 1988, to coincide with the promotion of *Ramones*

159

Mania, a compilation album. The eclectic music video features the Ramones (Joey, Johnny, Dee Dee, and Marky) looking extremely bored as they sit at a table eating generic corn flakes while a frenzy of activity takes place around them in the form of clowns, acrobats, ballerinas, monsters, cheerleaders, nuns, doctors, nurses, and schoolgirls dancing around. Look for Olivia Barash, who portrayed Leila in *Repo Man* (1984), as a Catholic school girl and a young Courtney Love dressed as a bride! Fishman also directed three other Ramones music videos—"Something to Believe In" (1986), "I Wanna Live" (1987), and "Pet Sematary" (1989)—as well as "Institutionalized" (1984) for Suicidal Tendencies and "Dream Warriors" (1987) for Dokken.

"TV PARTY"—BLACK FLAG   "We've got nothing better to do/Than watch TV and have a couple of brews." According to Henry Rollins, the song is "about people who stay inside their house and live in a TV kinda world." *Spin* magazine referred to "TV Party" as the "greatest ode to the slacker sloth." The raucous music video for "TV Party" features Black Flag band members downing brews in front of the TV while shouting out their favorite shows. Among the beer-swilling partiers is the video's director Glen E. Friedman, who served as coproducer and consultant for the 2001 skateboarding documentary *Dogtown and Z-Boys*. Friedman also photographed the back cover and insert photos for the 1981 self-titled debut album of the Adolescents, as well as the front cover of Minor Threat's 1985 EP *Salad Days*. He also self-published a punk zine, *My Rules: Photozine*, in 1982. "TV Party" appeared on the soundtrack of *Repo Man* in 1984 (Emilio Estevez's character Otto can be heard singing the song at one point in the film).

"INSTITUTIONALIZED"—SUICIDAL TENDENCIES   "They say they're gonna fix my brain/Alleviate my suffering and my brain." Los Angeles hardcore punk/crossover thrash band Suicidal Tendencies possessed quite a sense of humor, as evidenced in their "Institutionalized" music video, which received heavy rotation on MTV in 1984. Directed by Bill Fishman, the video features the band's lead singer, Mike Muir, wandering through the streets and skate parks of his

A cult classic, Suicidal Tendencies' music video for "Institutionalized" featured cameos by the likes of Jack Nance from *Eraserhead* and Mary Woronov from *Rock 'n' Roll High School*. BY SELBYMAY, OWN WORK/WIKIMEDIA COMMONS

hometown. His parents turn his room into a makeshift padded cell, which he escapes from with the help of fellow band members. Tom Araya of Slayer appears in the video, along with Jack "Eraserhead" Nance and Mary Woronov (who portrayed evil Principal Togar in *Rock 'n' Roll High School*). One of the band's most popular songs, "Institutionalized" appeared on their 1983 self-titled debut album, as well as the *Repo Man* soundtrack in 1984. *REVOLVER* magazine called the song "quite possibly the greatest song ever written about growing up frustrated and alienated in the Reagan Era."

"NEW ROSE"—THE DAMNED "I got a feeling inside of me/It's kind of strange like a stormy sea." Notable as the first single by a British punk-rock band, "New Rose" was released on October 22, 1976, and appears on the band's debut album, *Damned Damned Damned*. Written by guitarist Brian James, the track features a deadpan intro by lead singer Dave Vanian—"Is she really going out with him?"— that parodies "Leader of the Pack," the 1964 Shangri-Las song. The accompanying music video for "New Rose" features an energetic

performance by the Damned filmed in the basement of the legendary Hope & Anchor pub in Islington, London (just down the street
from Pathway Studios where the song was recorded). First opened
in 1880, the Hope & Anchor was a leading venue for both pub
rock and punk rock during the 1970s. The pub hosted the Hope
& Anchor Front Row Festival in 1977, which featured a variety of
pub-rock, punk, and new-wave bands. The pub was also featured in
the 1980 punk musical *Breaking Glass*.

"ROCK THE CASBAH"—THE CLASH   "Degenerate the faithful/With that
crazy Casbah sound." Armadillos, oil wells, a sheik in a Cadillac,
mohawks, and total insanity make up this classic music video by
the Clash that humorously parodies the energy crisis. Directed by
Don Letts, the "Rock the Casbah" music video was primarily filmed
in Austin, Texas. "Rock the Casbah" appeared on the Clash's fifth
studio album, *Combat Rock* (1982), which reached no. 30 on the
UK charts. Letts directed seven other music videos for the Clash:
"White Riot" (1977), "Tommy Gun" (1978), "London Calling"
(1979), "Bankrobber" (1980), "The Call Up" (1980), "This Is Radio
Clash" (1981), and "Should I Stay or Should I Go?" (1982). He also
directed music videos for the Psychedelic Furs, the Pretenders,
Elvis Costello, Musical Youth, and Fun Boy Three. In 1984, Letts
cofounded (with Clash guitarist Mick Jones) the band Big Audio
Dynamite.

"BANNED IN DC"—BAD BRAINS   "Banned in DC with a thousand more
places to go." The title of this Bad Brains signature song relates to
the fact that the pioneering hardcore band was blacklisted from
just about every Washington, DC, live music venue due to their
raucous and destructive fan base. The band soon relocated to New
York City and became a mainstay at area clubs such as CBGBs,
where they recorded a live album and DVD called *Live at CBGB
1982*. The music video of Bad Brains performing "Banned in DC"
captures the intensity of the band's live shows in all their glory.

"THIS AIN'T NO PICNIC"—MINUTEMEN   "Punch in punch out, eight
hours, five days a week/Sweat, pain, and agony, on Friday I'll get

paid." In 1984, punk trio Minutemen released their third album,
Double Nickels on the Dime,
which is generally acknowledged
as the band's crowning achievement. The band released two
music videos to accompany the
album: "This Ain't No Picnic"
and "Ain't Talkin' 'bout Love"
(a Van Halen cover). Made for
just $440 by UCLA graduate
Anthony Johnson, the music
video for "This Ain't No Picnic" features the band performing
amid an apocalyptic wasteland
as they get attacked by a fighter
plane piloted by none other than
Ronald Reagan (the footage was
taken from a 1943 World War II

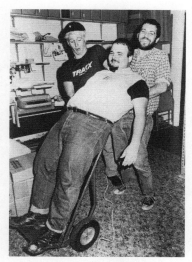

Made for just $440, Minutemen's
music video for "This Ain't No Picnic" has evolved into a punk rock
classic. PHOTOFEST

training film starring the future president titled *Recognition of the
Japanese Zero Fighter*).

"STREAMS OF WHISKEY"—THE POGUES   "I am going, I am going/Where
streams of whiskey are flowing." Released on October 15, 1984,
Red Roses for Me served as the debut album for Celtic punk band
the Pogues. The band released a humorous music video to accompany the eighth track on the album, "Streams of Whiskey," which
features the lyrics: "When the world is too dark/And I need the light
inside of me/I'll walk into a bar/And drink fifteen pints of beer."
The video features plenty of the usual debauchery associated with
the Pogues, especially that of lead singer and all-around hell-raiser
Shane MacGowan.

"PUNK ROCK GIRL"—DEAD MILKMEN   "Let's travel round the world/
Just you and me, punk rock girl." *Trouser Press* once referred to
Philadelphia punk band the Dead Milkmen as "a homegrown insult
machine with a snotty attitude and a grasp of modern society's

cultural monstrosities." These traits are all evident in the band's pop-punk-style "Punk Rock Girl," the first single released from their fourth album, *Beelzebubba* (1988). Directed by Adam Bernstein, the lively music video for "Punk Rock Girl" quickly became a staple on MTV. It was partly filmed at the abandoned (and reputedly haunted) Eastern State Penitentiary in Philadelphia. An episode of *Beavis and Butt-Head* riffed on the "Punk Rock Girl" video, with Butt-Head exclaiming, "This is horrible," "Something's wrong with these guys," and "A real punk rock girl would eat this guy alive."

"SEEING DOUBLE AT THE TRIPLE ROCK"—NOFX "I'm a religious drunk and this is where I pray." The music video for NOFX's "Seeing Double at the Triple Rock" was shot at the Triple Rock Social Club in Minneapolis, Minnesota. The legendary club, which closed its doors in 2017, was co-owned by Gretchen Funk and Erik Funk of the punk band Dillinger Four. The club's name was taken from the 1980 film *The Blues Brothers*, which had a scene at the Triple Rock Baptist Church featuring pastor James Brown as Jake (John Belushi) and Elwood (Dan Aykroyd) declare they are on a "mission from God." The track "Seeing Double at the Triple Rock" appeared on NOFX's tenth studio album, *Wolve in Wolves' Clothing* (2006). Fiercely independent, NOFX has sold over eight million records worldwide without ever being signed to a major label.

"STREETS OF LONDON"—ANTI-NOWHERE LEAGUE "So how can you tell me you're lonely/Don't say to me that your sun don't shine." Formed in 1979, the English punk band Anti-Nowhere League featured lead singer Animal (Nick Culmer), guitarist Magoo (Chris Exall), bassist Chris Elvy, and drummer Bones (Tony Shaw). The band's first single, a cover of Ralph McTell's "Streets of London," peaked at no. 48 on the UK charts. The B-side, "So What," would become the band's anthem. The music video for "Streets of London" features a blistering assault on the senses in typical Anti-Nowhere League fashion.

"ALL TWISTED"—KRAUT "They're gonna get you anyway/Anyway they can." Formed in 1981, New York City hardcore-punk band Kraut featured the original lineup of lead singer Davy Gunnar, guitarist/ vocalist Doug Holland, bassist/vocalist Don Cowan, and drummer/ vocalist Johnny Feedback. "All Twisted" served as the opening track of Kraut's debut album, *An Adjustment to Society* (1982). With their high-energy music video accompanying the song, Kraut reportedly became the first independent band ever to be put into rotation on MTV. With its frantic pace and intensity, the video has since become recognized as one of the definitive punk music videos.

"TIME HAS COME TODAY"—ANGRY SAMOANS   "My mind is blown/The truth is unknown." Formed in 1978 in Los Angeles, Angry Samoans recorded a cover of the Chambers Brothers' classic "Time Has Come Today" for their 1982 debut album, *Back from Samoa*, which was released by Bad Trip Records. The nonsensical but highly entertaining music video for "Time Has Come Today" features alternate shots of a pool party, the band performing on stage, and a very nervous U.S. president who accidentally hits the red doomsday button and sets off a nuclear holocaust. The Ramones later covered "Time Has Come Today" for their 1983 *Subterranean Jungle* album.

"BASKET CASE"—GREEN DAY   "Sometimes I give myself the creeps/ Sometimes my mind plays tricks on me." The setting for the "Basket Case" music video is, appropriately enough, a mental ward straight out of the Academy Award–winning film *One Flew Over the Cuckoo's Nest* (filming took place at the abandoned Agnews Developmental Center in Santa Clara County, California). Directed by Mark Kohr, the video, which was filmed in black and white and then colorized, even features a Nurse Ratched wannabe passing out pills to patients, as well as a reenactment of Chief Bromden's famous escape at the end of the 1975 movie. Although the video was nominated for eight MTV Video Music Awards in 1995— Video of the Year, Best Group Video, Best Metal/Hard Rock Video, Best Alternative Video, Breakthrough Video, Best Direction, Best Editing, and Best Cinematography—Green Day went home empty-handed. The third single from the band's extraordinarily popular third album, *Dookie* (1994), "Basket Case" spent five weeks at the top of Billboard's Alternative Songs chart and ranked no. 150

on *Rolling Stone*'s list of the "500 Greatest Songs of All Time." In 2017, Green Day frontman Billie Joe Armstrong said of "Basket Case" in *Rolling Stone*: "It's an anthem for weirdos. It's about losing your mind. Most people have had that experience."

18

Color Me Impressed
Iconic Punk-Rock Album Covers

> Radical ideas will always get appropriated. The establishment will rob everything they can, because they lack the ability to be creative. That's why you always have to keep moving. —Jamie Reid

Behind every great punk-rock album cover lies a memorable story like when the Clash's Paul Simonon famously smashed his Fender Precision bass guitar in total disgust during a show at New York's Palladium on September 21, 1979, and immortalized for the band's third studio album, *London Calling*. Not known for such sudden outbursts of anger, Simonon was simply pissed off that concert security was holding back the raucous crowd and trying to keep them in their seats. And how about English artist (and anarchist) Jamie Reid's signature pink and yellow cover for *Never Mind the Bollocks, Here's the Sex Pistols* with its frequently imitated ransom-note cutout lettering—making it arguably the most influential and imitated artwork in punk history. Here are some prime examples of punk-rock album covers that have achieved legendary status over the years.

RAMONES (1976)—RAMONES The cover of the Ramones' debut album was originally intended to emulate the famous *Meet the Beatles!* album cover from 1964. However, the results of that photo shoot

The Ramones (pictured in concert) released their 1976 self-titled debut album, which featured a famous cover shot at Albert's Garden in Bowery. MAGNOLIA/PHOTOFEST

were reportedly dismal. Fortunately, the backup plan involved using an iconic photo of the band taken by Roberta Bayley, a renowned *Punk* magazine photographer. The black-and-white photo features band members Johnny Ramone, Tommy Ramone, Joey Ramone, and Dee Dee Ramone casually leaning against a brick wall. Each of the Ramones is wearing what would soon become their distinctive look: a leather jacket, T-shirt, and faded and/or ripped jeans. The legendary photo shoot took place at Albert's Garden, a private community garden located at 16 East 2nd Street in the Bowery district of Manhattan. Frequently imitated, the album cover was even copied by the Chipmunks for their 1980 album, *Chipmunk Punk*.

DAMNED DAMNED DAMNED (1977)—THE DAMNED Recognized as the first full-length album released by a UK punk band, *Damned Damned Damned* was produced by Nick Lowe and released by Stiff Records on February 18, 1977. The eclectic cover of the album photographed by Peter Kodick (aka Peter Gravelle) depicts the four band members—Dave Vanian, Brian James, Captain Sensible, and Rat Scabies—all getting hit in the face with pies. According to James: "[Stiff Records] had assigned [Kodick] to do the thing. They thought it was a jolly wheeze to surprise us with a few cream cakes, little knowing that we would relish it, get into it and enjoy the whole experience."

NEVER MIND THE BOLLOCKS, HERE'S THE SEX PISTOLS (1977)—SEX PISTOLS   Legendary English artist and anarchist Jamie Reid served as an integral part in defining the image of the Sex Pistols through his use of engaging and thought-provoking visuals, especially his bright, ransom-note-style design that graces the front and back covers of the band's first and only album, *Never Mind the Bollocks* (which was originally going to be titled *God Save Sex Pistols*). Reid also designed the iconic single covers for "Anarchy in the UK," "God Save the Queen" (featuring Queen Elizabeth II with a safety pin through her nose and swastikas in her eyes), "Pretty Vacant," and "Holidays in the Sun." In his essay, "Too Low to Be Low: Art Pop and the Sex Pistols," critic and theorist Robert Garnett comments, "Reid's work became even more than a visual equivalent of the music; his visuals inflected the experience of listening to the music to the extent that they became a part of it."

PARALLEL LINES (1978)—BLONDIE   Blondie's third album—which was released by Chrysalis Records on September 23, 1978, and reached no. 1 on the UK charts and no. 6 on the U.S. charts (spawning the hit single "Heart of Glass")—represents a true turning point for the band as Debbie Harry moved toward center stage, both literally and figuratively on the album cover itself. The cover illustration features the glamorous lead singer posing defiantly, dressed in white, and standing in front of her fellow band members—all indistinguishably dressed in identical black suits set against a black-and-white piano background. The photo taken by Edo Bertoglio was reportedly rejected by the band but later chosen for the cover by manager Peter Leeds.

CUT (1979)—THE SLITS   The controversial cover for the debut album of all-female English punk band the Slits depicted the three band members—Ari Up, Viv Albertine, and Tessa Pollitt—posing topless and clad only in mud and loincloths. Produced by Dennis Bovell, the album itself reached no. 30 on the UK charts. A favorite of Kurt Cobain of Nirvana, *Cut* was voted no. 58 on the *Observer's* list of the "100 Greatest British Albums." In addition, *Rolling Stone* ranked the album no. 260 on its list of the "500 Greatest Albums of All Time."

***LONDON CALLING* (1979)—THE CLASH**   The iconic image of Clash bassist Paul Simonon smashing his Fender Precision bass guitar on stage perfectly captures the spirit of punk rock. Considered one of the greatest rock 'n' roll images of all time, it was taken by photographer Pennie Smith during a September 21, 1979, Clash concert at the Palladium in New York City during the band's "Take the Fifth Tour" of the United States. Ironically, Smith objected to using the image for the album cover because she felt it was too out of focus!

  The design of the *London Calling* album cover itself paid tribute to the cover of Elvis Presley's legendary 1956 self-titled debut album, the first rock 'n' roll record to reach no. 1 on the

The Clash's third album, *London Calling*, which features the iconic image of bassist Paul Simonon (center) smashing his guitar on stage, has sold more than 5 million copies worldwide. PHOTOFEST

U.S. charts. *Q* magazine named the Simonon image as the best rock 'n' roll photograph of all time for capturing "the ultimate rock 'n' roll moment—total loss of control." By the way, the remnants of Simonon's bass guitar are now on permanent display at the Museum of London.

UNKNOWN PLEASURES (1979)—JOY DIVISION Renowned English art director and graphic designer Peter Saville created the amazingly innovative cover for Joy Division's debut album, which was released by Factory Records on June 15, 1979. Regarded as a classic of minimalist sleeve design, it features an illustration that originally appeared in the 1977 *Cambridge Encyclopedia of Astronomy* depicting an image of radio waves from a pulsar. Saville decided to reverse the image from black-on-white to white-on-black.

In a review of *Unknown Pleasures* for BBC Online, Susie Goldring wrote, "The duochrome Peter Saville cover of this first Joy Division album speaks volumes. Its white on black lines reflect a pulse of power, a surge of bass, and raw angst." Saville designed many record sleeves for Factory Records—including Joy Division's second and final album, *Closer* (1980). Believe it or not, in 2007, sportswear company New Balance commissioned a pair of "Unknown Pleasures" training shoes sporting the distinctive cover design.

FRESH FRUIT FOR ROTTING VEGETABLES (1980)—DEAD KENNEDYS Never strangers to controversy, the Dead Kennedys chose an image taken during the so-called White Night Riots to grace the cover of their debut album, *Fresh Fruit for Rotting Vegetables*, which was released on September 2, 1980. The White Night Riots, which took place in San Francisco on May 21, 1979, stemmed from the light sentence of voluntary manslaughter given to city supervisor Dan White (who used the notorious "Twinkie defense") for the murder of both Mayor George Moscone and supervisor Harvey Milk (one of the first openly gay elected officials in the country at the time).

The image of burning police cars perfectly accompanies an album that features such powerful and controversial tracks as "Holiday in Cambodia," "California uber alles," and "Kill the Poor." Lead singer-songwriter Jello Biafra later altered the lyrics to the song "I Fought the Law" to relate the story of the assassinations from White's perspective. The track appears on the Dead Kennedys' 1987 compilation album, *Give Me Convenience or Give Me Death*.

LOS ANGELES (1980)—X   Los Angeles punk-rock band X released their powerful debut album, *Los Angeles*, via Slash Records on April 26, 1980. Featuring some of the band's best known tracks—such as "Your Phone's off the Hook, But You're Not," "Johny Hit and Run Paulene," and "Nausea"—the album was produced by former Doors keyboardist Ray Manzarek (the album includes a cover of the 1967 Doors song "Soul Kitchen").

Both provocative and striking, the album cover consists of a huge fiery X amid a completely black background with the album title in all caps in bright red in the upper left corner. In his 2008 book *A Brief History of Album Covers*, Jason Draper states,

> A simple, burning wooden "X" is an obvious ground zero-style manifesto from the position of Los Angeles punk, but also mimics the burning cross symbolism often associated with the Ku Klux Klan. There is no suggestion whatsoever that X had anything to do with KKK sentiments (in fact, very much the opposite), but as far as arresting images go, the burning cross is one of the more inflammatory (no pun intended). Considering the fact that Los Angeles would be set ablaze by race riots just 12 years later, it is also remarkably prescient.

DAMAGED (1981)—BLACK FLAG   The cover art for Black Flag's debut album, *Damaged*, by punk-rock photographer Edward Colver features Black Flag lead singer Henry Rollins smashing his fist through a mirror. The powerful image—which was reportedly accomplished by cracking a mirror with a hammer and using a mixture of coffee and red ink to create "blood"—perfectly complements one of the classic hardcore-punk albums of all time.

A celebrated photographer of the hardcore-punk-rock scene during the 1980s, Colver also has made artistic contributions to the following album covers: *Group Sex* (1980, the Circle Jerks), *Danger Zone* (1981, China White), *Let Them Eat Jellybeans!* (1981, various artists), *Reagan's In* (1981, Wasted Youth), *T.S.O.L.* (1981, T.S.O.L.), *Dance with Me* (1981, T.S.O.L.), *Welcome to Reality* (1981, Adolescents), *How Could Hell Be Any Worse?* (1982, Bad Religion), and *Mommy's Little Monster* (1983, Social Distortion). In addition, his work was featured extensively in the 2001 book *American Hardcore: A Tribal History* and its accompanying 2006 documentary, *American Hardcore*.

GROUP SEX **(1980)—CIRCLE JERKS**   Released by Frontier Records on October 1, 1980, the Circle Jerks' debut album remarkably consists of fourteen songs clocking in at just over fifteen minutes. The equally impressive album cover by graphic designer Diane Zincavage features a colorized image taken by punk photographer Edward Colver of the aftermath of a Circle Jerks/Adolescents show at the Marina del Rey Skatepark (aka "The Dog Bowl"). Milling around in the photo are various members of the Los Angeles hardcore-punk scene, including Circle Jerks bassist Roger Rogerson and Adolescents drummer Casey Royer.

LET IT BE **(1984)—THE REPLACEMENTS**   Released by Twin/Tone Records on October 2, 1984, the third album by this legendary Minneapolis, Minnesota, punk/alternative-rock band features a classic image taken by Daniel Corrigan of the four band members—Chris Mars, Bob Stinson, Tommy Stinson, and Paul Westerberg—just chilling out on roof of the Stinson family house. Now widely considered one of the greatest rock albums of the 1980s, *Let It Be* ranked 241 on *Rolling Stone*'s list of the "500 Greatest Albums of All Time."

Original titles for the album included both *Whistler's Mammy* and *Stunk*. However, according to legend, the band decided that the next song they heard on the radio would be the album title, which turned out to be "Let It Be" by the Beatles. According to Westerberg, it was "our way of saying that nothing is sacred, that the Beatles were just a fine rock 'n' roll band."

MINOR THREAT **(1984)—MINOR THREAT**   For their 1984 self-titled compilation album (aka *First Two Seven Inches*), Washington, DC, hardcore-punk band (and pioneers of the straight-edge movement)

Minor Threat chose to feature an iconic image of lead singer Ian MacKaye's brother Alec (of the bands Untouchables and the Faith)—sitting on a staircase with his head bowed. Rancid copied the image (with the addition of a mohawk) for their third album, . . . *And Out Come the Wolves* (1995). In 2005, Nike launched a "Major Threat" ad campaign for its 2005 East Coast Tour using the Minor Threat album cover image without asking permission. The company was forced to retract the ad and issue an apology to both Minor Threat and Dischord Records (the band's own record label).

RUM SODOMY AND THE LASH (1985)—**THE POGUES**   Considered their masterpiece, the second album by Celtic punk band the Pogues reached no. 14 on the UK charts and spawned the hit single "A Pair of Brown Eyes." The cover artwork features a modified version of French artist Theodore Gericault's famous 1819 Romantic-era painting, *The Raft of the Medusa* (originally titled *Shipwreck Scene*), with the heads of band members replacing those of various individuals on the raft. The original painting depicts the aftermath of the wreck of the *Meduse*, a French naval frigate that ran aground off the coast of West Africa in 1816. All but 15 of the 147 set adrift survived the thirteen-day ordeal on the raft.

DOOKIE (1994)—**GREEN DAY**   Green Day's breakthrough album, *Dookie*, was released by Reprise Records on February 1, 1994, and went on to sell twenty million copies on the strength of such pop-punk classics as "Basket Case," "Longview," "When I Come Around," "She," and "All by Myself." The somewhat-controversial *Dookie* album cover featured colorful artwork by legendary East Bay musician and artist Richie Bucher that depicted bombs dropping on a replica of Berkeley's Telegraph Avenue and Green Day exploding out of all the wreckage. According to Green Day lead singer Billie Joe Armstrong, "I wanted the artwork to look really different. I wanted it to represent the East Bay and where we come from, because there's a lot of artists in the East Bay scene that are just as important as the music."

Incidentally, the album's title, which was originally supposed to be *Liquid Dookie*, referred to Green Day band members constantly suffering from bouts of diarrhea while on tour. *Dookie* won a 1995 Grammy Award for Best Alternative Album—beating out the likes of Tori Amos (*Under the Pink*), Crash Test Dummies (*God Shuffled His Feet*), Sarah McLachlan (*Fumbling Towards Ecstasy*), and Nine Inch Nails (*The Downward Spiral*).

19

All the Small Things
Punk Flyers and Zines

> The word "punk" seemed to sum up the thread that con-
> nected everything we liked—drunk, obnoxious, smart
> but not pretentious, absurd, funny, ironic, and things
> that appealed to the darker side. —Legs McNeil

Punk zines served as the embodiment of the DIY ethic of the
punk-rock movement. According to rock historian Dave Laing,
"[Punk] was the first musical genre to spawn fanzines in any significant number." One of the earliest and arguably the best zine,
Punk championed the early punk-rock scene at CBGBs in New
York City by profiling such bands as the Ramones, Blondie, Television, Johnny Thunders and the Heartbreakers, the Dictators, Patti
Smith, and many others. In London, *Sniffin' Glue* had much the
same impact—promoting the likes of the Sex Pistols, the Damned,
and the Clash. According to *Sniffin' Glue* founder Mark Perry,
"Punk was like a bomb going off. By issue four, we were talking
about taking over the music business."

PUNK FLYERS Long before the internet and social media, simple
hand-drawn and Xeroxed flyers pasted on walls, telephone poles,
phone booths, and traffic lights served as the most effective way to
promote punk shows. Today, some of best punk flyers are considered
collectible artwork from the likes of Jamie Reid (who designed most

of the iconic images associated with the Sex Pistols) and Raymond Pettibon (the renowned flyer artist from SST Records and Black Flag leader Greg Ginn's brother). It was Pettibon who suggested the name Black Flag and designed the band's distinctive four bars logo. *Fucked Up and Photocopied: Instant Art of the Punk Rock Movement* (1999) by Bryan Ray and Christopher Miller serves as the definitive history of punk flyer art.

ZIGZAG (1969–1986)   Started by Pete Frame, *ZigZag* was named after the Captain Beefheart song "Zigzag Wanderer" (and also rolling papers!). In 1974, the zine was taken over by Charisma Records founder Tony Stratton-Smith, who appointed Kris Needs as editor in 1977. At this point, the zine switched its focus entirely on the punk-rock scene with features on such musical artists as the Stranglers, Sex Pistols, Dr. Feelgood, Ian Dury, Buzzcocks, the Clash, and Blondie.

BACK DOOR MAN (1975–1978) Started by Phast Phreddie (Fred Patterson) in 1975, this highly influential Los Angeles fanzine (subtitled "For Hardcore Rock

True pioneers of hardcore punk, Los Angeles-based Black Flag was established by guitarist Greg Ginn in 1976.

Crudely hand-drawn and Xeroxed flyers served as the most effective way to promote early punk shows such as this one that showcased pioneering Washington, DC-based hardcore band Bad Brains.

'n' Rollers Only") covered the early punk scene as it evolved on the West Coast. It was copublished by Don Waller, lead singer of Los Angeles proto-punk band the Imperial Dogs. A reaction against the boring, "insipid pop of the Johns"—Elton John, Olivia Newton-John, and John Denver—the zine got its name after the Howlin' Wolf classic that was covered by the Doors on their self-titled debut album in 1967. The first issue of *Back Door Man* in March 1975 featured a cover story on Iggy Pop. The zine also published features on such bands as the Ramones, the Clash, the Weirdos, the Zeros, X, and the Last.

PUNK (1975–1979)   Founded in 1975 by cartoonist John Holmstrom, Ged Dunn, and Legs McNeil, *Punk* focused heavily on the CBGBs scene and occupied a nearby office at 365 Tenth Avenue dubbed the "Punk Dump." According to Holmstrom, "Punk rock had to come along because the rock scene had become so tame that [acts] like Billy Joel and Simon and Garfunkel were being called rock and roll when to me and other fans, rock and roll meant this wild and rebellious music."

To promote the arrival of *Punk*, the magazine's founders plastered flyers all over the streets of New York City that announced, "Watch Out! Punk is Coming!" The first issue of *Punk* in January 1976 sold for fifty cents and featured a cartoon cover of Lou Reed, a "Death to Disco Shit!" editorial, an article on Marlon Brando as "the original punk," and a quirky interview with the Ramones. Later issues of *Punk* offered interviews with the likes of Johnny Rotten, Iggy Pop, David Johansen, Debbie Harry, Patti Smith, Brian Eno, and Bob Geldof, as well as two special "film features" comprised of photos and cartoon special effects: *The Legend of Nick Detroit* (featuring Richard Hell and Debbie Harry) and *Mutant Monster Beach Party* (featuring Debbie Harry and Joey Ramone).

McNeil went on to coauthor *Please Kill Me: The Uncensored Oral History of Punk* in 1996 with Gillian McCain. In that book, McNeil remarked, "Holmstrom wanted [*Punk*] magazine to be a combination of everything we were into—television reruns, drinking beer, getting laid, cheeseburgers, comics, grade-B movies, and this weird rock 'n' roll that nobody but us seemed to like: the

Velvets, the Stooges, the New York Dolls, and the Dictators." *Punk* featured some outrageous reviews and opinions, like when Holmstrom proclaimed Lou Reed's 1975 album *Metal Machine Music*, which consisted of nothing but feedback, as "the ultimate punk album." Edited by Holmstrom and Bridget Hurd, *Punk: The Best of Punk Magazine* (2012) serves as an essential compendium of this prototypical punk zine.

BONDAGE (1976) A true do-it-yourself project, *Bondage* was created by future Pogues lead singer Shane MacGowan (aka "Shane O'Hooligan") in 1976. According to MacGowan in his 2001 memoir, *A Drink with Shane MacGowan*, *Bondage* served as the first graphic fanzine: "It was covered in graphics. Like, each page was covered in safety pins and chains and stuff." MacGowan only created one issue of the zine, which consisted of six pages scrawled in pen and then photocopied and stapled together. A photo of the Sex Pistols glommed from one of the band's gig flyers graced the front cover. The hard-partying MacGowan quickly turned his attention away from the zine and soon formed his first band, the Nipple Erectors (aka the Nips).

NEW YORK ROCKER (1976–1982) Founded by Alan Betrock and edited by Andy Schwartz, this punk-rock/new-wave zine published fifty-four issues and reached a peak circulation of 35,000. Tom Verlaine of Television was featured on the cover of the first issue of *New York Rocker*, which sold for seventy-five cents and also included features on Iggy and the Stooges, the Ramones, Wayne County, Patti Smith, Johnny Thunders and the Heartbreakers, Talking Head, Blondie, and the Flamin' Groovies. *New York Rocker* was immortalized in the song "I Read *New York Rocker*" by the dB's.

SNIFFIN' GLUE (1976–1977) Although this monthly London-based punk zine (full title: *Sniffin' Glue and Other Rock 'n' Roll Habits*) only lasted about a year, it proved highly influential. Started by Mark Perry in July 1976 with a circulation of just fifty copies, the zine took its name from the Ramones song "Now I Wanna Sniff Some Glue." The last issue of *Sniffin' Glue* sold twenty thousand copies. *NME* proclaimed the zine to be "the nastiest, healthiest, and funniest piece of press in the history of rock 'n' roll habits." Perry went on to form the experimental post-punk band Alternative TV. The anthology *Sniffin' Glue: The Essential Punk Accessory* was published in 2000.

FLIPSIDE (1977–2000)   Originally known as *Los Angeles Flip Side*, this punk zine was started by five high school students from Whittier and Pasadena, California. Between 1979 and 1989, *Flipside* was co-owned and coedited by Hudley "Hud" Flipside (Holly Duval Cornell). *Flipside* covered such bands as Black Flag, Social Distortion, Redd Kross, Dead Kennedys, the Germs, the Bags, the Skulls, Operation Ivy, Mr. T Experience, L7, and the Dickies. The zine also started Flipside Records, which signed the likes of Sluts for Hire, Doggy Style, Detox, Sandy Duncan's Eye, and Bulemia Banquet.

DAMAGE (1979–1981)   Started by Brad Lapin and based out of San Francisco, *Damage*, which published only thirteen issues, concentrated its coverage on the early California hardcore punk scenes. The zine's first issue featured Jello Biafra of the Dead Kennedys on the cover, along with features on the Bags, Noh Mercy, and MX-80 Sound. Other musical artists featured in the pages of *Damage* included the Mutants, John Cale, Lene Lovich, the Plastics, the Cramps, PiL, Crime, Stiff Little Fingers, Black Flag, D.O.A., Magazine, the Circle Jerks, Echo and the Bunnymen, Roky Erickson, and the Plugz.

SEARCH & DESTROY (1977–1979)   An immensely popular San Francisco punk zine that began publishing in 1977, *Search & Destroy* set the bar high in terms of DIY graphics and attitude. In its two short years of publication, *Search & Destroy* featured such musical artists and influencers as Iggy Pop (the zine took its name from the famous Stooges song), Patti Smith, Vivienne Westwood, Nico, the Ramones, Throbbing Gristle, and Devo, alongside renowned writers and filmmakers such as David Lynch, William S. Burroughs, J. G. Ballard, Russ Meyer, David Lynch, and John Waters. *Search &*

Destroy was the brainchild of photographer Richard Peterson and writer/publisher V. Vale, who later created RE/Search Publications, which published such classics as *Freaks: We Who Are Not as Others* (1976), *William S. Burroughs/Brion Gysin/Throbbing Gristle* (1982), *J. G. Ballard* (1984), *Incredibly Strange Films* (1986), and *Pranks!* (1986), among others. The *Search & Destroy* zine took shape only after Peterson and Vale received a $100 donation from Beat poet Allen Ginsberg, along with a matching donation from poet and cofounder of City Lights Bookstore Lawrence Ferlinghetti.

SLASH (1977–1988) Founded by Philomena Winstanley, Steve Samiof, Melanie Nissen, and Claude "Kickboy Face" Bessy, *Slash* enthusiastically covered the early Los Angeles punk scene, following the antics of such bands as the Weirdos, X, Fear, the Germs, the Skulls, Nervous Gender, the Bags, and the Screamers.

MAXIMUM ROCKNROLL (1982–2019) An influential nonprofit monthly zine based in San Francisco that originated as a weekly punk radio show on Berkeley's KPFA in 1978, *Maximim Rocknroll* (aka *MRR*) covered the gamut of punk subculture. Between 1992 and 2011, the zine also published a guide called *Book Your Fuckin' Life*.

PROFANE EXISTENCE (1989–2013) Based in Minneapolis, *Profane Existence* served as the zine for an anarcho-punk collective of the same name whose slogan was "Making Punk a Threat Again." The zine specialized in covering the anarcho-punk, crust-punk, and grindcore scene, as well as highlighting the punk lifestyle, and antifascism, in addition to animal, women's, and minority rights.

20

Pull My Strings
Punk Fashion, Trends, and Styles

> The only reason I'm in fashion is to destroy the word "conformity." —Vivienne Westwood

Influenced by the look of French writers Arthur Rimbaud and Antonin Artaud, along with the Antoine Doinel character in Francois Truffaut's 1959 classic *The 400 Blows*, punk icon Richard Hell developed the archetypal disheveled punk style. Sex Pistols manager Malcolm McLaren took the "ripped and slashed" look of Hell and brought it back to London. According to McLaren in *Please Kill Me,*

> Here was a guy all deconstructed, torn down, looking like he'd just crawled out of a drain hole, looking like he was covered with slime, looking like he hadn't slept in years, looking like he hadn't washed in years, and looking like no one gave a fuck about him. . . . By being inspired by it, I was going to imitate it and transform it into something more English.

In his memoir, *Massive Pissed Love*, Hell notes, "Without a doubt, the single most important thing I've ever done was my haircut."

BONDAGE PANTS Developed and popularized by Vivienne Westwood and Malcolm McLaren at their famous London boutique, SEX, bondage pants (aka bondage trousers) feature zippers, straps,

183

chains, rings, and/or buckles that give them an appearance of BDSM style. Punks, ravers, and goths have all adopted the bondage pants style.

GOBBING   One of the absolute worst trends in punk was the practice of gobbing (spitting) from the crowd directed toward band members onstage. Fred Schneider of the B-52's called gobbing "awful," while Robert Quine of Richard Hell and the Voidoids referred to it as "a horrible experience." Quine reportedly smacked an audience member with his guitar after getting gobbed on. Steve Diggle of Buzzcocks got gobbed straight in the mouth while doing backing vocals, while Joe Strummer of the Clash allegedly picked up hepatitis via gobbing during one gig, and Adam Ant reportedly used his pirate-themed eyepatch to cover up gob-induced conjunctivitis. Ironically, gobbing was meant as a means for fans to show appreciation for the band. No one is exactly sure when or how gobbing began, but some have pointed the finger to either Steve Jones of the Sex Pistols, Rat Scabies of the Damned, or Iggy Pop of the Stooges.

MOHAWKS   Mohawks have been traditionally associated with punk rockers, their hardcore fans, and other rebels. Paratroopers of the Seventeenth Airborne Division in World War II wore mohawks as a form of intimidation, as did jazz musicians like saxophonist Sonny Rollins. Peter Gabriel sported a mohawk while on tour with Genesis in 1973. Robert De Niro's deranged Travis Bickle character sported a mohawk briefly in Martin Scorsese's classic 1976 film *Taxi Driver*. Punk bands like the Germs, the Exploited,

Full of nihilism and rage, Martin Scorsese's 1976 psychological thriller, *Taxi Driver*, foreshadowed the coming of punk and even featured a Mohawk-sporting Travis Bickle (Robert De Niro). COLUMBIA PICTURES/PHOTOFEST

and several others featured mohawk-wearing band members. In addition, Wendy O. Williams of the Plasmatics famously wore a mohawk, as did Travis Barker of Blink-182. The Clash's sixth and final studio album, *Cut the Crap* (1985), which is generally regarded as their worst, features a mohawk-sporting punk on the cover. During the May Day 2000 anti-capitalist protests in London, a statue of Winston Churchill was defaced with a Mohawk.

POGOING   A precursor to moshing, the pogo was a simple dance initiated among crowds at early punk shows where the dancer jumps up and down like on a pogo stick. Shane MacGowan of the Pogues has claimed that he invented the pogo at the 100 Club (although most punk-rock historians claim that Sid Vicious started it). In fact, Viv Albertine of the Slits claimed in her 2014 autobiography that the pogo was inspired by the way Vicious jumped up and down as he played saxophone while a member of the band Flowers of Romance. The 1982 Men Without Hats hit single, "Safety Dance," was reportedly penned as a defense of pogoing.

SAFETY PINS   Richard Hell reportedly started the safety pin look that became a standard of punk-rock fashion after it was adopted by British punks. Johnny Rotten disputed this assertion, claiming that safety pins were incorporated for practical reasons to prevent "the arse of your pants falling out." Regardless, punk fans quickly incorporated safety pins as a clothing accessory or for piercings. In her 2009 book *Punks: A Guide to an American Subculture*, Sharon M. Hannon asserts that punk fashion consists of "black straight-leg pants, black leather jackets, short spiky hair, and torn T-shirts held together with safety pins."

SLAM DANCING   Slam dancing (aka moshing or slamming) is a ritualistic style of dancing common at hardcore punk shows where participants slam into each other in a designated area near the stage called the mosh pit. The infamous Cuckoo's Nest club in Costa Mesa, California, became known as the "Birthplace of Slam Dancing" in the late 1970s. Believe it or not, actor Tim Robbins (*The Shawshank Redemption*) was a slam-dancing punk fan in

Los Angeles during the early 1980s and attended shows by the likes of X, Fear, Black Flag, and the Circle Jerks. In *More Fun in the New World*, Robbins states, "In the mosh pit, as crazy as it got sometimes, I saw more people taking care of each other than I saw people who wanted to hurt others. We were a disparate, anarchic community. There was a strange family in those sweaty clubs." In his 2016 memoir *My Damage*, Keith Morris remarks, "In my mind skaters like Tony Alva and the Dogtown guys invented slam dancing and stage diving. The movement of someone in a circle pit looks like someone grinding away on a skateboard. If you don't know what you're seeing, it can look brutal and crude, but it's actually graceful and athletic."

A famous shot of skateboarder Chuck Burke stage diving at a 1981 Stiff Little Fingers/ Adolescents/DOA show was used on the cover of the 2006 documentary *American Hardcore* DVD cover. SONY PICTURES CLASSICS/PHOTOFEST

WALL OF DEATH   An extreme and extremely dangerous form of moshing, the infamous wall of death features audience members dividing into two halves on either side of a venue and rushing toward each other. The wall of death was reportedly invented by NYC hardcore band Sick of It All in the late 1980s and also became associated with Philadelphia crust punk band R.A.M.B.O., who even released a 2001 album titled *Wall of Death the System*. The wall of death was also called the "Braveheart" after the style of battle depicted in the 1995 Academy Award–winning film of the same name.

21

Strange Notes
Memorable Punk Literature

Rock and Roll adolescent hoodlums storm the streets of
all nations. —William Burroughs, *Naked Lunch*

The worlds of punk rock and literature intersected in strange and
wonderful ways during the 1970s. Known as the "Godfather of
Punk," legendary *Naked Lunch* author William S. Burroughs hung
out with Lou Reed, Debbie Harry, Patti Smith, Richard Hell, Joe
Strummer, and other musicians at the so-called "Bunker," his
windowless apartment at 222 Bowery just down the street from
CBGBs. In her 2010 memoir, *Just Kids*, Smith described a visit to
the Bunker: "It was the street of winos and they would often have
five cylindrical trash cans to keep warm, to cook, or light their cigarettes. You could look down the Bowery and sees these fires glowing
right to William's door. . . . He camped in the Bunker with his type-
writer, his shotgun and his overcoat." Burroughs's Beat Generation
compatriot, "Howl" poet Allen Ginsberg, later collaborated with the
Clash on the song "Ghetto Defendant."

In addition, a new punk style of writing was spawned—exemplified by such groundbreaking works as Kathy Acker's *Blood and
Guts in High School* and Jim Carroll's *The Basketball Diaries*. Last
but not least, Henry Rollins started his own publishing company,
2.13.61, which published works by Iggy Pop, Exene Cervenka of X,
Nick Cave, and others.

THE BASKETBALL DIARIES (1978)—JIM CARROLL   Jim Carroll's harrowing autobiographical novel documents his descent into the sordid world of drug addiction. An Irish bartender's son, Carroll attended the prestigious Trinity School in Manhattan on scholarship and was an All-City basketball star (as well as a hustler and heroin addict). The novel was made into a film of the same name in 1995 starring Leonardo DiCaprio, Lorraine Bracco, James Madio, and Mark Wahlberg. Carroll makes a cameo as a drug addict named Frankie Pinewater.

In the late 1970s, Carroll was encouraged by his friend and roommate, Patti Smith, to form a punk-rock/new-wave band called the Jim Carroll Band. His most memorable song, "People Who Died," appeared on the 1980 album *Catholic Boy*. In 1987, Carroll published a sequel to *The Basketball Diaries* called *Forced Entries: The Downtown Diaries: 1971–1973*. According to *The Encyclopedia of Punk*, "Along with Richard Hell and Tom Verlaine, Carroll brought a literary sensibility to punk and was able to use his druggy past to evocative effect in chronicling a life almost wasted, but in which a true poetic talent was somehow nurtured through an opiate haze." Carroll died of a heart attack at the age of sixty in 2009.

BLOOD AND GUTS IN HIGH SCHOOL (1978)—KATHY ACKER   Influenced by the likes of the Black Mountain School of progressive poets and William S. Burroughs, postmodernist writer Kathy Acker developed a writing style during the 1970s that evoked a strong punk sensibility with themes that addressed childhood trauma, rebellion, and sexuality. Born on April 18, 1947, in New York City, Acker studied classics at Brandeis University and the University of California, San Diego. *Blood and Guts in High School*, Acker's most popular novel, has been described as a masterpiece of surrealist fiction and deals with the then taboo subjects of human trafficking, incest, and sexual violence. Interspersed into the narrative are poems, letters, dream visions, and pornographic drawings. According to *The Outlaw Bible of American Literature*, "Acker invented the postmodern novel with genius and aplomb." Acker died of breast cancer at the age of fifty on November 30, 1997.

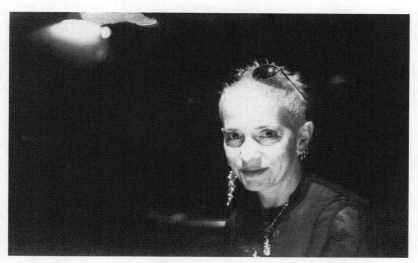

Considered a masterpiece of surrealist fiction with a strong punk sensibility, Kathy Acker's 1978 novel, *Blood and Guts in High School*, features poems, letters, dream visions, and pornographic drawings. By CorkyPleasures, Own work/Wikimedia Commons

***HIGH-RISE* (1975)—J. G. BALLARD**   A luxury high-rise building housing affluent residents in a London suburb descends into violent, *Lord of the Flies*–type chaos in this dystopian work from English novelist J. G. Ballard (1930–2009), who has been dubbed "punk's poet laureate" for his post-apocalyptic novels, which also include *The Atrocity Exhibition* (1970), *Concrete Island* (1974), and *Hello America* (1981), among others. None other than Joy Division lead singer Ian Curtis cited *High-Rise* as one of his favorite books, and English rock band Hawkwind used the book as the basis of one of the tracks of the same name that appears on their 1978 album, *PXR5*, and features the lyrics: "It's a human zoo/A suicide machine." In 2015, a film adaptation of *High-Rise* was released to generally positive reviews. Directed by Ben Wheatley, it stars Tom Hiddleston, Jeremy Irons, Sienna Miller, Luke Evans, and Elisabeth Moss.

***STARBURN: THE STORY OF JENNI LOVE* (1979)—ROSALYN DREXLER**   Primarily known for her innovative pop art paintings, Bronx-born visual artist Rosalyn Drexler penned this outrageous look at the trials and travails of "female funk/punk queen" Jenni Love and her band "The Great Mother Goddess Cult." Love must stand trial for the murder of a music critic. Drexler's other works include *I Am the Beautiful Stranger* (1965), *One or Another* (1970), *To Smithereens* (1972), *The Cosmopolitan Girl* (1974), *Unwed Widow* (1975), *Bad Guy* (1982), *Art Does (Not!) Exist* (1996), and *Vulgar Lives* (2007). During the 1950s, Drexler was a professional wrestler under the character of "Rosa Carlo, the Mexican Spitfire."

THE WILD BOYS: A BOOK OF THE DEAD (1971)—WILLIAM S. BURROUGHS

Billed as "a futuristic tale of global warfare," *The Wild Boys* depicts "a guerrilla gang of boys dedicated to freedom" battling "the organized armies of repressive police states." According to author Ted Morgan in his 1988 biography *Literary Outlaw: The Life and Times of William S. Burroughs*, the novel served as "Burroughs' Utopian vision of an alternative society, and, like all his writing, a search for a way to escape social conditioning, time, and his own body."

Glam rocker David Bowie reportedly based the look of his "Ziggy Stardust" on a character from the novel, and Malcolm McDowell's "Alex" character in Stanley Kubrick's 1971 film *A Clockwork Orange* reveals the novel's influence as well. In addition, Joy Division lead singer Ian Curtis often cited *The Wild Boys* and *Naked Lunch* as two of his favorite books. English post-punk/neo-psychedelic band the Soft Boys (originally known as Dennis and the Experts), which formed in 1976, took their name from a hybrid of *The Wild Boys* and *The Soft Machine*. A sample of the band's songs include "The Pig Worker," "The Return of the Sacred Crab," "Sandra's

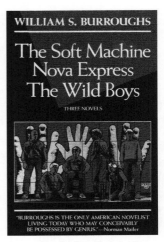

Known as the "Godfather of Punk," Beat Generation legend William S. Burroughs proved highly influential to the early NYC punk rock scene with such classic novels as *Naked Lunch* and *The Wild Boys*, among others.

Having Her Brains Out," "Old Pervert," "Fatman's Son," and "I Wanna Destroy You."

THE VOIDOID (1973)—RICHARD HELL   First written in 1973, Richard Hell's novella *The Voidoid* was finally published by 38th Street Publishers in 1996. The book's title served as inspiration for the name of Hell's band Richard Hell and the Voidoids, which formed in 1976. According to Hell, *"The Voidoid* was written in 1973 in a little furnished room on East 10th St. . . . Every day I'd take a bottle of wine with me across the street to the $16-a-week room I'd rented for writing. The method was I'd keep going till I got to the end of a single-spaced page, which was pretty far. I'd wake up an hour later and have to drink a whole lot of water."

Other works by Hell include *I Was a Spiral on the Floor* (1988), *Artifact: Notebooks from Hell 1974–1980* (1990), *Go Now* (1996), *Weather* (1998), *Hot and Cold* (1998), *Rabbit Duck* (2005, with David Shapiro), *Godlike* (2005), *The Toilet Paper Columns* (2007), *Psychopts* (2008, with Christopher Wool), *Disgusting* (2010), *I Dreamed I Was a Very Clean Tramp* (2013), and *Massive Pissed Love: Nonfiction 2001–2014* (2015).

PSYCHOTIC REACTIONS AND CARBURETOR DUNG (1987)—LESTER BANGS
Edited by Greil Marcus (*Lipstick Traces*), this celebrated collection of rock 'n' roll essays was released five years after brilliant rock critic Lester Bangs died of an accidental overdose at the age of thirty-three on April 30, 1982. Bangs served as editor for *CREEM* magazine between 1971 and 1976. He also wrote reviews for *Rolling Stone* and freelanced for *NME* and several other music publications over the years.

In his introduction to *Psychotic Reactions and Carburetor Dung*, Marcus comments, "Perhaps what this book demands from a reader is a willingness to accept that the best writer in America could write nothing but record reviews." The title of the book comes from a 1971 essay on garage rock that contains one of the first references to punk as a type of rock music: "Punk bands started cropping up who were writing their own songs but taking the Yardbirds' sound." Essays also include "Iggy Pop: Blowtorch in Bondage," "Richard

Hell: Death Means Never Having to Say You're Incomplete," "Sham 69 Is Innocent," and "A Reasonable Guide to Horrible Noise." Pertaining to punk rock, Bangs writes, "You see, dear reader, so much of what's doled out as punk merely amounts to saying I suck, you suck, the world sucks, and who gives a damn—which is, er, ah, somehow *insufficient.*"

***PARADOXIA: A PREDATOR'S DIARY* (1997)—LYDIA LUNCH**   One of the founding members of New York City "no wave" band Teenage Jesus and the Jerks, Lydia Lunch is also a prolific writer and published *Paradoxia: A Predator's Diary*, which has been billed as "an uncensored, novelized account of one woman's assault on men." A loose autobiography, *Paradoxia* explores Lunch's early life with graphic details about her sexual history, substance abuse, and mental health struggles. In a review of the book, *Popmatters* magazine wrote that *Paradoxia* is for those "who thrill to the exploits of sociopaths and revel in sex as both the ultimate means and metaphor for power itself. This means that its tedium is hard for any adult to sit through without skimming and groaning." For example, a typical line from *Paradoxia* reads, "I beg for his fuck, beg to be power-slammed against the wall, squashed by his slippery prick, annihilated." Other Lunch works to seek out (or deliberately avoid) include *Adulterers Anonymous* (1982 with Exene Cervenka of X), *Bloodsucker* (1992, with Bob Fingerman), *Incriminating Evidence* (1992), *The Gun Is Loaded* (2007), *Will Work for Drugs* (2009), and *So Real It Hurts* (2019, featuring an introduction by Anthony Bourdain).

***CHELSEA HORROR HOTEL* (2001)—DEE DEE RAMONE**   When Dee Dee Ramone departed the Ramones in 1989, he embarked on a thankfully short-lived career as rap singer "Dee Dee King" while continuing to write songs for his former band. He also turned to writing his memoirs, as well as working on this highly eclectic, fictionalized account of living in the legendary Chelsea Hotel with his wife Barbara and their dog Banfield. Released just thirteen months before his fatal heroin overdose on June 5, 2002, *Chelsea Horror Hotel* documents Dee Dee's day-to-day life in the hotel (which revolves primarily on his attempts to score drugs and walk Banfield, with whom he can "magically communicate"). In addition, the book occasionally descends into the paranormal as Dee Dee becomes tormented by the deaths of his punk rock buddies Johnny Thunders, Stiv Bators, Jerry Nolan, and Sid Vicious.

Chelsea Horror Hotel features a foreword by director Joe Dante (*Gremlins*) and crudely drawn cover art of the Chelsea by Dee Dee himself. Dante quite hyperbolically refers to the novel as a "phantasmagoric acid trip" from a "punk Lovecraft" with "surreal echoes of *Naked Lunch*." Dee Dee's other published works include *Legend of a Rock Star* (2001) and *Lobotomy: Surviving the Ramones* (2000), which was originally published in 1998 as *Poison Heart: Surviving the Ramones*.

JUST KIDS (2010)—PATTI SMITH An award-winning memoir by the so-called "punk poetess" details her relationship with celebrated (and often controversial) photographer Robert Mapplethorpe, who died of complications due to HIV/AIDS at the age of forty-two on March 9, 1989. In the late 1960s, the aspiring and unknown bohemian artists shared a Brooklyn apartment together and became soulmates for life. According to Smith, "I didn't write [*Just Kids*] to be cathartic. I wrote it because Robert asked me to. . . . Our relationship was such that I knew what he would want and the quality of what he deserved." It was Mapplethorpe who took the iconic photograph that appears on the cover of Smith's 1975 debut album, *Horses*. Other Mapplethorpe photo subjects included Iggy Pop, Debbie Harry, Andy Warhol, and Kathy Acker, among many others. *Just Kids* won the 2010 National Book Award for Nonfiction.

22

When the Shit
Hits the Fan
Hollywood Goes Punk

> Punk is about not giving a shit and being angry and
> doing what you want and living your own life and being
> a shithead, but like, you know, a great shithead. —Jared,
> *The House of Tomorrow* (2017)

The punk film genre offers plenty of rewards for the adventurous
explorer! Many of the earliest punk-themed films were gritty, low-
budget independent efforts such as *The Foreigner* (1977), *Breaking
Glass* (1980), *Smithereens* (1982, which starred punk rock iconoclast Richard Hell), and *Suburbia* (1984). The punk film genre has
also produced at least three legitimate cult classics: *Rock 'n' Roll
High School* (1979) starring the Ramones; *Repo Man* (1984) with
its outstanding soundtrack that features classic tracks from Iggy
Pop, Black Flag, Circle Jerks, Suicidal Tendencies, the Plugz, and
others; and *SLC Punk!* (1998), which deftly explores the counter-
culture scene in Utah (!). Last but not least, worthy punk biopics to
seek out include *Sid & Nancy* (1986), *24 Hour Party People* (2002,
the rise and fall of Factory Records), *Control* (2007, tragic life of
Joy Division's Ian Curtis), *What We Do Is Secret* (2007, tragic life
of the Germs' Darby Crash), *The Runaways* (2010, the 1970s all-
girl hard-rock band), *Good Vibrations* (2012, Terri Hooley and the
Belfast punk scene), and *CBGB* (2013, NYC's punk hot spot during the 1970s).

***THE FOREIGNER* (1977)**   "When we dream that we dream, we are beginning to wake up." Directed by Amos Poe, one of the founders of No Wave Cinema, and filmed entirely in New York City (including at CBGBs, where punk band the Mumps are seen performing), this black-and-white curiosity involves a secret agent known only as Max Menace (Eric Mitchell) from Europe who arrives in New York City and encounters a variety of odd characters. The rest of the cast includes Debbie Harry of Blondie as Dee Trick, Patti Astor as Fili Harlow, Terens Severine as Zazu Weather, and Anya Phillips as Doll.

Poe's filmography also includes *Night Lunch* (1975, codirected with Ivan Kral), a compilation of live onstage performances by Queen, David Bowie, Patti Smith, Blondie, and the Ramones; *Unmade Beds* (1976), a quirky remake of Jean-Luc Godard's *Breathless*; *The Blank Generation* (1976), early punk performances filmed at CBGBs; *Subway Riders* (1981), a thriller involving a murderous saxophonist named Ant Zindo (played by John Lurie); and *Alphabet City* (1984), a NYC crime drama starring Vincent Spano and Jami Gertz; among others.

***JUBILEE* (1978)**   "It will excite your senses and terrify your soul!" Now considered somewhat of a cult classic, *Jubilee* was directed by Derek Jarman and scored by Brian Eno. An aimless mess, *Jubilee* serves mainly as a curiosity to anyone curious enough to view early performances by punk and new-wave icons such as Adam Ant, Wayne/Jayne County, the Slits, and Siouxsie and the Banshees. The movie's title refers to the Silver Jubilee celebration of Queen Elizabeth II the previous year.

The *Jubilee* soundtrack features "Deutscher Girls" and "Plastic Surgery" by Adam and the Ants, "Paranoia Paradise" by Jayne County and the Electric Chairs, "Right to Work" by Chelsea, "Nine to Five" by Maneaters, "Wargasm in Pornotopia" by Amilcar, "Slow Water" and "Dover Beach" by Brian Eno, and "Love in a Void" by Siouxsie and the Banshees, among others.

***OVER THE EDGE* (1979)**   "A real story of teenage rebellion." A bunch of bored, stoned young punks raise hell in a planned suburban community called "New Granada" in this forgotten movie classic notable for its punk sensibilities. It's all here: booze, pot, guns, vandalism, and sex—"a real story of teenage rebellion," according to the film's tagline. Shot in just thirty-six days and notable as Matt Dillon's film debut, *Over the Edge* was reportedly based on an actual incident that occurred at a planned community in Foster City, California, in the early 1970s. Directed by Jonathan Kaplan (who had briefly been tapped to direct the unfinished Sex Pistols movie *Who Killed Bambi*), the film also stars Michael Eric Kramer, Pamela Ludwig, Harry Northup, and Vincent Spano.

All the mayhem is accompanied by some classic tunes, including "Teenage Lobotomy" (The Ramones), "You Really Got Me" (Van Halen), and "Just What I Needed" (The Cars). In his 2007 self-titled autobiography, Slash of Guns N' Roses stated, "In its aggressive and most realistic moments, [*Over the Edge*] was a true representation of teenage culture at the time."

Over the Edge was allegedly Kurt Cobain's favorite film and served as the inspiration for Nirvana's iconic "Smells Like Teen Spirit" video. In addition, the film reportedly influenced Director Richard Linklater's 1993 coming-of-age comedy, *Dazed and Confused*.

ROCK 'N' ROLL HIGH SCHOOL (1979)   "Will your school be NEXT?" Produced by the "King of B-Movies," Roger Corman, and directed by Allan Arkush (*Caddyshack II*), this cheesy, over-the-top cult film featured the Ramones along with a flimsy plot about a rebellious teenager named Riff Randell (P. J. Soles), the biggest Ramones fan at Vince Lombardi High School, who writes the title song in hopes that the band will agree to record it. Vince Van Patten, Clint Howard, Dey Young, Paul Bartel, and Mary Woronov (as evil Principal Togar) round out the eclectic cast. Believe it or not, the film's working titles included *Disco High*, *Heavy Metal Kids*, and *Girl's Gym*. In addition, the Ramones were reportedly the third choice for the film, behind Cheap Trick and Todd Rundgren (!).

By far the best thing about *Rock 'n' Roll High School* is the Ramones medley that takes place in the middle of the movie and consists of "Blitzkrieg Bop," "Teenage Lobotomy," "California Sun,"

The Ramones steal the show in the 1979 cult film *Rock 'n' Roll High School* although the band was the third choice behind Cheap Trick and Todd Rundgren. NEW WORLD/ PHOTOFEST

"Pinhead," and "She's the One." The performance was recorded live at the legendary Roxy nightclub in Los Angeles. The *Rock 'n' Roll High School* soundtrack also consists of "Come Back Jonee" by Devo, "School's Out" by Alice Cooper, "School Days" by Chuck Berry, "Smokin' in the Boys Room" by Brownsville Station, "Teenage Depression" by Eddie and the Hot Rods, "Energy Fools the Magician" by Brian Eno, and "So It Goes" by Nick Lowe.

Look for Darby Crash of the Germs very briefly as an extra in the Ramones concert audience. The movie was shot primarily in California at the now-defunct Mount Carmel High School in South Central, Los Angeles. According to Dee Dee Ramone in his 2000 memoir *Lobotomy*, making the movie "was horrible, real low-budget. I didn't like Vince Van Patten or the other extras in the movie. They weren't bad people or anything, but they just came from a totally different world than the Ramones. . . . They weren't even Ramones fans, except for Allan the director."

Make sure to stay clear of the dismal 1991 "sequel" titled *Rock 'n' Roll High School Forever*, which stars none other than Corey Feldman.

BREAKING GLASS (1980)   "It will tear your heart out." A British cult film written and directed by Brian Gibson, *Breaking Glass* stars Hazel O'Connor as a young and talented punk club singer who is willing to do just about everything to achieve stardom—with tragic consequences, of course! According to critic Danny Peary in *Guide for the Film Fanatic*, "This is a sad, thematically bewildering film—and if you don't like either O'Connor's singing or her make-up and weird outfits, you won't get much satisfaction." Surprisingly, the *Breaking Glass* soundtrack, which features songs performed by O'Connor, reached no. 5 on the UK charts and includes the hits "Eighth Day" and "Will You?"

OUT OF THE BLUE (1980)   "She's 15. The only adult she admires is Johnny Rotten." Directed by Dennis Hopper, this intense and disturbing Canadian drama stars Linda Manz (*Days of Heaven*) as a troubled and rebellious teenager named Cebe whose only two interests are Elvis Presley and punk rock. Hopper portrays her psychopathic ex-convict father, along with Sharon Farrell as her junkie mother. The movie's title is taken from Neil Young's classic song "My, My, Hey, Hey (Out of the Blue)."

TIMES SQUARE (1980)   "Go Sleaze! . . . in Times Square." A rather mediocre drama directed by Allan Moyle about two teenage runaways (Trini Alvarado and Robin Johnson) set amok in New York City, *Times Square* (original title: *She's Got the Shakes*) has gained a growing cult over the years—mostly for its great punk- and new-wave-inspired soundtrack. Look for Tim Curry as radio DJ Johnny LaGuardia. Critic Roger Ebert wrote, "*Times Square* rarely comes together into anything more than a good idea that fails, but there are times when it seems on the brink of wonderful things. Of all the bad movies I've seen recently, this is the one that projects the real sense of a missed opportunity—of potential achievement gone wrong."

The stellar *Times Square* soundtrack features "Dangerous Type" by the Cars, "Grinding Halt" by the Cure, "Flowers in the City" by David Johansen and Robin Johnson, "Down in the Park" by Gary Numan, "Talk of the Town" by the Pretenders, "Rock Hard" by Suzi Quatro, "I Wanna Be Sedated" by the Ramones, "Walk on the Wild Side" by Lou Reed, "Same Old Scene" by Roxy Music, "Babylon's Burning" by the Ruts, "Pissing in the River" by the Patti Smith Group, "Life Before Wartime" by Talking Heads, and "Take This Town" by XTC, among others.

LADIES AND GENTLEMEN: THE FABULOUS STAINS (1982)   "She can't fool all of the fans all of the time." Directed by music mogul Lou Adler, this musical satire (with a working title of *All Washed Up*) reportedly sat on Paramount's shelf for a couple of years but has since evolved into somewhat of a cult classic. The plot (such as it is) concerns an all-female punk band comprised of Corinne Burns (Diane Lane), Jessica McNeil (Laura Dern), and Tracy Burns (Marin Kanter). A happy MTV video ending was reportedly tacked on in a desperate attempt to please the masses. The cast includes Paul Cook and Steve Jones of the Sex Pistols, Paul Simonon of the Clash, and Fee Waybill and Vince Welnick of the Tubes, who make up a fictional punk band called the Looters.

SMITHEREENS (1982)   "Everyone's a little weird these days. It's normal." Another extremely low-budget film about a young teenager (a rather unpleasant Susan Berman) trying to make it in the Big Apple, *Smithereens* is notable as being the directorial debut of Susan Seidelman (*Desperately Seeking Susan*) and for casting punk-rock icon Richard Hell of Television, the Heartbreakers, and the Voidoids in a prominent role. In fact, the soundtrack features two songs by Richard Hell and the Voidoids: "Another World" and "The Kid with the Replaceable Head."

VALLEY GIRL (1983)   "Crush that fly!" One of the best of the plethora of teen comedies from the early 1980s and a true artifact of the era, this "totally tubular" flick loosely based on *Romeo and Juliet* (but actually inspired by Frank Zappa's immensely popular 1982 novelty hit of the same name that features his daughter, Moon Unit) concerns a brief love affair between a popular valley chick from the San Fernando Valley named Julie (Deborah Foreman) and Randy (Nicolas Cage), a punker from the seedy streets of Hollywood. Julie spouts such memorable lines as "Man, he's like tripendicular, ya know?" while Randy casually remarks, "That techno-rock you guys listen to is gutless."

Directed by Martha Coolidge, *Valley Girl* also stars Michael Bowen as Julie's douchebag boyfriend "Tommy," Cameron Dye as Randy's idiotic sidekick "Fred Bailey," and Frederic Forrest and Colleen Camp as Julie's parents—two stoner hippie refugees from the 1960s who now operate a health food restaurant.

For better or worse, *Valley Girl* pretty much launched Cage's film career (he appeared very briefly in a thankless role as "Brad's Bud" in *Fast Times at Ridgemont High*). The eclectic *Valley Girl* soundtrack features such gems as "A Million Miles Away" (the Plimsouls), "Angst in My Pants" (Sparks), "I Melt with You" (Modern English), "Love My Way" (Psychedelic Furs), and "She Talks in Stereo" (Gary Myrick & the Figures).

REPO MAN (1984) "I'd rather die on my feet than live on my knees." An outrageous science fiction black comedy, *Repo Man* somehow blends the seedy world of automobile repossession with punk rock and science fiction (there's an anti-nuclear-war subtext thrown in as well!). The cult classic stars Harry Dean Stanton as seasoned repo veteran Bud and Emilio Estevez as the young upstart Otto, a punk rocker and former supermarket stock clerk.

The duo has run-ins with ruthless government agents, UFO cultists, hired killers, a lobotomized nuclear scientist, and the infamous Rodriguez brothers—all in search of a mysterious '64 Chevy Malibu. Everyone drinks generic beer. As Bud, Stanton gets to deliver some truly unforgettable lines, such as "A repo man spends his life getting into tense situations" and "I don't want no commies in my car. No Christians either."

Directed by Alex Cox (*Sid & Nancy*), *Repo Man* features a great soundtrack, including the likes of Iggy Pop ("Repo Man"), Black Flag ("TV Party"), Circle Jerks ("When the Shit Hits the Fan"), Fear

Dubbed the "quintessential cult film of the 1980s" by the Criterion Collection, *Repo Man* (1984) features an amazing soundtrack full of punk classics and great performances from the likes of Harry Dean Stanton. UNIVERSAL PICTURES/PHOTOFEST

("Let's Have a War"), Suicidal Tendencies ("Institutionalized"), Burning Sensations (cover of Jonathan Richman's "Pablo Picasso"), and the Plugz ("El Clavo y la Cruz"). In addition, Zander Schloss, who portrays "Kevin the Nerd," went on to play bass for the Circle Jerks and the Weirdos. Over the years, he has also collaborated with the likes of Joe Strummer, Thelonious Monster, Die Hunns, Mike Watt of Minutemen, and Stan Ridgway from Wall of Voodoo, among other musical acts.

Beat Generation aficionados will want to pay attention in the hospital scene where a "Dr. Benway" and a "Mr. Lee" are paged—an indirect tribute to *Naked Lunch* author William S. Burroughs.

STRANGER THAN PARADISE (1984) "You know it's funny. You come to someplace new and everything looks just the same." Dull Willie (John Lurie of the Lounge Lizards) and his even duller buddy Eddie (Richard Edson, Sonic Youth's original drummer) decide to liven up their excruciatingly dull lives by taking a vacation . . . to Cleveland! Once they arrive, they hang out with Willie's Hungarian cousin Eva

(Eszter Balint) during an exceptionally bleak winter. Cecilla Stark practically steals the show as Aunt Lotte, who constantly exclaims, "Son of a beetch." Nothing much happens, and that is the brilliance of this film.

Director Jim Jarmusch filmed this static black-and-white masterpiece for just $120,000. Music was provided by Lurie and the Lounge Lizards. The soundtrack also features "I Put a Spell on You" by Screamin' Jay Hawkins. Also look for character actor Rockets Redglare (Michael Morra) as a very disgruntled poker player. In his November 12, 1984, diary entry, Andy Warhol wrote, "Went to see *Stranger Than Paradise*. It isn't good."

Jarmusch has remarked that his work has been inspired by the early New York City punk scene because "you didn't have to be a virtuoso musician to form a rock band. Instead, the spirit of the music was more important than any kind of technical expertise on the instrument, which of course was—in New York—first Patti Smith and Television, and then Heartbreakers, the Ramones, Mink de Ville, Blondie, Talking Heads—all those bands."

SUBURBIA (1984) "A New Movie . . . about a New Generation." Also known as *The Wild Side* and *Rebel Streets*, this gritty coming-of-age drama was written and directed by Penelope Spheeris (*The Decline of Western Civilization* trilogy) and depicts the sordid lives of a bunch of homeless punks who take refuge in an abandoned suburban tract home in Los Angeles. Spheeris recruited her actors among street kids and punk rockers, one of whom is portrayed by none other than Flea of the Red Hot Chili Peppers.

One of the highlights of this dreary but memorable film is live performance footage from the likes of D.I. ("Richard Hung Himself"), T.S.O.L. ("Wash Away," "Darker My Love"), and the Vandals ("The Legend of Pat Brown").

SID & NANCY (1986) "Never trust a junkie." Brilliant performances by Gary Oldman as Sid Vicious (Daniel Day Lewis had originally been considered for the role!) and Chloe Webb as Nancy Spungen elevate this outstanding drama directed by Alex Cox that premiered at the 1986 Cannes Film Festival.

Courtney Love of Hole has a small role in the film as one of the couple's junkie friends (she had auditioned for the part of Spungen). In addition, Slash of Guns N' Roses appears as an extra in a club scene. According to critic Michael Weldon in *The Psychotronic Encyclopedia of Film,* "This is the best 'punk rock' movie, and it has the best Thanksgiving dinner scene since *Eraserhead.*"

Although *Sid & Nancy* (aka *Sid & Nancy: Love Kills*) received critical acclaim, John Lydon had some harsh words for the film in his 1994 autobiography, *Rotten: No Irish, No Black, No Dogs:* "To me this movie is the lowest form of life. I honestly believe that it celebrates heroin addiction. It definitely glorifies it at the end when that stupid taxi drives off into the sky. That's such nonsense. . . . It was so off and ridiculous."

Directed by Alex Cox, *Sid & Nancy* (1986) features outstanding performances by Gary Oldman and Chloe Webb in the title roles although John Lydon called the film's ending "ridiculous." New Line Cinema/ Photofest

The *Sid & Nancy* soundtrack includes "Love Kills" and "Dum Dum Club" (Joe Strummer), "Haunted" and "Junk" (the Pogues), "Pleasure and Pain" (Steve Jones), "Chinese Choppers" and "Burning Room" (Pray for Rain), "Love Kills" (Circle Jerks), "She Never Took No for an Answer" (John Cale), and "I Wanna Be Your Dog" and "My Way" (Gary Oldman).

DUDES (1987) "New York City is tough, but the country is really murder." A very minor and forgettable effort directed by Penelope Spheeris, this punk rock comedy/drama involves the struggles of three punk rockers to make their way from New York City to

California. When one of them is murdered in the desert by a sadistic gang leader (portrayed by none other than Lee Ving of Fear), the other two vow to seek revenge. Jon Cryer, Catherine Mary Stewart, Daniel Roebuck, and Flea of the Red Hot Chili Peppers round out the cast. John Densmore of the Doors and Axxel G. Reese of the Gears also appear in small roles. In addition, California punk-rock band the Vandals appear as themselves.

THE BASKETBALL DIARIES (1995) "The true story of the death of innocence and the birth of an artist." Directed by Scott Kalvert (*Deuces Wild*) and starring Leonardo DiCaprio, Lorraine Bracco, James Madio, Mark Wahlberg, Ernie Hudson, Michael Imperioli, and Bruno Kirby, *The Basketball Diaries* captures all the glory and depravity of the sordid, heroin-laced life of writer and musician Jim Carroll (who makes a cameo as a strung-out drug addict named Frankie Pinewater).

Based on Carroll's 1978 autobiographical novel of the same name, the film, which premiered at the Sundance Film Festival, documents his descent into the harrowing world of drug addiction after the initial promise of attending prestigious Trinity School on scholarship as an All-City basketball star.

The film's soundtrack consists of "Star" by the Cult, "I've Been Down" by Flea, "Riders on the Storm" by the Doors, "Catholic Boy" by Carroll (with Pearl Jam), and "Blind Dogs" by Soundgarden. Controversy has shrouded the legacy of *The Basketball Diaries* due to a fantasy scene where DiCaprio's character imagines himself shooting up the school that eerily recalls the Columbine tragedy. As for Carroll, he formed the Jim Carroll Band in the late 1970s and scored a hit with the song "People Who Died."

TRAINSPOTTING (1996) "Living like this is a full-time business." A gritty British black comedy-drama directed by Danny Boyle about a gang of heroin addicts in Edinburgh, Scotland, *Trainspotting* was based on the 1993 novel of the same name by Irvine Welsh. The strong cast features Ewan McGregor, Jonny Lee Miller, Ewen Bremner, Kevin McKidd, Robert Carlyle, and Kelly Macdonald.

The film's outstanding soundtrack includes "Lust for Life" and "Nightclubbing" by Iggy Pop, "Deep Blue Day" by Brian Eno, "Trainspotting" by Primal Scream, "Temptation" by New Order, "Sing" by Blur, and "Perfect Day" by Lou Reed, among others.

SLC PUNK (1998)   "'Anarchy in the UK'? What the fuck's that? What good is that to those of us in Utah?" Directed by James Merendino, *SLC Punk* depicts the adventures of "Stevo" Levy (Matthew Lillard), a young punk-rock fan living in Salt Lake City. Michael Goorjian portrays Stevo's best buddy, "Heroin" Bob. An inferior sequel, *Punk's Dead: SLC Punk 2*, was released on iTunes in 2016.

The film boasts an amazing soundtrack that features "I Never Promised You a Rose Garden" by the Suicide Machines, "Sex and Violence" by the Exploited, "I Love Livin' in the City" by Fear, "1969" by the Stooges, "Too Hot" and "Gangsters" by the Specials, "Cretin Hop" by the Ramones, "Dreaming" by Blondie, "Kiss Me Deadly" by Generation X, "Rock N' Roll" by the Velvet Underground, "Gasoline Rain" by Moondogg, "Mirror in the Bathroom" by Fifi, "Amoeba" by the Adolescents, "Kill the Poor" by Dead Kennedys, and "Look Back and Laugh" by Minor Threat.

24 HOUR PARTY PEOPLE (2002)   "The truly unbelievable story of one man, one movement, the music and madness that was Manchester." Directed by Michael Winterbottom and starring Steve Coogan as music mogul Tony Wilson, this superb British biographical comedy-drama showcases Manchester's music scene through the rise and fall of legendary Factory Records. The *24 Hour Party People* soundtrack consists of such classics as "Anarchy in the UK" (the Sex Pistols), "Love Will Tear Us Apart" (Joy Division), "Ever Fall in Love" (Buzzcocks), "Janie Jones" (the Clash), and "New Dawn Fades" (New Order), among others.

CONTROL (2007)   "The past is now part of my future. The present is well out of hand." Shot in black and white, *Control* is a critically acclaimed British biopic about Joy Division singer-songwriter Ian Curtis (Sam Riley), a creative genius who suffered from epilepsy and depression and committed suicide in 1980 at the age of twenty-three. Directed by Anton Corbijn, the film was based on the 1995 biography *Touching from a Distance* by Curtis's widow, Deborah (who is portrayed by Samantha Morton). It premiered at the Cannes Film Festival. The film's title comes from the Joy Division song "She's Lost Control."

Highlights of the film's soundtrack include "Love Will Tear Us Apart" by Joy Division, "Exit" by New Order, "What Goes On" by the Velvet Underground, "Shadowplay" by the Killers, "Boredom" by Buzzcocks, "Autobahn" by Kraftwerk, and "Sister Midnight" by Iggy Pop.

WHAT WE DO IS SECRET (2007) "It All Started with a Germ." In this disturbing biopic directed by Rodger Grossman, Shane West stars as Darby Crash, the self-destructive lead singer of highly influential Los Angeles punk band the Germs who committed suicide via intentional heroin overdose in 1980 at the age of twenty-two. Highlights of the film's soundtrack include "You Drive Me Nervous" by Alice Cooper, "Five Years" by David Bowie, "We Are the One" by Avengers, "Survive" by the Bags, "Life of Crime" by the Weirdos, "Nausea" by X, and "Manimal" by the Germs.

THE RUNAWAYS (2010) "It's 1975 and they're about to explode." Based on the 1989 book *Neon Angel: A Memoir of a Runaway* by the band's lead vocalist Cherie Currie, *The Runaways* was directed by Floria Sigismondi and stars Dakota Fanning as Currie, Kristen Stewart as Joan Jett, and Michael Shannon as sleazy record producer Kim Fowley.

The Runaways soundtrack features "It's a Man's Man's Man's World" by MC5, "Rebel Rebel" by David Bowie, "I Wanna Be Your Dog" by the Stooges, "Pretty Vacant" by the Sex Pistols, and "Don't Abuse Me" by Joan Jett, as well as "Hollywood," "You Drive Me Wild," and "I Wanna Be Where the Boys Are" by the Runaways.

GOOD VIBRATIONS (2012) "Based on a true rock 'n' roll story." A highly entertaining and uplifting comedy/drama, *Good Vibrations* depicts the life and times of Terri Hooley (Richard Dormer), a record store owner instrumental in promoting the burgeoning punk-rock scene in Belfast, North Ireland, that featured the likes of the Undertones ("Teenage Kicks"), the Outcasts ("Justa Nother Teenage Rebel"), and Rudi ("The Pressure's On").

CBGB (2013)   "50,000 Bands and 1 Disgusting Bathroom." A rather mediocre, disappointing, and forgettable biographical drama that follows the history of a true New York City landmark, the legendary dive bar CBGBs, which has since been dubbed the "Birthplace of Punk." Alan Rickman portrays the club's eccentric owner, Hilly Kristal, whose initial concept for the club was to highlight country, bluegrass, and blues music. However, punk rock quickly reigned supreme at CBGBs, as bands like Television, Blondie, Patti Smith, Talking Heads, the Dead Boys, and, of course, the Ramones took the stage there regularly.

Universally panned by critics, the film was also a box-office bomb, grossing just $40,400 during its brief run in U.S. movie theaters. One bright spot was the film's soundtrack, which features "Life during Wartime" by the Talking Heads, "Kick Out the Jams" by MC5, "Chatterbox" by the New York Dolls, "Careful" by Television, "Blank Generation" by Richard Hell and the Voidoids, "Slow Death" by the Flamin' Groovies, "I Can't Stand It" by the Velvet Underground, "Out of Control" by Wayne County & the Electric Chairs," "Psychotic Reaction" by Count Five, "All for the Love of Rock 'n' Roll" by Tuff Darts, "All by Myself" by the Heartbreakers, "California Sun" by the Dictators, "Caught with the Meat in Your Mouth" by the Dead Boys, "I Got Knocked Down (but I'll Get Up)" by Joey Ramone, "Get Outta My Way" by the Laughing Dogs, "Sunday Girl" by Blondie, "I Wanna Be Your Dog" by the Stooges, "Sonic Reducer" by the Dead Boys, and "Roxanne" by the Police.

THE HOUSE OF TOMORROW (2017)   "Make Your Own Future." A greenhaired teenage punk (Alex Wolff) with a heart condition befriends a sheltered loner (Asa Butterfield) who lives with his grandmother (Ellen Burstyn) in one of those dated roadside futuristic house attractions. The two alienated outsiders form a punk-rock band called the Rash.

Written and directed by Peter Livolsi and based on the 2010 novel of the name by Peter Bognanni, *The House of Tomorrow* features a stellar soundtrack that includes "We Must Bleed" by the Germs, "Alternative Ulster" by Stiff Little Fingers, "Rise Above" by Black Flag, "Strange Little Girl" by the Stranglers, "Blank Generation" by Richard Hell and the Voidoids, and "I Wish It Would Rain" by Wreckless Eric.

23

Beyond and Back
Legendary Punk Documentaries

> I was always into music. I think everyone is when they're
> a teenager, as a way to drown out the world. —Penelope
> Spheeris

The earliest punk documentaries were DIY home-movie-type
productions such as *The Blank Generation* (1976) and *The Punk
Rock Movie* (1978). However, director Penelope Spheeris set the
standard for the genre with her groundbreaking *The Decline of
Western Civilization* (1981), which perfectly captured the burgeoning West Coast punk scene in all of its fascinating depravity. The
following punk documentaries cover the entire gamut, featuring the
good (*End of the Century: The Story of the Ramones*), the bad (*Kill
Your Idols*), and the ugly (*Hated: GG Allin and the Murder Junkies*).
Watch at your own risk!

THE BLANK GENERATION (1976)   "The Birth of Punk." One of the earliest punk films, this raw and gritty documentary of the early New
York City punk scene was directed by Amos Poe and Ivan Kral in
the true DIY fashion of a home movie. The film features some great
(but rather disorienting!) footage of then up-and-coming performers, such as the Ramones, Television, New York Dolls, the Heartbreakers, Blondie, and Patti Smith, as well as bands that have faded

from memory over time, such as Tuff Darts ("Your Love Is Like Nuclear Waste") and the Shirts ("Tell Me Your Plans").

THE PUNK ROCK MOVIE (1978)   "Oh, some decent fucking music at last!" Also known as *The Punk Rock Movie from England*, this British documentary features some excellent grainy Super 8 camera footage shot by Roxy Club DJ Don Letts depicting London's early punk-rock scene in 1977. Featured bands include the Sex Pistols ("God Save the Queen"), the Clash ("White Riot"), Generation X ("Walking in the City"), the Slits ("Vaseline"), Siouxsie and the Banshees ("Bad Shape"), X-Ray Spex ("Oh Bondage! Up Yours!"), Eater ("No Brains"), Slaughter and the Dogs ("Cranked Up Really High"), and Johnny Thunders and the Heartbreakers ("Born to Lose").

THE DECLINE OF WESTERN CIVILIZATION (1981)   "See it in a theater . . . where you can't get hurt." Directed by Penelope Spheeris (*Wayne's World*), this fascinating documentary takes an uncompromising

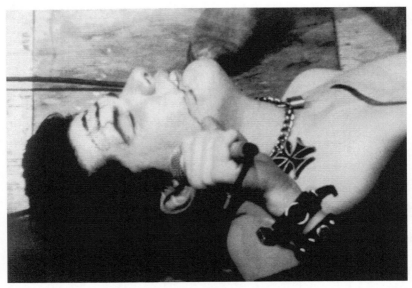

The Germs featuring self-destructive lead singer Darby Crash were one of the notable Los Angeles punk bands showcased in the 1981 documentary *The Decline of Western Civilization*. Photofest/Spheeris Films

look at the early Los Angeles punk scene with interviews and performances by Black Flag ("Depression," "Revenge," and "White Minority"), the Germs ("Manimal," "Shutdown"), X ("Beyond and Back," "Johny Hit and Run Paulene," "Nausea," "Unheard Music," and "We're Desperate"), Circle Jerks ("Back against the Wall," "Beverly Hills," "I Just Want Some Skank," "Red Tape," and "Wasted"), Alice Bag Band ("Gluttony," "Prowlers in the Night"), Fear ("Beef Bologna," "I Don't Care about You," "I Love Livin' in the City," "Let's Have a War," and "Fear Anthem"), and Catholic Discipline ("Barbee Doll Lust," "Underground Babylon"). The most compelling punk depicted in the documentary, Darby Crash of the Germs, died from a heroin-induced suicide shortly before the documentary was released.

The Decline of Western Civilization is part 1 of a trilogy by Spheeris that includes The Decline of Western Civilization Part II: The Metal Years (1988) and The Decline of Western Civilization III (1998). In 2016, The Decline of Western Civilization was selected by the Library of Congress for preservation in the U.S. National Film Registry for being "culturally, historically or aesthetically significant."

D.O.A.: A RIGHT OF PASSAGE (1981) "When I saw Johnny Rotten's face I thought I would vomit it's so beautiful." Lech Kowalski's highly entertaining rockumentary of the early punk scene features interviews and concert footage of Sham 69 ("Rip Off"), X-Ray Spex ("Oh Bondage! Up Yours!"), the Rich Kids ("Pretty Vacant" cover), Generation X ("Kiss Me Deadly"), the Dead Boys ("All This and More") and, of course, the Sex Pistols ("Anarchy in the UK," "God Save the Queen," "Liar," "I Wanna Be Me," "Pretty Vacant," "No Fun," "New York," "Holidays in the Sun," "E.M.I.," and "Bodies"). In addition, D.O.A. includes some great footage of the band's disastrous 1978 U.S. tour, which culminated in their last performance at Winterland Ballroom in San Francisco on January 14, 1978. D.O.A. also features an infamous, disturbing, but compelling interview with a zoned-out Sid Vicious and his girlfriend Nancy Spungen. D.O.A. premiered at the 1980 Festival of Festivals in Toronto. In Guide *for the Film Fanatic*, critic Danny Peary calls *D.O.A.* "an arresting, upsetting social document about the punk scene at its peak."

ANOTHER STATE OF MIND (1984)   "Under the makeup. Over the edge. An incredible journey through the underground." Filmed in the summer of 1982, *Another State of Mind* highlights the punk bands Social Distortion and Youth Brigade as they embark on their first (rather chaotic) international tour. It also includes footage of Washington, DC–based hardcore band Minor Threat. It was written and directed by Adam Small and Peter Stuart.

X: THE UNHEARD MUSIC (1986)   "Play This Movie Loud!" Directed by W. T. Morgan, this lively rockumentary showcases Los Angeles punk band X and its members: Exene Cervenaka, John Doe, Billy Zoom, and D. J. Bonebrake. Songs performed include "Los Angeles," "Year One," "We're Desperate," "Because I Do," "Come Back to Me," "Soul Kitchen," "White Girl," "The Once Over Twice," "Motel Room in My Bed," "The Unheard Music," "Real Child of Hell," "Johny Hit and Run Paulene," "I Must Not Think Bad Thoughts," "The World's a Mess; It's in My Kiss," and "The Have Nots."

1991: THE YEAR PUNK BROKE (1992)   "It's just fuckin' live man!" Directed by Dave Markey, this critically acclaimed rockumentary follows Sonic Youth as they tour Europe in 1991. It also features compelling footage of Nirvana, the Ramones, Dinosaur Jr., Babes in Toyland, and Gumball.

THE DECLINE OF WESTERN CIVILIZATION III (1998)   "Spare a quarter for disorder?" Part 3 of director Penelope Spheeris's award-winning trilogy depicts the desperate plight of "gutter punks" in Los Angeles. The documentary features revealing interviews with Keith Morris of Black Flag and Circle Jerks fame and Flea of Red Hot Chili Peppers, as well as such gutter punks as "Why Me," "Spoon," "Squid," "Filth," "Pinwheel," and "Hamburger." One of the punks remarks, "People who decide to live on the streets, they know they can't exist in regular society. They can't go on. It's not because of them. It's because what society has become. It's in decline. It's falling apart."

In addition, *Decline* highlights performances from the Resistance, Naked Aggression, Litmus Green, and Final Conflict. The film won the Freedom of Expression Award when it premiered at the 1998 Sundance Film Festival.

HATED: GG ALLIN AND THE MURDER JUNKIES (1993)   "A Rock 'n' Roll Overdose." Simply one of the most disturbing documentaries of all time, *Hated* explores the depraved world of shock rocker GG Allin. It was directed by Todd Phillips, who went on to more innocuous fare, such as the raunchy comedies *Road Trip* (2000), *Old School* (2003), and *The Hangover* (2009). Not for weak stomachs!

THE FILTH AND THE FURY (2000)   "A Sex Pistols Film . . . Uncut . . . Unseen . . . Unbelievable." An outstanding British rockumentary directed by Julien Temple, *The Filth and the Fury* traces the rise and fall of the Sex Pistols through interviews and rare concert footage. The film's title references an infamous headline in the *Daily Mirror* on December 2, 1976, following the Sex Pistols' notorious televised interview on the *Today* show with Bill Grundy. Temple had previously documented the band in *The Great Rock and Roll Swindle* (1980).

AFRO-PUNK (2003)   "The Movie That Sparked the Movement." Directed by James Spooner, *Afro-Punk* documents the lives of several Black punk artists among the predominantly White punk scene in the United States. Featured bands in this award-winning documentary include Bad Brains, Cipher, Ten Grand, and Tamar-kali. *Afro-Punk* inspired the annual Afropunk Festival, which began in 2005.

END OF THE CENTURY: THE STORY OF THE RAMONES (2003)   "That was the weird thing about it. They stayed together, but they hated each other." Produced and directed by Jim Fields and Michael Gramaglia, *End of the Century* explores the history of the Ramones from the band's modest beginnings in Forest Hills, Queens, during the early 1970s to their acrimonious 1996 breakup to their induction into the Rock and Roll Hall of Fame, and the tragic deaths of both

Joey Ramone and Dee Dee Ramone in the early 2000s. A rough version of the documentary premiered at the Slamdance Film Festival in 2003. Sadly, a third original member, Johnny Ramone, died a year after the film's release.

KILL YOUR IDOLS (2004)   "You Are a Target Market." Produced and directed by Scott Crary, *Kill Your Idols* highlights three decades of the art-punk and "no-wave" scene in New York City. Featured bands include Suicide, Teenage Jesus and the Jerks, DNA, Theoretical Girls, Sonic Youth, Swans, and Foetus. The film captured the Best Documentary Award at the 2004 Tribeca Film Festival. In 2013, *Kill Your Idols* was accepted into the permanent archives of the Rock and Roll Hall of Fame.

NEW YORK DOLL (2005)   "One Man. Two Journeys." Directed by Greg Whiteley, *New York Doll* depicts the fascinating life and career

The 2005 documentary, *New York Doll*, showcases the weird and wonderful life of New York Dolls bassist Arthur "Killer" Kane. First Independent Pictures/ Photofest

of Arthur "Killer" Kane, a founding member of the New York Dolls. Kane struggled for years with drug abuse and alcoholism. Miraculously, Kane managed to clean up his act and somewhat improbably converted to The Church of Jesus Christ of Latter-Day Saints. He even found work as a librarian in the church's extensive genealogy collection at its Los Angeles Family History Center. The documentary follows Kane as he nervously prepares to embark on a New York Dolls reunion in London with former bandmates David Johansen and Sylvain Sylvain. Tragically, Kane died from leukemia shortly after the triumphant performance. *New York Doll* premiered at the 2005 Sundance Film Festival, where it was nominated for both a Satellite Award and a Grand Jury Prize.

AMERICAN HARDCORE: THE HISTORY OF AMERICAN PUNK ROCK 1980–1986 (2007) "A Raw Blast of Politics, Passion, and Rage." Produced and directed by Paul Rachman, *American Hardcore* is based on *American Hardcore: A Tribal History*, a 2001 book written by Steven Blush that traces the history of American hardcore punk rock. Featured performers include Black Flag, D.O.A., Bad Brains, Minor Threat, SSD, and Minutemen, among others. *American Hardcore* premiered at the 2006 Sundance Film Festival.

JOE STRUMMER: THE FUTURE IS UNWRITTEN (2007) "A Celebration of Joe Strummer: Before, During, and After the Clash." Directed by Julien Temple (*The Filth and the Fury*), this powerful documentary depicts the life and career of the rhythm guitarist/vocalist/cofounder/lyricist of the Clash. The film premiered at the 2007 Sundance Film Festival.

KING OF PUNK (2007) "The Relevance of a Three Chord Revolution." Produced and directed by Kenneth and Julie van Schooten, *King of Punk* documents the punk scene from the late 1970s through the early 1980s and features wide-ranging interviews with band members from the Ramones, Dead Boys, Avengers, UK Subs, Zeros, and Exploited, among others.

The 2007 documentary, *Joe Strummer: The Future Is Unwritten*, celebrates the life of the legendary member of the Clash. By JOHN COFFEY/WIKIMEDIA COMMONS

***CLOCKWORK ORANGE COUNTY* (2012)**   "I lot of crazy shit went down there." The controversial Cuckoo's Nest nightclub in Costa Mesa, California, served as headquarters for the West Coast hardcore-punk scene in the late 1970s, and this documentary directed by Jonathan W. C. Mills traces its rise and spectacular fall. Bands that performed at the Cuckoo's Nest included the likes of Black Flag, the Circle Jerks, Iggy Pop, Dead Kennedys, T.S.O.L., the Vandals, and even the Ramones. The documentary, which offers a wide range of interviews from those who lived through all the madness—such as Jello Biafra (Dead Kennedys), Henry Rollins (Black Flag), Chuck Dukowski (Black Flag), and Keith Morris (Black Flag, Circle Jerks)—also borrows some great gritty footage of the club from the hard-to-find 1981 documentary *Urban Struggle: The Battle of the Cuckoo's Nest.*

***THE PUNK SINGER* (2013)**   "Her critics wished she would just shut up, and her fans hoped she never would." Directed by Sini Anderson, *The Punk Singer* highlights the life and career of Kathleen Hanna, a central figure in the Riot Grrrl movement, who fearlessly fronted the bands Bikini Kill and Le Tigre, and for many years suffered from Lyme disease, which prevented her from performing. The documentary also explores Hanna's marriage to Adam "Ad-Rock" Horovitz of the Beastie Boys.

THE DAMNED: DON'T YOU WISH THAT WE WERE DEAD (2015) "I don't fuckin' care about your documentary. I don't care about being in a fuckin' group. All I care about is survival. It's fuckin' bollocks." Directed by Wes Orshoski, this high-energy documentary explores the history of the Damned, the "long-ignored pioneers of punk," through archival footage, interviews, and performances. The film, which premiered at the SXSW Film Festival in 2015, also features appearances from Mick Jones, Lemmy, and Chrissie Hynde, as well as members of Pink Floyd, Black Flag, Guns N' Roses, the Sex Pistols, Blondie, and Buzzcocks.

HR FINDING JOSEPH I (2016) "I think that creativity comes with a bit of madness." Directed by James Lathos, this fascinating documentary chronicles the life and career of Paul "HR" Hudson, the brilliant and eccentric lead singer of pioneering Washington, DC, hardcore-punk band Bad Brains who has struggled with schizophrenia.

CROCK OF GOLD: A FEW ROUNDS WITH SHANE MACGOWAN (2020) "A good musician has to put music before everything." *Crock of Gold* celebrates the life and eclectic career of notorious hell-raiser Shane McGowan, who is best known as the lead singer and songwriter of the Pogues. The film was produced by Johnny Depp and directed by Julien Temple, whose filmography includes *The Great Rock 'n' Roll Swindle* (1979), *UK Subs: Punk Can Take It* (1979), *The Filth and the Fury* (2000), *Joe Strummer: The Future Is Unwritten* (2007), and *The Sex Pistols: There'll Always Be an England* (2008), among others.

24

Pretty Vacant
Post-Punk and New-Wave Bands

What went wrong? How did a music of such unruly
origins end up so trivial and diffused? —Mikal Gilmore

In his brutally honest 1994 memoir, John Lydon exclaimed with
typical bravado, "After the Pistols that term New Wave was the kiss
of death! Elvis Costello into Joe Jackson into Tom Robinson. . . .
The first time I heard the term it sickened me and turned my
stomach. If you settle for something so flimsy and vacuous as New
Wave, you certainly don't deserve to buy anything I put out. I'd be
appalled if that was my audience." Punk historian Nicholas Rombes
in *A Cultural Dictionary of Punk* notes that "the term 'New Wave'
suggested the softening, the de-fanging, of punk's initial combus-
tive fury."

Either way you look at it, by the time MTV launched on August
1, 1981, with the first music video, "Video Killed the Radio Star"
by the Buggles, the Second British Invasion was underway on the
airwaves, while hardcore dominated at the punk clubs. In addition,
innovative and diverse post-punk bands emerged on the scene in
the late 1970s and early 1980s, such as the Psychedelic Furs, the
Fall, Echo and the Bunnymen, Gang of Four, Joy Division, Sonic
Youth, Killing Joke, and the Smiths, among many others.

221

ADAM AND THE ANTS   Formed in London in 1977, Adam and the Ants started as a pub-rock band called Bazooka Joe, which then briefly morphed into simply the Ants. The band featured Adam Ant (real name: Stuart Goddard, who dropped out of the Hornsey College of Art to pursue his music career), Lester Square (guitar), Andy Warren (bass), and Paul Flanagan (drums). According to Ant, quoted in *The Encyclopedia of New Wave*, "I really knew I wanted to be Adam, because Adam was the first man. Ant I chose because, if there's a nuclear explosion, the ants will survive." After Malcolm McLaren gutted the entire band except Ant to form Bow Wow Wow, the new, improved version of Adam and the Ants consisted of guitarist Marco Pirroni, bassist Kevin Mooney, and two drummers: Chris Hughes and Terry Lee Miall. The resulting album, *Kings of the Wild Frontier* (1980), reached no. 1 on the UK charts and spawned three hit singles: "Antmusic," "Dog Eat Dog," and "Kings of the Wild Frontier."

Always dressed in his signature pirate attire, Ant went on to enjoy a successful solo career, starting with the wildly successful album *Friend or Foe*, which featured such MTV-friendly hits as "Goody Two Shoes" (no. 1 on the UK charts) and "Desperate but Not Serious" (no. 33 on the UK charts), as well as a spirited cover of the Doors' "Hello, I Love You." According to the *Rolling Stone Album Guide*, "Ant was the campiest figurehead of the New Romantic movement that also enlisted Bow Wow Wow and Duran Duran." Ant even embarked on a rather lackluster acting career, appearing in such forgettable clunkers as *Nomads* (1986), *Slam Dance* (1987), and *Trust Me* (1989).

Essential Listening: *Kings of the Wild Frontier* (1980)

THE B-52'S   Formed in Athens, Georgia, in 1976, the B-52's were known for their quirky recordings such as "Rock Lobster," "Love Shack," and "Private Idaho," sky-high beehive hairdos, and all-around eccentricity. Drawing their inspiration primarily from trash culture, the band consisted of vocalist Fred Schneider, keyboard player Kate Pierson, singer Cindy Wilson, guitarist Ricky Wilson (who tragically died of AIDS-related complications at the age of thirty-two in 1985), and drummer Keith Strickland. Early influences on the band included the Sex Pistols, Ramones, Patti Smith, and Devo.

The B-52's headed to New York City in 1977 and played gigs at Max's Kansas City and CBGBs. None other than Sid Vicious was reportedly a huge fan of the band. The B-52's earned a reputation as the "World's Greatest Party Band" and eventually sold over twenty million albums. The band's second album, *Wild Planet* (1980), features such classics as "Private Idaho," "Give Me Back My Man," and "Strobe Light," while their fifth album, *Cosmic Thing* (1989), sold five million copies and yielded the hits "Love Shack," "Roam," and "Deadbeat Club."

Essential Listening: *The B-52's* (1979), *Wild Planet* (1980), *Cosmic Thing* (1989)

BOW WOW WOW   Formed in 1980 by Malcolm McLaren, who persuaded the musicians from Adam and the Ants to defect and start a new band, Bow Wow Wow featured talented lead singer Annabella Lwin, a thirteen-year-old Burmese immigrant whom the former Sex Pistols manager discovered while she was working in a London laundromat. Guitarist Matthew Ashman, bassist Leigh Gorman, and drummer David Barbarossa rounded out the band. Bow Wow Wow's 1981 debut album sported one of the worst titles in rock history: *See Jungle! See Jungle! Go Join Your Gang Yeah, City All Over! Go Ape Crazy!* The album also featured much controversy for showcasing a naked Lwin, who was just fourteen years old at the time, on the cover. A remake of the Strangelove's

Formed in 1980 by Malcolm McLaren, Bow Wow Wow consisted of former members of Adam and the Ants along with thirteen-year-old Burmese immigrant Anabella Lwin as lead singer. BY BRAUNOV/WIKIMEDIA COMMONS

classic 1965 tune "I Want Candy" appeared on the band's subsequent album, *The Last of the Mohicans*. It reached no. 9 on the UK charts and received heavy airplay on MTV.

Bow Wow Wow released a total of four studio albums before calling it quits in 1983. Lwin then embarked on an unsuccessful solo career. The group made an attempted comeback in 1998, rehashing its tired material to bored and unresponsive audiences throughout the United States and Europe.

Essential Listening: *See Jungle! See Jungle! Go Join Your Gang Yeah, City All Over! Go Ape Crazy!* (1981)

THE CARS   Singer and guitarist Ric Ocasek met bassist Benjamin Orr in Cleveland, Ohio, and they performed in several unsuccessful bands together (including Martin Mull and His Fabulous Furniture!). The musicians eventually made their way to Boston and recruited guitarist Elliot Easton, keyboardist Greg Hawkes, and drummer Dave Robinson (formerly of the Modern Lovers) to form the Cars in 1976. The band's self-titled debut album was released in 1978 and features such hits as "Just What I Needed" (which ranked no. 369 on *Rolling Stone*'s list of the "500 Greatest Songs of All Time") "My Best Friend's Girl," and "Good Times Roll."

New York Times music critic Robert Palmer commented on the band's appealing blend of styles, which included "punk minimalism, the labyrinthine synthesizer and guitar textures of art rock, the '50s rockabilly revival and the melodious terseness of power pop." Darlings of MTV, the Cars scored four top 10 hits: "Shake It Up" (1981), "You Might Think" (which won Video of the Year at the first MTV Video Music Awards in 1984), "Drive" (1984), and "Tonight She Comes" (1985). The Cars broke up in 1988 and were inducted into the Rock and Roll Hall of Fame in 2018.

Essential Listening: *The Cars* (1978), *Candy-O* (1979), *Heartbeat City* (1984)

THE CURE   Formed in 1976, the Cure—which have been variously described as post-punk, new wave, goth rock, and alternative rock—originally started out as Easy Cure and consisted of lead singer and guitarist Robert Smith, guitarist Porl Thompson, bassist Michael Dempsey, and drummer Laurence "Lol" Tolhurst. The Cure's first single, "Killing an Arab," was inspired by Albert Camus's 1942 existential novel, *The Stranger*. The band released their debut album, *Three Imaginary Boys*, in 1979. Their 1982 album, *Pornography*, featured such hits as "Let's Go to Bed," "Just Like Heaven," "Lovesong," and "Friday I'm in Love." The Cure have released thirteen studio albums, the latest being *4:13 Dream* in 2008. Known for his disheveled appearance, unruly jet-black hair, pale complexion, black eyeliner, and smeared red lipstick, Smith has remained the only constant member throughout the years. The Cure were inducted into the Rock and Roll Hall of Fame in 2019.

Essential Listening: *Seventeen Seconds* (1980), *Pornography* (1982), *The Head on the Door* (1985), *Kiss Me, Kiss Me, Kiss Me* (1987), *Disintegration* (1989)

DEPECHE MODE   One of the most influential and successful electronic music bands of all time, Depeche Mode formed in 1980. The trio consists of lead vocalist Dave Gahn, keyboardist/guitarist/ vocalist Martin Gore, and keyboardist Andy Fletcher. The band released its debut album, *Speak & Spell*, in 1981. It spawned the hit single "Just Can't Get Enough." Over the years, Depeche Mode has placed fifty-four songs on the UK charts and sold more than one hundred million records worldwide. The band, which was inducted into the Rock and Roll Hall of Fame in 2020, has influenced the likes of Coldplay, No Doubt, the Smashing Pumpkins, Arcade Fire, the Killers, A Perfect Circle, Linkin Park, Muse, and others.

Essential Listening: *Black Celebration* (1986), *Music for the Masses* (1987), *Violator* (1990), *Songs of Faith and Devotion* (1993)

DEVO   Originating from Akron, Ohio, in the early 1970s, Devo started out as a rather lighthearted art project by Kent State University students Gerald Casale and Bob Lewis. The band then added keyboardist Mark Mothersbaugh and soon developed a cult following with their wacky costumes, futuristic helmets, and totally bizarre lyrics (just listen to "Blockhead"). Devo took its name from the somewhat-muddled concept of "devolution," the idea that mankind was regressing into an earlier state. In a scathing review of an early Devo performance, music critic Charlotte Pressler remarked, "If they had been beer can collectors, it would have been a good gig. Probably there were some rare varieties among the ones the audiences threw at them."

In 1978, Devo released their debut album, *Q: Are We Not Men? A: We Are Devo!* which was produced by Brian Eno and featured such quirky hits as "Mongoloid," "Jocko Homo," and a truly bizarre cover of the Rolling Stones' "(I Can't Get No) Satisfaction." Devo scored another massive hit in "Whip It," an early MTV staple, from the band's 1980 *Freedom of Choice* album. Devo has been nominated for induction into the Rock and Roll Hall of Fame in 2018, 2021, and 2022—but hasn't received an invite.

Essential Listening: *Q: Are We Not Men? A: We Are Devo!* (1978), *Duty Now for the Future* (1979), *Freedom of Choice* (1980)

ECHO AND THE BUNNYMEN   An English post-punk group formed in Liverpool in 1978, Echo and the Bunnymen consisted of lead singer Ian McCulloch, guitarist Will Sergeant, and drummer Pete de Freitas (who left the band in 1986 and tragically died in a motorcycle accident in 1989). The band's critically acclaimed debut album, *Crocodiles*, was released in 1980 and was followed by *Heaven Up Here* (1981), which reached no. 2 on the UK charts. The band's third album, *Ocean Rain* (1984), spawned the hit singles "The Killing Moon," "Silver," and "Seven Seas." In 1987, McCulloch left the band to pursue a solo career, the same year that the band's cover of the Doors' "People Are Strange" appeared on *The Lost Boys* soundtrack. Echo and the Bunnymen reappeared under a new incarnation in 1990 and released an album called *Reverberation*, which was poorly received by critics and fans alike. They disbanded in 1993 but have periodically reunited since then.

Essential Listening: *Crocodiles* (1980), *Heaven Up Here* (1981), *Ocean Rain* (1984)

THE FALL   Led by former office worker Mark E. Smith, English post-punk band the Fall formed in 1976 in Manchester and featured an astounding revolving door of more than fifty band members over the years (Smith once remarked, "If it's me and your granny on bongos, then it's the Fall"). The band, which quickly developed a strong cult following, took its name from a 1956 Albert Camus novel. The Fall released an incredible thirty-one studio albums, starting with *Live at the Witch Trials* in 1979. In his book *Music's Cult Artists*, John Riordan refers to Smith as the "grizzled Captain Ahab of alternative music." Championed by legendary DJ John Peel, the Fall influenced the likes of the Pixies, Sonic Youth, Pavement, LCD Soundsystem, and others. The band released their final album, *New Facts Emerge*, in 2017. Smith died of cancer on January 24, 2018, at the age of sixty. *Vice* called the Fall "a firestorm of a band that fused post-punk, amphetamine rockabilly, inimitable lyrics, gargling electronics and anything else they decided to throw in along the way."

Essential Listening: *Live at the Witch Trials* (1979), *Hex Enduction Hour* (1982), *Perverted by Language* (1983), *This Nation's Saving Grace* (1985)

GANG OF FOUR   Formed in 1977, English post-punk band Gang of Four influenced the likes of R.E.M., Nirvana, Fugazi, and Flea of Red Hot Chili Peppers. The original band consisted of lead singer Jon King, guitarist Andy Gill, bassist Dave Allen, and drummer Hugo Burnham. The band's debut album, *Entertainment!* (1979), ranked no. 5 on *Rolling Stone's* list of the "40 Greatest Punk Albums of All Time," behind *Fun House* (the Stooges), *Never Mind the Bollocks* (the Sex Pistols), *The Clash* (the Clash), and *Ramones* (Ramones).

Essential Listening: *Entertainment!* (1979)

THE JAM   Formed in 1972, English mod-rock/punk band the Jam achieved four no. 1 hit singles in the UK: "A Town Called Malice," "Beat Surrender," "Going Underground," and "Start." The Jam lineup featured singer-guitarist Paul Weller, bassist Bruce Foxton, and drummer Rick Buckler. The band released their first single, "In the City," followed a month later by their debut album, *In the City*, in 1977. The following year, they toured the United States in support of Blue Oyster Cult. Shortly after releasing their sixth album, *The Gift*, which reached no. 1 on the UK charts, the band called it quits in 1982.

Essential Listening: *In the City* (1977), *All Mod Cons* (1978), *Setting Sons* (1979), *Sound Affects* (1980), *The Gift* (1982)

THE JESUS AND MARY CHAIN   Scottish alternative-rock band the Jesus and Mary Chain formed in 1983. The band consisted of brothers Jim and William Reid, along with bassist Douglas Hart and drummer Murray Dalglish. They released their critically acclaimed debut album, *Psychocandy*, in 1985. According to rock critic Mikal Gilmore in *Night Beat*,

> All these years later, [*Psychocandy*] is still a record that can thrill you—like the best and worst stolen orgasms of your life—or that can drive you into a bad, spooky corner of your mind and spirit, as

Formed in 1983, Scottish alternative rock band, the Jesus and Mary Chain, released their critically acclaimed debut album, *Psychocandy*, in 1985. By Paul Hudson, United Kingdom/Wikimedia Commons

if you finally realized how mad, worthless, wonderful, and disar-
rayed life truly is, regardless of your best efforts to impose hope
and design on to all its unbeatable final disorder.

Essential Listening: *Psychocandy* (1985)

JOY DIVISION   Originally named Warsaw (after David Bowie's 1977
song "Warszawa"), Joy Division was formed in Manchester in 1977
and consisted of brooding lead singer Ian Curtis (who wandered the
streets with "HATE" scrawled on the back of his jacket), guitarist/
keyboardist Bernard Sumner, bassist Peter Hook, and drummer
Stephen Morris. The band took its unfortunate name from Karol
Cetinsky's 1953 World War II novella, *The House of Dolls*, which
depicted forced brothels—dubbed "joy divisions"—set up inside
some Nazi concentration camps. After the band self-released their
1978 debut EP, *An Ideal for Living*, they were signed to independent label Factory Records. Joy Division's debut album, *Unknown
Pleasures* (1979), features such classics as "Disorder," "New Dawn
Fades," "She's Lost Control," and "Shadowplay."
    Curtis, who suffered from depression and epilepsy, committed
suicide by hanging himself on May 18, 1980, at the age of twenty-
three, just before the band was set to tour the United States.
The band's second and final album, *Closer*, was released just two
months later, reached no. 6 on the UK charts, and features the
haunting ballad "Love Will Tear Us Apart." The surviving band
members formed the successful band New Order. Joy Division figures prominently in the films *24 Hour Party People* (2002), about
the rise and fall of Factory Records, and *Control* (2007), a black-
and-white biopic about Curtis.

Essential Listening: *Unknown Pleasures* (1979), *Closer* (1980)

KILLING JOKE   An English post-punk/industrial-rock band, Killing
Joke formed in Notting Hill in 1979. The lineup featured lead
singer/keyboardist Jaz Coleman, guitarist Geordie Walker, bassist
Youth (Martin Glover), and drummer Paul Ferguson. The band's
self-titled debut was released in 1980. According to *Trouser Press*,
"Killing Joke are practitioners of intellectual dance-thrash-rock with

a penchant for apocalypse." Killing Joke has influenced the likes of Metallica, Nirvana, Soundgarden, and Nine Inch Nails.

Essential Listening: *Killing Joke* (1980)

NEW ORDER After the suicide of lead singer Ian Curtis on May 18, 1980, the rest of Joy Division—guitarist Bernard Sumner, bassist Peter Hook, and drummer Stephen Morris—decided to forge ahead under the band name New Order. They soon recruited Morris's girlfriend, Gillian Gilbert, as keyboardist. The band released their debut studio album, *Movement* (1981), followed by *Power, Corruption & Lies* (1983). In addition, they released the hit single "Blue Monday," which rose to no. 9 on the UK charts.

Essential Listening: *Power, Corruption & Lies* (1983)

NICK CAVE AND THE BAD SEEDS Formed in 1983, highly influential Australian rock band Nick Cave and the Bad Seeds featured Cave on vocals, multi-instrumentalist Mick Harvey, and guitarist Blixa Bargeld. Starting with *From Her to Eternity* (1984), which offered a unique blend of post-punk, gothic rock, and blues, the band has released seventeen studio albums, the latest being *Ghosteen* (2019).

Essential Listening: *Let Love In* (1994), *Murder Ballads* (1996), *The Boatman's Call* (1997), *Skeleton Tree* (2016)

PERE UBU Named in honor of Alfred Jarry's 1896 absurdist drama, *Ubu Roi*, experimental avant-garde band Pere Ubu formed in Cleveland, Ohio, in 1975. Pere Ubu was part of a thriving Cleveland rock scene in the mid-1970s that included Devo, the Mirrors, the Electric Eels, and Tin Huey, among others. The band's lineup featured lead singer Dave Thomas (formerly of Rocket from the Tombs), guitarist Tom Herman, keyboardist Allen Ravenstine, Tony Maimone, and drummer Scott Krauss. According to Thomas, "I was going to create a band that Herman Melville or William Faulkner or Raymond Chandler would have wanted to be in. It wasn't going to happen right away. It was going to take years and years but that was my plan."

Pere Ubu released its first single, "30 Seconds Over Tokyo," in 1975 with "Heart of Darkness" as the B-side. The band released their debut album, *The Modern Dance*, in 1978. In 2009, Pere Ubu released a studio album titled *Long Live Pere Ubu*, which served as a soundtrack to a musical adaptation of the play *Ubu Roi*. Pere Ubu has influenced the likes of Henry Rollins, Joy Division, Pixies, Husker Du, R.E.M., Sisters of Mercy, Bauhaus, Julian Cope, and Thomas Dolby, among many others.

Essential Listening: *The Modern Dance* (1978)

THE PSYCHEDELIC FURS   Led by vocalist Richard Butler and his brother, Tim Butler, on bass guitar, British post-punk band the Psychedelic Furs formed in London in 1977. Guitarist Roger Morris, saxophone player Duncan Kilburn, guitarist John Ashton, and drummer Vince Ely rounded out the band. With a name inspired by the Velvet Underground song "Venus in Furs," the band was known for their catchy singles, such as "Love My Way," "Heartbreak Beat," and "Heaven." In 1980, the band released their self-titled debut album, which features one of their signature songs, "Sister Europe." The hit single "Pretty in Pink" appeared on the album *Talk Talk Talk* (1981) and later inspired the John Hughes teen comedy *Pretty in Pink* (1986), which starred Molly Ringwald, Andrew McCarthy, Harry Dean Stanton, James Spader, and Jon Cryer as "Duckie Dale." The band's third studio album, *Forever Now* (1982), yielded the hit single "Love My Way." In 2020, the Psychedelic Furs released their eighth studio album, *Made of Rain*.

Essential Listening: *The Psychedelic Furs* (1980), *Talk Talk Talk* (1981), *Forever Now* (1982)

PUBLIC IMAGE LTD.   A brilliant and uncompromising experimentalist post-punk band, Public Image Ltd. (aka PiL) was formed by John Lydon (Rotten) after the spectacular collapse of the Sex Pistols following their disastrous U.S. tour in 1978. Lydon recruited his old buddy Jah Wobble (aka John Wardle) for bass player, along with guitarist Keith Levene and drummer Jim Walker. The band released its debut single, "Public Image," in 1978, followed by a debut album, *Public Image: First Issue*, which *Rolling Stone* dubbed as "postnasal drip monotony." PiL's second album, *Metal Box*, was released in 1979. A review of the album in the *Observer* declared that *Metal Box* "is made up of the bleached white bones of art rock, disco and reggae, reassembled into a gorgeous noise that defies easy description. It is also one of the best albums of all time." PiL broke up in 1992 but re-formed in 2009. The band has released ten studio albums, the latest being *What the World Needs Now* in 2015.

Essential Listening: *Public Image: First Issue* (1978), *Metal Box* (1979), *The Flowers of Romance* (1981)

THE SLITS   An all-female London punk band, the Slits formed in 1976 from the ashes of the Flowers of Romance and the Castrators. The band's classic lineup consisted of vocalist Ari Up (Ariana Forster), guitarist Viv Albertine, and bassist Tessa Pollitt. Drummer Palmolive (Paloma Romero) performed in the band between 1976 and 1978 before leaving to join the Raincoats. The Slits were known for their confrontational performance style and incorporating elements of reggae and dub into their sound. Along with Buzzcocks, Subway Sect, and the Prefects, the Slits supported the Clash on their 1977 White Riot tour and appeared in *The Punk Rock Movie* the following year. Palmolive departed the band to join the Raincoats. The Slits released their debut album, *Cut*, in 1979. The controversial cover art for the album featured the three topless, mud-covered band members clad only in loincloths. The Slits only released two more studio albums: *Return of the Giant Slits* (1981) and *Trapped Animal* (2009).

Essential Listening: *Cut* (1979)

THE SMITHS   One of the most important English rock bands of the 1980s, the Smiths formed in Manchester in 1982. The band's classic lineup featured lead singer Morrissey (Steven Patrick Morrissey), guitarist Johnny Marr, bassist Andy Rourke, and drummer Mike Joyce. They released their self-titled debut studio album, in 1984, followed by *Meat Is Murder* (1985), which reached no. 1 on the UK charts. The band's third studio album, *The Queen*

Is Dead, which reached no. 2 on the UK charts, includes the hit single "There Is a Light That Never Goes Out." After releasing their fourth studio album, *Strangeways, Here We Come* (1987), the Smiths broke up and Morrissey pursued a successful solo career. According to *Trouser Press*, "No other pop music act since Jonathan Richman ever raised blatant self-absorption to such a high level. The Smiths' ability to turn shameless solipsism into incalculable stardom, however, was their entirely unique accomplishment."

Essential Listening: *The Smiths* (1984), *Meat Is Murder* (1985), *The Queen Is Dead* (1986)

SONIC YOUTH   Formed in New York City in 1981 by Kim Gordon and Thurston Moore (who later married), along with Lee Ranaldo, Sonic Youth has been dubbed the "Godfathers of Grunge" for their strong impact on bands such as Nirvana. The band's name

Widely regarded as the "Godfathers of Grunge," Sonic Youth was formed in New York City in 1981 by Kim Gordon, Thurston Moore, and Lee Ranaldo. By GREG NEATE, SUSSEX, UK/WIKIMEDIA COMMONS

reportedly served as a tribute to Fred "Sonic" Smith of MC5. They were well known for their unorthodox use of alternate tunings, dissonance, and feedback. Sonic Youth broke into the mainstream with their hit single "Teenage Riot," which later ranked no. 157 on *Rolling Stone*'s list of the "500 Greatest Songs of All Time." In 1995, Sonic Youth headlined the Lollapalooza Festival. The band dissolved in 2011 after Gordon and Moore got divorced.

Essential Listening: *Confusion Is Sex* (1983), *Bad Moon Rising* (1985), *EVOL* (1986), *Daydream Nation* (1988)

TEARS FOR FEARS   Formed by Roland Orzabal and Curt Smith in Bath, England, in 1981, synth pop band Tears for Fears eventually sold more than thirty million records worldwide. The band's debut album, *The Hurting* (1983), reached no. 1 on the UK charts and features the hits "Mad World," "Pale Shelter," and "Change." Their second album, *Songs from the Big Chair* (1985), includes two hit singles, "Everybody Want to Rule the World" and "Shout," the music videos of which quickly became MTV staples. After the release of their third album, *The Seeds of Love* (1989), Tears for Fears split up but have reunited sporadically ever since.

Essential Listening: *The Hurting* (1983), *Songs from the Big Chair* (1985), *The Seeds of Love* (1989)

VIOLENT FEMMES   Formed in Milwaukee, Wisconsin, in 1980, this immensely popular folk-punk band featured the original lineup of singer-songwriter/guitarist Gordon Gano, bassist Brian Ritchie, saxophonist Blaise Garza, and keyboardist/drummer John Sparrow. The Violent Femmes released their self-titled debut album in 1983, which contains many of their best-known songs such as "Blister in the Sun," "Gone Daddy Gone," "Add It Up," and "Kiss Off." *Billboard* called the album "a seminal document of hormonal angst and black humor." The band has released a total of ten studio albums, the latest being *Hotel Last Resort* in 2019.

Essential Listening: *Violent Femmes* (1983)

WIPERS Considered to be the first Pacific Northwest punk band and a favorite of Nirvana's Kurt Cobain, the Wipers formed in Portland, Oregon, in 1976. The band featured lead singer/guitarist Greg Sage, bassist Dave Koupal, and drummer Sam Henry. The band's name was reportedly derived from a job Sage had cleaning windows at a movie theater. Their first album, *Is This Real?* (1978), quickly gained a regional cult following. The band's next two albums, *Youth of America* (1981) and *Over the Edge* (1983), also proved to be highly influential.

The Wipers influenced Mudhoney, the Melvins, Dinosaur Jr., Sonic Youth, and others. A Wipers tribute album, *Eight Songs for Greg Sage and the Wipers*, was released in 1992 and features "Potential Suicide" (Napalm Beach), "Astro Cloud" (M99), "Return of the Rat" (Nirvana), "Up Front" (Poison Idea), "On the Run" (Dharma Bums), "I Don't Know What I Am/Mystery" (Crackerbash), "Over the Edge" (Hole), and "Land of the Lost" (Whirlees).

Essential Listening: *Is This Real?* (1978), *Youth of America* (1981), *Over the Edge* (1983)

WIRE Formed in South London in 1976, Wire never achieved widespread fame but heavily influenced other punk- and alternative-rock bands such as Sonic Youth, R.E.M, Henry Rollins, Ian MacKaye of Minor Threat, Minutemen, Big Black, Spoon, and Boss Hog, among others. The band in turn claimed inspiration from Dadaists such as Marcel Duchamp. According to *Cult Artists*, Wire was "inspired by punk, but their artsy sensibilities set them apart from the more rabble-rousing scene centered on the Sex Pistols." *Rolling Stone* has referred to Wire as "punk's ultimate cult band."

The band's lineup consisted of lead singer/guitarist Bruce Gilbert, guitarist/vocalist Colin Newman, bassist Graham Lewis, and drummer Robert Gotobed (aka Robert Grey). *Pink Flag*, Wire's 1977 debut album, features no less than twenty-one tracks (six of which came in under the one-minute mark!). The band broke up in 1980 but re-formed in 1984 and released their fourth studio album, *The Ideal Copy*, in 1987. Overall, Wire has released eighteen studio albums, the latest being *10:20* in 2020.

Essential Listening: *Pink Flag* (1977), *Chairs Missing* (1978)

25

Surface Envy
The Riot Grrrl Movement and Punk-Rock Feminism

I would much rather be the 'obnoxious feminist girl' than be complicit in my own dehumanization. —Kathleen Hanna

Consisting of a loose affiliation of feminist punk bands, the Riot Grrrl movement exploded throughout the Pacific Northwest in the early 1990s, led by such pioneering groups as Bikini Kill, Bratmobile, 7 Year Bitch, and Sleater-Kinney, among others. A flyer distributed during a Bikini Kill tour captures the spirit of the movement: "Riot Grrrl is because we girls want to create mediums that speak to us. Because every time we pick up a pen, or an instrument, or get anything done, we are creating the revolution, We *are* the revolution." However, the Riot Grrrl's theme of female empowerment took inspiration from pioneering all-female punk bands from the 1970s such as the Slits, the Raincoats, and others.

7 YEAR BITCH   Formed in Seattle, Washington, in 1990, 7 Year Bitch was inspired by fellow Emerald City punk band the Gits. One of the most aggressive punk bands in the Pacific Northwest, 7 Year Bitch (named after the 1955 Marilyn Monroe romantic comedy, *The Seven Year Itch*) featured lead singer Selene Vigil, guitarist Stefanie Sargent, bassist Elizabeth Davis, and drummer Valerie Agnew. In October 1992, the band released their debut album,

Sick 'Em. Tragically, Sargent had died four months earlier of a heroin overdose at the age of twenty-four. Sargent was replaced by Roisin Dunne later that year.

In 1994, 7 Year Bitch released their second studio album, *¡Viva Zapata!* which served as a tribute to both Sargent and Gits lead singer Mia Zapata, who was raped and murdered at the age of twenty-seven while walking home from a Seattle music venue on July 7, 1993. The album contains a cover of Jim Carroll's "It's Too Late," which features the opening lyrics: "It's too late/To fall in love with Sharon Tate/But it's too soon/To ask me for the words I want carved on my tomb." In reaction to Zapata's brutal murder, Agnew cofounded Home Alive, an antiviolence and self-defense organization. After releasing their third album, *Gato Negro*, in 1996, 7 Year Bitch broke up the following year.

Essential Listening: *Sick 'Em* (1992), *¡Viva Zapata!* (1994)

BIKINI KILL Feminist punk band Bikini Kill pioneered the Riot Grrrl movement and were known for their confrontational live shows. Formed in 1990 in Olympia, Washington, Bikini Kill featured lead singer Kathleen Hanna, guitarist Billy Boredom (Billy Karren), guitarist/bassist Kathi Wilcox, and drummer Tobi Vail.

Pioneers of the Riot Grrrl movement, feminist punk band Bikini Kill were known for their confrontational live shows. By Raph_PH/Wikimedia Commons

The band took its name from the 1967 British spy film *The Million Eyes of Sumuru*. According to the band's official biography, "Bikini Kill believed that if all girls started bands the world would change. They actively encouraged women and girls to start bands as a means of cultural resistance." Bikini Kill's debut studio album, *Pussy Whipped*, was released in 1993 and features the band's signature song, "Rebel Girl." After releasing the 1996 album, *Reject All American*, Bikini Kill broke up in 1997 but has reunited for tours in 2019 and 2020. "Rebel Girl" later ranked no. 296 on *Rolling Stone*'s list of the "500 Greatest Songs of All Time."

Essential Listening: *Pussy Whipped* (1993)

BRATMOBILE   Along with Bikini Kill, Bratmobile spearheaded the Riot Grrrl revolution. Singer Allison Wolfe and drummer Molly Neuman met in 1989 while students at the University of Oregon and started Bratmobile along with guitarist Erin Smith. They also started a zine, *Girl Germs*, in 1990. The band made their performing debut at the 1991 International Pop Underground Convention in Olympia, Washington, and released their first album, *Pottymouth*, in 1993. *Pottymouth* featured the powerful anthem "Stab" as well as a cover of the Runaways' hit "Cherry Bomb." Bratmobile disbanded the following year, with Neuman joining the PeeChees and the Frumpies, while Wolfe and Smith reunited in Cold Cold Hearts. In 1998, the band re-formed and went on tour as the opening act for Sleater-Kinney. They also released a new album, *Ladies, Women and Girls* (2000), followed by *Girls Get Busy* (2003).

Essential Listening: *Pottymouth* (1993)

EMILY'S SASSY LIME   An all-Asian American teenage band that formed in Southern California in 1993, Emily's Sassy Lime (the name is a palindrome) featured the trio of sisters Wendy and Amy Yao, along with Emily Ryan. They became interested in the Riot Grrrl movement after sneaking out to catch a Bikini Kill and Bratmobile show. In true DIY punk spirit, the band members began making music by calling each other's answering machines and leaving each other pieces of songs. Also, early on, they had to borrow instruments to play gigs. In 1995, the band members appeared as dancers in the PeeChees' "Mad Doctor" music video. After releasing their debut album, *Right Is Here* (1996), Emily's Sassy Lime called it quits in 1997 after the band members graduated from high school and attended separate colleges. However, the band re-formed in 2000 to take part in the first Ladyfest in Olympia, Washington.

Essential Listening: *Right Is Here* (1996)

EXCUSE 17   Formed in Olympia, Washington, in 1993, Excuse 17 featured Becca Albee (lead singer and guitarist), Carrie Brownstein (guitarist and singer), and Curtis James (drummer). The band's first studio album, *Excuse Seventeen*, was released in 1994, followed by *Such Friends Are Dangerous* the following year. Excuse 17 supported Heavens to Betsy several times on tour. Brownstein later formed Sleater-Kinney with Corin Tucker of Heavens to Betsy.

Essential Listening: *Excuse Seventeen* (1994)

HEAVENS TO BETSY   Lead singer Corin Tucker met drummer Tracy Sawyer while students at Evergreen State College in Eugene, Oregon, and the duo formed Heavens to Betsy in 1991. The band made its performing debut at the International Pop Underground (IPU) Convention in Olympia, Washington, in August of that year. Other Riot Grrrl bands to perform at IPU included Bratmobile, 7 Year Bitch, and Jean Smith of Mecca Normal. When Heavens to Betsy broke up in the mid-1990s, Tucker teamed up with Carrie Brownstein of Excuse 17 to form Sleater-Kinney.

Essential Listening: *Calculated* (1994)

L7   One of the most influential female bands of all time, L7 was formed in Seattle, Washington, in the late 1980s. The original lineup featured Donita Sparks (vocals/guitar), Suzi Gardner (vocals/guitar), Jennifer Finch (vocals/bass), and Dee Plakas (drums). They counted the Ramones, Motorhead, and the Runaways among their main influences. The band released the critically acclaimed album *Smell the Magic* in 1991, followed by *Bricks Are Heavy* (1992), which spawned the hit single, "Pretend That We're Dead." After a restless crowd at the 1992 Reading Festival started throwing mud onto the stage during a L7 performance, Sparks threw a used tampon at the festival crowd, yelling, "Eat my used tampon, fuckers!" In addition, the band even raffled off an "intimate meeting" with Plakas on the tour bus in London in 2000. L7 is featured in a hilarious 1999 documentary directed by Krist Novoselic titled *The Beauty Process*, as well as a 2016 documentary, *L7: Pretend We're Dead*.

Essential Listening: *Smell the Magic* (1991), *Bricks Are Heavy* (1992), *Scatter the Rats* (2019)

SLEATER-KINNEY Formed by Corin Tucker (Heavens to Betsy) and Carrie Brownstein (Excuse 17) in Olympia, Washington, in 1994, Sleater-Kinney was named after Sleater Kinney Road in Lacey, Washington. Drummer Janet Weiss joined the band in 1996. Highly influential, the band has released ten studio albums: *Sleater-Kinney* (1995), *Call the Doctor* (1996), *Dig Me Out* (1997), *The Hot Rock* (1999), *All Hands on the Bad One* (2000), *One Beat* (2002), *The Woods* (2005), *No Cities to Love* (2015), *The Center Won't Hold* (2019), and *Path of Wellness* (2021). Brownstein is also well

Formed in Olympia, Washington, in 1994, Sleater-Kinney consisted of Corin Tucker (Heavens to Betsy), Carrie Brownstein (Excuse 17), and Janet Weiss (Quasi). By RAPH_P /WIKIMEDIA COMMONS

known for her performance in the quirky satirical comedy TV series *Portlandia* (2011–2018) along with *Saturday Night Live* alumnus Fred Armisen.

Essential Listening: *Call the Doctor* (1996), *The Woods* (2005), *No Cities to Love* (2015)

26

When I Come Around
The Rise of Pop Punk

Punk is not just the sound, the music. Punk is a lifestyle.
—Billie Joe Armstrong

The pop-punk sound has been around since the early days of punk, with bands like Buzzcocks, Undertones, Generation X, the Jam, and even the Ramones leading the way. For better or worse, the pop-punk genre dragged punk rock into the mainstream during the 1990s and early 2000s with the astounding success of such ground-breaking albums as Green Day's *Dookie* (1994), the Offspring's *Smash* (1994), Blink-182's *Enema of the State* (1999), and Sum 41's *All Filler, No Killer* (2001).

Characterized by pop melodies with fast tempos, loud guitars, and power chord changes, pop punk served to bridge several musical styles and managed to appeal to a much wider audience base in the process. Although pop punk has its naysayers, a lot of highly talented bands such as those highlighted below that fall under the mantle truly rocked at their peak.

ALKALINE TRIO Formed in Chicago in 1996 by lead singer/guitarist Matt Skiba, bassist Rob Doran, and drummer Glenn Porter, Alkaline Trio (known for their distinctive Heart & Skull logo) released their debut single, "Sundials," in 1997. Doran soon departed the band and was replaced by Dan Andriano. In 1998, the band released both an EP, *For Your Lungs Only*, and a debut studio album, *Goddamnit* (1998), followed by *Maybe I'll Catch Fire* (2000). Porter departed the band and was replaced by Mike Felumlee on drums for the next album, *From Here to Infirmary* (2001), which features the singles "Stupid Kid" and "Private Eye." Alkaline Trio's ninth album, *Is This Thing Cursed?* was released in 2020.

Essential Listening: *Maybe I'll Catch Fire* (2000), *From Here to Infirmary* (2001), *Crimson* (2005)

ALL TIME LOW   Starting out as a cover band in high school, All Time Low was formed in 2003 in Towson, Maryland, by lead singer/rhythm guitarist Alex Gaskarth, lead guitarist Jack Barakat, bassist Zack Merrick, and drummer Rian Dawson. Influenced by the catchy pop-punk sounds of Blink-182 and New Found Glory, the band released their debut EP, *The Three Words to Remember in Dealing with the End EP*, in 2004, followed by eight studio albums, the latest being *Wake Up, Sunshine* (2020).

Essential Listening: *So Wrong, It's Right* (2007), *Nothing Personal* (2009), *Don't Panic* (2012)

THE ATARIS   An alternative-rock band from the unlikely city of Anderson, Indiana, the Ataris formed in 1996 and released five studio albums between 1997 and 2007. The band's best-selling album, *So Long, Astoria* (2003), features a popular cover of Don Henley's "The Boys of Summer." In addition, the Ataris song "The Night the Lights Went Out in NYC" appeared on the *Spider-Man 2* soundtrack in 2004. The Ataris are known for extensively referencing pop culture in their songs, such as *The Karate Kid*, *The Goonies*, and *Bill and Ted's Excellent Adventure*. Singer-songwriter/guitarist Kris Roe has been the only constant member of the Ataris through the years. The band was named after Roe's extensive Atari video game collection.

Essential Listening: *Anywhere but Here* (1997), *Blue Skies, Broken Hearts . . . Next 12 Exits* (1999), *End Is Forever* (2001), *So Long, Astoria* (2003)

Denizens of the Southern California skate-punk scene, pop-punk band Blink-182 has sold over fifty million records worldwide. BY KERRY KEY, SAN DIEGO/WIKIMEDIA COMMONS

BLINK-182 Formed in Poway, California, in 1992, Blink-1982 is known for its catchy and fast-paced songs such as "All the Small Things," "Dammit," "I Miss You," and "What's My Age Again?" Spawned from the suburban SoCal skate-punk scene, the band has sold over fifty million records worldwide. The current Blink-182 lineup features guitarist/vocalist Matt Skiba, bassist/vocalist Mark Hoppus, and drummer Travis Barker. The band has cited such influences as Descendents, the Ramones, the Cure, Stiff Little Fingers, Depeche Mode, NOFX, Dinosaur Jr., the Vandals, Bad Religion, and the Queers, among others. Blink-182 has released eight studio albums over the years, the latest being *Nine* in 2019.

Essential Listening: *Enema of the State* (1999), *Take Off Your Pants and Jacket* (2001)

BOWLING FOR SOUP Bowling for Soup (aka BFS) is known for their quirky singles, such as "Punk Rock 101," "1985" (a SR-71 cover that reached no. 23 on the U.S. charts), "Girl All the Bad Guys Want," "Almost," and "High School Never Ends." They also performed the intro to the popular Disney Channel animated TV show *Phineas and Ferb*. Formed in Wichita Falls, Texas, in 1994, the band's lineup features lead singer/guitarist Jaret Reddick, guitarist Chris Burney, bassist Rob Felicetti, and drummer Gary Wiseman.

Essential Listening: *Drunk Enough to Dance* (2002), *A Hangover You Don't Deserve* (2004), *The Great Burrito Extortion Case* (2006)

FALL OUT BOY   Formed in Wilmette, Illinois, in 2001, Fall Out Boy traces their origins from Chicago's hardcore punk scene and features lead singer/songwriter Patrick Stump, guitarist Joe Trohman, bassist/songwriter Pete Wentz, and drummer Andy Hurley. The band's first gig was opening for a Black Sabbath cover band in the DePaul University cafeteria. The band's pop-punk-style debut album, *Take This to Your Grave,* became an underground hit in 2003, and they quickly developed a dedicated fan base.

Fall Out Boy's second release, *From Under the Cork Tree* (2005), served as their breakthrough album, going double platinum and spawning two hit singles: "Sugar, We're Going Down" and "Dance, Dance." As the band's principal songwriter, Wentz has acknowledged his debt to such writers as Ernest Hemingway, Charles Bukowski, and JT LeRoy. According to legend, the band got their name after they were performing in a club and asked the audience what they should be called and someone shouted, "Fall Out Boy" (the name of Radioactive Man's sidekick in *The Simpsons*).

Essential Listening: *Take This to Your Grave* (2003), *From Under the Cork Tree* (2005), *Infinity on High* (2007), *Save Rock and Roll* (2013)

GOOD CHARLOTTE   Formed in 1996 in Waldorf, Maryland, Good Charlotte features a current lineup of Joel Madden (lead vocals), Benji Madden (guitar and vocals), Paul Thomas (bass), Bill Martin (guitar/keyboards), and Dean Butterworth (drums). The band released their self-titled debut album in 2000, followed by their breakthrough album, *The Young and the Hopeless* (2002), which sold five million copies worldwide and spawned the hit singles

"Lifestyles of the Rich and Famous," "The Anthem," and "Girls & Boys." Good Charlotte's latest album, *Generation Rx*, was released in 2018.

Essential Listening: *Good Charlotte* (2000), *The Young and the Hopeless* (2002), *The Chronicles of Life and Death* (2004)

GREEN DAY More than any other 1990s rock band, the phenomenally successful Green Day helped return punk to the mainstream for better or worse. The origins of Green Day can be traced back to 1988, when childhood friends Billie Joe Armstrong (vocals, guitar) and Mike Dirnt (bass) created a band called Sweet Children. The band was influenced by the likes of Bad Religion, Stiff Little Fingers, and Buzzcocks. They then added drummer Al Sobrante (he was soon replaced by Tre Cool). Green Day honed its skills at the legendary 924 Gilman Street Project in Berkeley.

After releasing two albums, *39/Smooth* (1990) and *Kerplunk* (1991), Green Day skyrocketed to stardom with *Dookie* (1994),

Green Day frontman Billie Joe Armstrong released a compilation album of cover songs called *No Fun Mondays* in 2020. By Daniel Åhs Karlsson, Own work/Wikimedia Commons

which sold ten million copies and earned the band a Grammy Award for "Best Alternative Music Performance." The band's follow-up album, *Insomniac* (1995), sold a very respectable two million copies. In 1997, Green Day released the album *Nimrod*, which featured the hit "Time of Your Life (Good Riddance)." The catchy song allegedly took just ten minutes to write. Dubbed by the band as a "punk-rock opera," Green Day's seventh studio album, *American Idiot*, reached no. 1 on the U.S. charts, won a Grammy Award for "Best Rock Album," and eventually sold an astounding sixteen million copies worldwide. *American Idiot* contains some of Green Day's best-loved songs, such as the title track, "Jesus of Suburbia," "Boulevard of Broken Dreams," "Wake Me Up When September Ends," and "Holiday," which Armstrong referred to as a "big fuck you to all the politicians."

At least one disgruntled punk legend never jumped on the Green Day bandwagon. In a 1996 press conference announcing a Sex Pistols reunion, John Lydon referred to Green Day as "childish prattle. It's the same old shit, really. Nothing's changed. Through the years, we've all gone off and done different things and left it up to others to make waves, but nobody out there has done bollocks all to change this world. So here it is: part two." Green Day was inducted into the Rock and Roll Hall of Fame in 2015 and released their thirteenth studio album, *Father of All Motherfuckers* (aka *FOAMF*), in 2020.

Essential Listening: *Dookie* (1994), *Insomniac* (1995), *Nimrod* (1997), *American Idiot* (2004)

JAWBREAKER   Punk trio Jawbreaker was formed in 1986 by New York University students Blake Schwarzenbach, Chris Bauermeister (bassist), and drummer Adam Pfahler. After relocating to Los Angeles, the band released their debut album, *Unfun* (1990), followed by *Bivouac* (1992), and then toured in support of Nirvana in 1993. After releasing their third album, *24 Hour Revenge Therapy*, in 1994, Jawbreaker signed a $1 million contract with DGC Records and released their fourth album, *Dear You* (1995). This created quite a backlash from their hardcore fans, who accused the band of selling out. Tensions from inside and outside the band led to a breakup the following year. In 2017, Jawbreaker reunited and embarked on an extensive tour in 2019. *Rolling Stone* has called Jawbreaker a "legendary and absolutely incredible emotional punk rock band."

Essential Listening: *Unfun* (1990), *Bivouac* (1992), *24 Hour Revenge Therapy* (1994), *Dear You* (1995)

THE OFFSPRING   Formed in 1984 in Orange County, California, the Offspring (original name: Manic Subsidal) helped revive mainstream interest in punk rock, along with Green Day and Rancid. The quintessential SoCal pop-punk band of the 1990s, the Offspring featured Bryan "Dexter" Holland (guitar/vocals), lead guitarist Kevin "Noodles" Wasserman, Greg Kriesel (bass), and Ron Welty (drums). The band was influenced by such bands as Bad Religion, Social Distortion, and Husker Du.

Fueled by the smash hit single "Come Out and Play (Keep 'Em Separated)," the Offspring's third album, *Smash* (1994), sold four million copies. Believe it or not, "Come Out and Play" was reportedly inspired by the 1979 film *The Warriors* and addressed the issue of gang violence in schools. In 1995, the band recorded a version

Led by lead singer/vocalist Dexter Holland, the Offspring released their breakthrough single, "Come Out and Play (Keep 'Em Separated)," in 1994. By Livioandronico2013, Own work/Wikimedia Commons

of the Damned's "Smash It Up" for the *Batman Forever* soundtrack. The Offspring's 1998 song "Pretty Fly (for a White Guy)" received a "Weird Al" Yankovic parody titled "Pretty Fly for a Rabbi." Over the years, the Offspring have released ten studio albums (the latest being *Let the Bad Times Roll* in 2021) and sold over forty million records.

Essential Listening: *Ignition* (1992), *Smash* (1994), *Ixnay on the Hombre* (1997), *Americana* (1998)

RANCID   Arguably the most authentic of the post-grunge punk bands, Rancid was formed in Berkeley, California, by former members of Operation Ivy and evoked the independent spirit of East Bay punk. The classic lineup included Lars Frederikson (guitar), Matt Freeman (vocals/bass), Tim Armstrong (guitar/vocals), and Brett Reed (drums). The band has sold more than four million records worldwide.

Essential Listening: *Let's Go* (1994), *. . . and Out Come the Wolves* (1995), *Life Won't Wait* (1998)

SUM 41   Originally called Kaspir, this highly successful Canadian rock band from Ajax, Ontario, formed in 1996 and has sold over fifteen million records worldwide. The band's lineup features Deryck "Bizzy D" Whibley (vocals/guitar), Steve "Stevo32" Jocz (drums), Jay "Cone" McCaslin (bass), and Dave "Brownsound" Baksh (guitar). Sum 41 has cited such various influences as Devo, Rancid, Weezer, the Police, Foo Fighters, the Vandals, Green Day, NOFX, Nirvana, Beastie Boys, Guns N' Roses, and Metallica. They released their debut studio album, *All Killer No Filler*, in 2001. The first single from the album, "Fat Lip," reached no. 1 on the Billboard Modern Rock Tracks chart. The band's second studio album, *Does This Look Infected* (2002), spawned the hit singles "Still Waiting" and "The Hell Song." Sum 41 has released seven studio albums, the latest being *Order in Decline* (2019).

Essential Listening: *All Killer No Filler* (2001), *Does This Look Infected?* (2002), *Chuck* (2004)

WEEZER One of the most successful of the pop-punk bands of the 1990s, Weezer formed in Los Angeles in 1992. The band signed with Geffen Records the following year and released their self-titled debut album in 1994. Also known as the "Blue Album" and produced by Ric Ocasek of the Cars, it contains some of the band's most well-known tracks, such as "Buddy Holly," "Undone—the Sweater Song," and "Say It Ain't So." Weezer's quirky music videos received heavy MTV airplay. The current Weezer lineup consists of Rivers Cuomo (lead vocals, lead guitar, keyboards), Patrick Wilson (drums), Brian Bell (rhythm guitar), and Scott Shriner (bass/keyboards). The band has sold over thirty-five million records worldwide.

Essential Listening: *Weezer (Blue Album)* (1994), *Pinkerton* (1996), *Weezer (Green Album)* (2001)

YELLOWCARD Formed in Jacksonville, Florida, in 1997, this punk-inspired quintet (which includes a violinist!) has produced such hits as "Ocean Avenue" (which reached no. 37 on the U.S. charts), "Only One," and "Lights and Sounds." The band has released ten studio albums, the first being *Midget Tossing* in 1997 and the latest being *Yellowcard* in 2016. The band's lineup features vocalist/guitarist Ryan Key, vocalist/violinist Sean Mackin, guitarist Ben Harper, bassist Warren Cooke, and drummer Longineu Parsons.

Essential Listening: *Ocean Avenue* (2003), *Lights and Sounds* (2006), *When You're through Thinking Say Yes* (2011)

27

Straight to Hell
Later Artists and Movements
Influenced by Punk

Punk rock should mean freedom. —Kurt Cobain

Interviewed before an upcoming tour in 1977, Iggy Pop was asked what he thought of the term *punk rock,* and he responded, "Punk rock is a word used by dilettantes and heartless manipulators, about music that takes up the energies and the bodies and the hearts and the souls and the time and the minds of young men who give what they have to it and give everything they have to it." The reason that punk proves to be so undefinable and resistant to categorization is that it continually morphs into a myriad of new directions and styles. Below are some of the musical genres that punk has helped spawn for better or worse. Once you get past grunge, punk blues, and psychobilly, listen at your own risk!

GRUNGE Often referred to as the "Seattle sound," grunge had its earliest origins in the Pacific Northwest during the mid-1980s and blended elements of punk rock and heavy metal. Grunge was known for its angst-ridden and introspective lyrics. Founded in 1986, Seattle-based Sub Pop Records signed bands like Nirvana, Mudhoney, and Soundgarden during the early 1990s. Nirvana band members were influenced by the garage punk of the Melvins and the innovative sound of Sonic Youth, while Pearl Jam were hard-core Ramones fans.

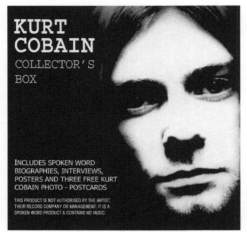

Punk rock strongly influenced the grunge sound that originated in the Pacific Northwest in the mid-1980s by the likes of Kurt Cobain of Nirvana.

Notable grunge albums include Nirvana's *Nevermind* (1991), which eventually sold thirty million copies worldwide, as well as Pearl Jam's *Ten* (1991), Soundgarden's *Badmotorfinger* (1991), Alice in Chains' *Dirt* (1992), and Stone Temple Pilots' *Core* (1992). Other notable grunge bands include Green River, Temple of the Dog, Mother Love Bone, Tad, Skin Yard, and Screaming Trees. John Lydon of the Sex Pistols dismissed Nirvana as "a dismal folk band with some squalling thrown in to bump up the revenue."

CROSSOVER THRASH   A subgenre of thrash metal, crossover served as a fusion of hardcore punk and thrash metal, becoming popular in the 1980s and 1990s. Characterized by absolutely blistering guitar riffs and high-speed drumming, crossover shares similarities with thrashcore, grindcore, and crust punk. Notable crossover thrash bands include Agnostic Front, Cro-Mags, Suicidal Tendencies, Attitude Adjustment, Carnivore, Excel, Crumbsuckers, S.O.D. (Stormtroopers of Death), and Cryptic Slaughter.

THRASHCORE   Not to be confused with crossover thrash or thrash metal, thrashcore (aka fastcore) emerged in the early 1980s and served as a faster, more intense style of hardcore punk. Notable thrashcore bands include Cryptic Slaughter, Hype, Electro

Hippies, Septic Death, Municipal Death, Dropdead, Vitamin X, D.R.I. (Dirty Rotten Imbeciles), and Siege.

GRINDCORE   *Kerrang!* refers to grindcore as "arguably the most unrepentantly violent music on the planet" and "the bastard offspring of hardcore punk," while *Loudwire* describes the genre as "fast as hell, ridiculously loud and best performed in rundown basements." Notable grindcore bands include Napalm Death, Extreme Noise Terror, Discordance Axis, Repulsion, Terrorizer, Carcass, Brutal Truth, Pig Destroyer, Nasum, Trap Them, and Agoraphobic Nosebleed. By the way, Napalm Death holds the record for the shortest song of all time—the 1.316-second "You Suffer" from the band's debut studio album, *Scum* (1987).

PSYCHOBILLY   Also known as horrorbilly, this loud and frantic genre fuses elements of punk rock and rockabilly (which itself blends elements of rock 'n' roll and bluegrass). Notable psychobilly bands include the Cramps (who pioneered the genre in New York City during the mid-1970s), the Meteors, Nekromantix, Demented Are Go, the Quakes, Mad Sin, Tiger Army, HorrorPops, the Reverend Horton Heat, Mad Sin, the Creepshow, Koffin Kats, the Brains, and the Living End.

PUNK BLUES   Fusing elements of punk rock and the blues, punk blues has antecedents in the garage-rock sound of the 1960s and the avant-garde style of Captain Beefheart. Notable punk-blues bands include the Gun Club (which released the pioneering punk-blues album *Fire of Love*, in 1981), Jon Spencer Blues Explosion, the Gories, the Dicks, Psychoterror, Social Distortion, T-Model Ford, the Gibson Brothers, the Oblivians, the Black Keys, the Kills, and the White Stripes.

Babylon's Burning

Legendary Punk-Rock Festivals

> Originality was prime and technique was second
> place. . . . We called this music "street rock" and later
> punk. Come as you are and do your own thing rock and
> roll. —Hilly Kristal

Three early punk festivals—the CBGB Festival of the Top 40 New
York Unrecorded Rock Bands in New York City in 1975, the 100
Club Festival in London in 1976, and the European Punk Rock
Festival in 1976—all helped serve as catalysts that spread the
punk-rock movement around the world. These were raw, gritty, DIY
events, as opposed to the slickly produced punk-related festivals to
come such as Vans Warped Tour. However, the DIY spirit of independent punk festivals lives on in such lively events as the Fest in
Gainesville, Florida.

CBGB FESTIVAL OF THE TOP 40 UNRECORDED NEW YORK BANDS (1975)

Known as the "Birthplace of Punk," CBGBs hosted a festival of
unsigned rock bands during the summer of 1975. The club's owner,
Hilly Kristal, dubbed it "The Top 40 New York Unrecorded Rock
Bands." According to Kristal, "The coverage of the festival started
making things happen. . . . The record companies started coming
down, mainly Sire Records, but also others." The CBGB festival
featured up-and-coming bands about to hit the big time, such as

CBGBs hosted a festival of unsigned rock bands such as Talking Heads during the "Top 40 New York Unrecorded Rock Bands" festival in the summer of 1975. ROLLING STONE/PHOTOFEST

the Heartbreakers, Television, Ramones, Blondie, and Talking Heads, as well as some musical acts that have been lost to history such as Tuff Darts, White Lightning, Jelly Roll, Seven Wind, Sting Rays, Hambone Sweets, Pretty Poison, Sniper, Day Old Bread, Rainbow Daze, Demons, Marbles, Ruby & the Rednecks, and Uneasy Sleeper, among others. In January 1976, the Ramones were the first of the unsigned bands to actually sign with a label, Sire Records.

100 CLUB FESTIVAL (1976)   Sex Pistols manager Malcolm McLaren and concert promoter Ron Watts organized a stellar lineup for the legendary 100 Club Festival (aka "100 Club Punk Special") that included the Sex Pistols, the Clash, the Damned, Buzzcocks, Siouxsie and the Banshees (making their performing debut and featuring Sid Vicious on drums), Chris Spedding and the Vibrators, and French punk band Stinky Toys. The 100 Club Festival took place at the 100 Club at 100 Oxford Street in London on September 20 and 21, 1976.

Siouxsie and the Banshees took the stage for the first time at the 100 Club Festival in London in 1976 with none other than Sid Vicious filling in on drums. COLUMBIA PICTURES/PHOTOFEST

During the Damned's set, Vicious got arrested for allegedly throwing a glass at the stage that shattered and injured a fan in the crowd. In her review of the festival for *Melody Maker*, Caroline Coon wrote, "The 600 strong line that stretched across two blocks was indisputable evidence that a new decade in rock is about to begin." Several audience members would go on to form their own bands, such as Shane MacGowan (the Nips and the Pogues), Viv Albertine (the Slits), and Chrissie Hynde (the Pretenders), among others. According to Vic Godard, lead singer of Subway Sect, "Before the 100 Club festival, punk was like a secret society. Afterwards it got hijacked by everybody."

EUROPEAN PUNK ROCK FESTIVAL (1976)   Mont-de-Marsan in the southwest of France served as the site of the first European Punk Rock Festival in August 1976. The Sex Pistols were supposed to perform but got dropped from the bill after reportedly making too many demands. The Clash backed out in solidarity with the Pistols. So it was left up to London pub-rock band Eddie and the Hot Rods to headline the event. Organized by Marc Zermati, the cofounder of Skydog Records, the European Punk Rock Festival took place at the Arenes de Plumacon, a legendary bullfighting ring. Performers included the Damned and the Pink Fairies, along with French punk bands Bijou, Il Biaritz, and Shakin' Street. Ian Curtis of Joy Division and his wife attended the festival. The Damned and Eddie and the Hot Rods returned the following year, along with the Clash, the Police, Lou Reed, and Dr. Feelgood.

ROCK AGAINST RACISM (1978)   A powerful political and cultural movement, Rock Against Racism (RAR) emerged in London in 1976 as a reaction to the increasing number of racist attacks on the streets of the United Kingdom coinciding with the disturbing rise of the far-right National Front. On April 30, 1978, Rock Against Racism joined forces with the Anti-Nazi League to organize a 100,000-person march from Trafalgar Square to the East End of London (which served as a hotbed of National Front support at the time) followed by an open-air Carnival at Victoria Park in Hackney. The event featured performances by the Clash, Steel Pulse, X-Ray Spex, Tom Robinson Band, Jimmy Pursey from Sham 69, Patrik Fitzgerald, and Southall-based reggae band Misty in Roots.

A second RAR Carnival took place at Brockwell Park in Brixton on July 15, 1978, featuring Stiff Little Fingers, Elvis Costello, and British reggae band Aswad. RAR also hosted a Northern Carnival at Alexandra Park in Manchester. The free music concert drew forty thousand people and featured performances by Steel Pulse, Buzzcocks, China Street, and Exodus. A 2019 documentary called *White Riot* highlights the history and achievements of the RAR movement.

INTERNATIONAL POP UNDERGROUND CONVENTION (1991)   A six-day punk- and alternative-rock festival, the International Pop Underground Convention (IPU) was held August 20–25, 1991, at the historic Capitol Theater in Olympia, Washington. IPU featured fifty bands, including Bikini Kill, Fastbacks, Melvins, L7, Unwound, Built to Spill, Some Velvet Sidewalk, and Fugazi. Other activities at IPU included poetry readings, cakewalk dances, and even a *Planet of the Apes* movie marathon. IPU helped bring the Riot Grrrl movement into public prominence. Conspicuously absent from the event? Nirvana, who were on tour at the time.

YOYO A GO GO (1994) A celebration of the Pacific Northwest punk/ grunge sound, this independent music festival (aka Yoyo) took place July 12–16, 1994, in Olympia, Washington, and featured dozens of punk and indie rock acts. The festival's mission statement read, "Punker than punk punk that will punk you like you've never been punked before." According to *SPIN* magazine, "The first Yoyo blossomed in the damp head that followed Seattle's grunge explosion." Yoyo featured performances from the likes of Bikini Kill, Heavens to Betsy, Beck, Team Dresch, Go Sailor, Neutral Milk Hotel, Bloodthirsty Butchers, Tattle Tale, Unwound, the Halo Benders, Cub, Slant 6, Mecca Normal, the Spinanes, Deerhoof, and Mary Lou Lord. In addition, Nirvana's Krist Novoselic and Dave Grohl made their first public performance together since the death of Kurt Cobain just a little over three months before on April 5, 1994.

WARPED TOUR (1995) A legendary traveling rock extravaganza, Warped Tour took place each summer from 1995 until 2019. The largest traveling music festival in the United States, the Warped Tour became Vans Warped Tour during its second year, after the shoe manufacturer became the main sponsor of the event. Known as a "punk-rock summer camp," the first Warped Tour blended skateboard culture with live music from CIV, Deftones, Face to Face, Fluf, Guttermouth, Integrity, L7, No Doubt, No Use for a Name, Orange 9mm, Quicksand, Seaweed, Shyster, Sick of It All, Sublime, Supernova, Swingin' Utters, Tilt, and Wizo. Year 2 of the Warped Tour in 1996 featured the likes of NOFX, Pennywise, Rocket from the Crypt, and Fishbone.

HOLIDAYS IN THE SUN (1996) A popular British punk-rock festival, Holidays in the Sun (later called the Wasted Festival and then the Rebellion Festival) was first held in 1996 at the Winter Gardens in Blackpool, England. The four-day festival featured three hundred acts such as X-Ray Spex (without Poly Styrene), Sham 69, Vibrators, UK Subs, the Lurkers, Anti-Nowhere League, Slaughter & the Dogs, Jayne County & the Electric Chairs, Buzzcocks, the Damned, and Walking Abortions. In addition to live music, Holidays in the Sun offered a literary stage, workshops, and a punk art gallery.

THE FEST (2002)   A funky annual music festival held in Gainesville, Florida, the Fest was the brainchild of Tony Weinbender of No Idea Records. Held each year during the weekend of the Florida–Georgia college football game in Jacksonville, the Fest hosts punk-rock and pop-punk bands, as well as hardcore-punk, indie-rock, metal, and ska acts. Established in 2002 with just sixty bands, the Fest had grown to 319 musical acts, 29 comedians, and 50 professional wrestlers by 2019. Bands such as Against Me!, Jawbreaker, Melvins, Stiff Little Fingers, Descendents, Dwarves, Government Issue, Hot Water Music, Leatherface, Diarrhea Planet, and many more have taken the stage at the Fest over the years. A documentary about the Fest titled *Fested: A Journey to Fest 7* was released in 2010.

DROP DEAD FESTIVAL (2003)   Originally held in CBGBs, the Drop Dead Festival was billed as a DIY festival for "art-damaged" music. The original festival featured Cinema Strange, Antiworld, Cult of the Psychic Fetus, the Brides, Memphis Morticians, Funeral Crashers, Alphabet Bombers, Cancerslug, the Secret Cervix, and Famous in Vegas. In later years, the Drop Dead Festival was moved to the Knitting Factory, a larger venue also located in Lower Manhattan.

RIOT FEST (2005)   An annual three-day music festival, Riot Fest was first held in 2005 at Douglass Park in Chicago, Illinois, and hosted a diverse range of rock, punk, alternative-rock, and hip-hop acts. The first Riot Fest featured the likes of the Dead Kennedys, Misfits, the Bouncing Souls, Suicide Machines, the Dickies, the Germs, Angry Samoans, Agent Orange, and others. It has since grown into one of the largest independent music festivals in the United States.

29

Institutionalized

Punk in the Rock and Roll Hall of Fame

> Next to the Sex Pistols rock and roll and that hall of
> fame is a piss stain. Your museum. Urine in wine. We're
> not coming. —John Lydon

The whole idea behind the Rock and Roll Hall of Fame seems like
an anathema to the true spirit of punk. According to rock critic
John Strausbaugh in *Rock 'Til You Drop*, "The Hall of Fame is
about old and dead people; rock 'n' roll is about the young and living. The Hall of Fame tries to reform rock 'n' roll, tame it, reduce
it to bland, middle-American family entertainment; it drains all the
sexiness and danger and rebelliousness out of it." For that reason,
the Sex Pistols declined the honor, with John Lydon scribbling a

The Rock and Roll Hall of
Fame has received much
controversy over the years for
snubbing the likes of MC5,
Bad Brains, Dead Kennedys,
Joy Division, Sonic Youth, and
Black Flag, among many oth-
ers. BY ERIK DROST, ROCK AND
ROLL HALL OF FAME/WIKIME-
DIA COMMONS

"cordial" note to the Hall of Fame basically telling the powers to be to "fuck off."

In addition, many deserving proto-punk and punk bands have been totally snubbed by the Rock and Roll Hall of Fame, such as Black Flag, Dead Kennedys, the Cramps, New York Dolls, MC5, Sonic Youth, Joy Division, the Damned, Bad Brains, the Jam, Devo, Minor Threat, the B-52's, the Replacements, and Johnny Thunders and the Heartbreakers, among many others.

THE VELVET UNDERGROUND (1996)   "Not everyone bought their album, but everyone who did started a band." The surviving members of the Velvet Underground—Lou Reed, John Cale, and Maureen "Moe" Tucker—were inducted into the Hall of Fame by Patti Smith. The award ceremony served as a tribute to band member Sterling Morrison, who was inducted posthumously after dying of non-Hodgkin lymphoma on August 30, 1995, at the age of fifty-three. According to Smith in her induction speech, "They are the Velvet Underground and their work is the clipper ship. We salute them and mourn with them their captain, Sterling Morrison." During his

Legendary proto-punk band the Velvet Underground were inducted into the Rock and Roll Hall of Fame in 1996 by Patti Smith. PHOTOFEST

acceptance speech, Cale said the band's induction served as "an astonishing point to all the musicians in the world that sales are not the be-all-and-end-all of rock and roll."

The trio performed a brand-new composition, "Last Night I Said Goodbye to My Friend," as a tribute to Morrison. Other 1996 inductees into the Rock and Roll Hall of Fame included David Bowie, Gladys Knight and the Pips, Jefferson Airplane, Little Willie John, Pink Floyd, and the Shirelles. In 2015, Reed was posthumously inducted into the Rock and Roll Hall of Fame for his solo work.

RAMONES (2002)   "The Ramones took punk rock on its maiden voyage." The Ramones—Joey (who had passed away of lymphoma less than a year before the induction ceremony), Dee Dee, Johnny, Tommy, and Marky—were inducted into the Hall of Fame by Eddie Vedder of Pearl Jam (complete with mohawk haircut and Ramones T-shirt) at the seventeenth-annual induction ceremony. Even though C. J. Ramone served as the band's bassist from 1989 to 1996, he was not invited to be inducted into the Hall of Fame.

During his speech, Vedder exclaimed that the Ramones "were armed with two-minute songs that they rattled off like machine-gun fire, and it was enough to change the Earth's revolution. Now it's Disney kids singing songs written by old men and being marketed to six- and seven-year-olds, so some kind of change might have to happen again soon."

Always a political conservative, Johnny reportedly infuriated the other band members when he exclaimed during his acceptance speech, "God bless President Bush and God bless America." Dee Dee gave a more laid-back speech, stating, "I'd like to congratulate myself and thank myself and give myself a big pat on the back." Green Day performed the Ramones classics "Teenage Lobotomy," "Rockaway Beach," and "Blitzkrieg Bop." Other 2002 inductees into the Rock and Roll Hall of Fame included Isaac Hayes, Brenda Lee, Gene Pitney, Talking Heads (see next entry), and Tom Petty and the Heartbreakers.

TALKING HEADS (2002)   "Artsy and experimental, Talking Heads created an oeuvre of funky New Wave hits." The four original Talking Heads band members—David Byrne, Tina Weymouth, Jerry Harrison, and Chris Frantz—put their long-standing differences aside to reunite for the induction ceremony. During his acceptance speech, drummer Frantz remarked, "I'd like to thank the Rock and Roll Hall of Fame for giving this band a happy ending." The band managed to pull off an outstanding set that featured "Psycho Killer," "Life during Wartime," "Burning Down the House," and "Take Me to the River."

THE CLASH (2003)   "Quite simply, the Clash were among the most explosive and exciting bands in rock and roll history." The Clash—Joe Strummer (who had died of a heart attack at the age of fifty on December 22, 2002), Mick Jones, Paul Simonon, Topper Headon, and Terry Chimes)—were inducted in the Hall of Fame by Edge of U2 and Tom Morello of Rage Against the Machine. During his impassioned speech, Morello remarked,

> The Clash perform with passion, commitment, purpose, righteousness, and an unflinching political fire. . . . In fact, the Clash aren't really gone at all. Because whenever a band cares more about its fans than its bank account, the spirit of the Clash is there. Whenever a band plays as if every single person's soul in the room is at stake, the spirit of the Clash is there. And whenever a stadium band or little garage band has the guts to put their beliefs on the line to make a difference, the spirit of the Clash is there. And whenever people take to the streets to stop an unjust war, the spirit of the Clash is definitely there.

During the Edge's speech, he commented that if the Clash "had been around ten years earlier, they would have given the Beatles, the Kinks, and the Stones a run for their money. If they had arrived ten years later, they might have resolved their inner conflicts and stayed the course." According to music critic Simon Reynolds in his 2011 book *Retromania*, "At the 2003 ceremony, Mick Jones—balding, clad in black suit and tie—didn't look like a rock 'n' roll soldier getting a medal so much as a stoop-shouldered clerk shuffling to the podium to receive his retirement gift for forty-five years' loyal service to the firm." Other 2003 inductees into the Rock and Roll Hall of Fame included Elvis Costello and the Attractions (see entry below), the Police, the Righteous Brothers, Jackson Browne, the Dells, and George Harrison.

ELVIS COSTELLO AND THE ATTRACTIONS (2003)   "Elvis Costello took the literacy of folk music and broke it wide open against the ragged edges of punk." Accompanying the Clash in the 2003 lineup of Rock and Roll Hall of Fame inductees was Elvis Costello and the Attractions, inducted by Elton John. Costello and his band the Imposters (basically the Attractions without original bass player, a disgruntled Bruce Thomas) performed "(What's So Funny 'bout) Peace, Love and Understanding." One critic in attendance called the song "a good choice but only mediocre performance." As for Thomas, after he was presented with his trophy, he remarked, "Thanks for the memories, that's it," and then made a beeline for the exits.

THE PRETENDERS (2005)   "Punk professors and pop crossover phenoms. The Pretenders' music is simultaneously melodic and bristling with rebellion." The Pretenders—Chrissie Hynde, Martin Chambers, Pete Farndon (1952–1983), and James Honeyman-Scott (1956–1982)—were inducted into the Rock and Roll Hall of Fame by Neil Young. In his speech, Young remarked, "This is one of the greatest rock 'n' roll bands that ever lived. They went through all the heartache that rock 'n' roll is built on. They lost two key members and they never gave up."

During her acceptance speech, Hynde stated, "I know that the Pretenders have looked like a tribute band for the last twenty years. And actually they are a tribute band. And we're paying tribute to James Honeyman-Scott and Pete Farndon, without whom we wouldn't be here. And on the other hand, without us, they might have been here, but that's the way it works in rock 'n' roll." Young then joined the band for a rendition of "My City Was Gone." Other 2005 inductees into the Rock and Roll Hall of Fame included Buddy Guy, the O'Jays, Percy Sledge, and U2.

BLONDIE (2006)   "The vanguard of the new wave. Blondie have experimented with nearly every genre on record—reggae, rap, punk, disco, etc." Blondie—Debbie Harry, Chris Stein, Clem Burke, Jimmy Destri, Nigel Harrison, Frank Infante, and Gary Valentine— were inducted into the Rock and Roll Hall of Fame by Shirley Manson of alternative-rock band Garbage. However, the evening was not without controversy, as two former band members—bassist Harrison and guitarist Infante—were recognized but not invited to perform with the other band members at the induction ceremony. The bad blood between the band members originated in 1996 when Blondie re-formed without inviting either Harrison or Infante.

During his acceptance speech, Infante remarked, "I'd like to thank the Hall of Fame for recognizing us and not writing [us] out of rock 'n' roll history. One thing that could really make it better is if we could actually perform for you tonight, but for some reason some of us are not allowed to do that." Infante then pleaded with a visibly agitated Harry for the opportunity to perform with the band: "We'd like to play with you guys—me and Nigel. Pretty please! Pretty please, Debbie!" Harry replied, "Not tonight. Can't you see my band is up there?" Infante responded, "Oh, your band! I thought Blondie was being inducted tonight." During Harrison's acceptance speech, he remarked, "It's nice to see everyone out of the court-room. That's the first positive thing. I got to say, after watching all that footage of us tonight, I felt I was going to my own funeral. It's messed up for us. We want to play. Obviously, we were part of it. We've been led to believe we weren't part of it. It sucks. Welcome to bingo night." Blondie ended up playing a set that featured "Call Me," "Rapture," and "Heart of Glass." Other 2006 inductees into the Rock and Roll Hall of Fame included Black Sabbath, Miles Davis, Lynyrd Skynyrd, and the Sex Pistols (see entry below).

SEX PISTOLS (2006)   "The Sex Pistols triggered the punk-rock movement by running a scorched earth campaign, calling out everyone from the music industry to the queen." Was there any doubt that the Sex Pistols would refuse their induction to the Rock and Roll Hall of Fame and decline to attend the ceremony?

In a crudely written handwritten letter faxed to the Rock and Roll Hall of Fame, John Lydon explained why the band had decided to refuse the honor:

> Next to the Sex Pistols, rock 'n' roll and that Hall of Fame is a piss stain. Your museum. Urine in wine. We're not coming. We're not your monkey and so what? Fame at $25,000 if we paid for a table, or $15,000 to squeak up in the gallery, goes to a non-profit organization selling us a load of old famous. Congratulations. If you voted for us, hope you noted your reasons. You're anonymous as judges, but you're still music industry people. We're not coming. You're not paying attention. Outside the shit-stem is a real Sex Pistol.

The Sex Pistols still made it into the Rock and Roll Hall of Fame because *Rolling Stone* founder and Hall of Fame cofounder Jann Wenner inducted them and even read part of Lydon's rejection letter at the induction ceremony.

PATTI SMITH (2007)   "The high priestess of punk-poetry. Rock was getting too slick for its own good when Patti Smith burst on the scene and tore it apart." Patti Smith was inducted into the Rock and Roll Hall of Fame by Zack de la Rocha of Rage Against the Machine. During his induction speech, de la Rocha remarked,

> Patti's spirit ultimately proved too restless for radio, and far too threatening. She seemed far more interested in creating transcendent poetic moments than fashionable hits, because she had already carved her legacy in something much deeper. The movement she helped define explained why people like me related to Bad Brains than we did to the Eagles, why we championed the Clash and hated Ronald Reagan, and why we dropped our textbooks and picked up Sonia Sanchez, Allen Ginsberg, and Langston Hughes.

Smith performed "Gloria," "Because the Night," and "People Have the Power" during the ceremony. Other 2007 inductees into the Rock and Roll Hall of Fame included Grandmaster Flash and the Furious Five, R.E.M., the Ronettes, and Van Halen.

The Stooges—featuring Iggy Pop, Dave Alexander, Scott Asheton, Ron Asheton, and James Williamson (pictured)—were inducted into the Rock and Roll Hall of Fame in 2010. By Eddy BERTHIER, Brussels, Belgium/Wikimedia Commons

THE STOOGES (2010)   "The Stooges were punk before punk existed. In a time when hippie idealism was popular, the Stooges threw down the gauntlet in the form of provocative, high-octane rock and roll." The Stooges—Iggy Pop, Dave Alexander (1947–1975), Ron Asheton (1948–2009), Scott Asheton, and James Williamson— were inducted into the Rock and Roll Hall of Fame by Billie Joe Armstrong of Green Day.

With a shirtless Iggy goading the lifeless audience members to join him onstage, the Stooges performed a raucous set that featured "Search and Destroy" and "I Wanna Be Your Dog." At one point during the performance, Iggy exclaimed, "Come on rich people! Show us you're not too rich to be cool!" Other 2010 inductees into the Rock and Roll Hall of Fame included ABBA, Genesis, Jimmy Cliff, and the Hollies.

NIRVANA (2014)   "Nirvana accidentally kicked off a cultural revolution with 1991's Nevermind, an album that brought rock & roll kicking and screaming into the modern world." Nirvana—Kurt

Cobain (1967–1994), Dave Grohl, and Krist Novoselic—was inducted into the Rock and Roll Hall of Fame by Michael Stipe of R.E.M. During his induction speech, Stipe stated,

> I embrace the use of the word "artist" rather than "musician" because the band Nirvana were artists in every sense of the word. It is the highest calling for an artist, as well as the greatest possible privilege to capture a moment, to find the zeitgeist, to expose our struggles, our aspirations, our desires. To embrace and define a period of time. That is my definition of an artist. Nirvana captures lightning in a bottle.

Various female rockers were enlisted to join Nirvana (Grohl, Novoselic, and Pat Smear, who was touring guitarist for the band in 1993 and 1994) onstage to perform, such as Joan Jett ("Smells Like Teen Spirit"), Kim Gordon of Sonic Youth ("Aneurysm"), St. Vincent ("Lithium"), and Lorde ("All Apologies"). Other 2014 inductees into the Rock and Roll Hall of Fame included Peter Gabriel, Hall & Oates, KISS, Linda Ronstadt, and Cat Stevens.

GREEN DAY (2015)   "Green Day yanked punk rock out from the underground and into the mainstream." Green Day—Billie Joe Armstrong, Tre Cool, and Mike Dirnt—was inducted into the Rock and Roll Hall of Fame in their first year of eligibility by Fall Out Boy. In his acceptance speech, Armstrong remarked,

> So we come from this place called Gilman Street. It's a club. It's in Berkeley. We are so fortunate to be able to play there because it's all ages and it was nonprofit. It was just all of these goofballs. It was like Romper Room for degenerates. It was so great. And what a great scene. We got to watch our friends' bands, and they got to watch us play, and they got to heckle us. We tried to heckle back, but they had one better. So, then I got to see Operation Ivy, and I got to see Crimpshrine, and I got to see Sewer Trout, Nasal Sex. These far out there bands. I'm truly fortunate.

Other 2015 inductees into the Rock and Roll Hall of Fame included Lou Reed (see next entry), Joan Jett and the Blackhearts, the Paul Butterfield Blues Band, Bill Withers, and Stevie Ray Vaughn and Double Trouble.

LOU REED (2015)   "Frank, brutal, and brilliant." Reed, who had passed away in 2013 and was previously inducted into the Rock and Roll Hall of Fame in 1996 as a member of the Velvet Underground, was posthumously inducted into the Rock and Roll Hall of Fame by Patti Smith. During her eloquent induction speech, Smith remarked,

> I made my first eye contact with Lou dancing to the Velvet Underground when they were playing upstairs at Max's Kansas City in the summer of 1970. The Velvet Underground were great to dance to because they had this sort of transformative, like a surf beat. And then somewhere along the line, Lou and I became friends. It was a complex friendship, sometimes antagonistic and sometimes sweet. Lou would sometimes emerge from the shadows at CBGBs. If I did something good, he would praise me. If I made a false move, he would break it down. . . . True poets must often stand alone. As a poet, he must be counted as a solitary artist. And so, Lou, thank you for brutally and benevolently injecting your poetry into music.

THE GO-GO'S (2021)   "The Go-Go's catchy, well-crafted songs formed a bridge between the brash urgency of L.A. punk and the dark melodies of new wave pop." The Rock and Roll Hall of Fame finally got around to recognizing the first—and only—all-female rock band to ever earn a no. 1 album (*Beauty and the Beat*, 1981). The Go-Go's—Belinda Carlisle, Charlotte Caffey, Gina Schock, Kathy Valentine, and Jane Wiedlin—were inducted into the Rock and Roll Hall of Fame by Drew Barrymore. During her acceptance speech, Valentine remarked, "By recognizing our achievement, the Rock Hall celebrates possibility—the kind of possibility that creates hopeful dreamers. The Go-Go's will be advocating for the inclusion of more women [into the Rock and Roll Hall of Fame]." The band performed three of their most recognizable hits during the ceremony: "Vacation," "Our Lips Are Sealed," and "We Got the Beat." Other 2021 inductees into the Rock and Roll Hall of Fame included Tina Turner, Carole King, Jay-Z, the Foo Fighters, and Todd Rundgren.

30

Here We Are Nowhere

Famous (and Infamous) Punk Landmarks

Legendary punk clubs in NYC like CBGBs and Max's Kansas City are long gone, but the spirit of punk can still be found in the Big Apple (if you look hard enough!) at such popular tourist sites as Joey Ramone Place and the Joe Strummer Mural. In addition, the morbidly curious can seek out the final resting places of self-destructive punks such as Darby Crash of the Germs and shock rocker GG Allin, among others.

For the adventurous traveler who wishes to further explore punk-rock landmarks, two books come highly recommended: *Led Zeppelin Crashed Here: The Rock and Roll Landmarks of North America* (2007) by Chris Epting and *Rock and Roll Explorer Guide to New York City* (2018) by Mike Katz and Crispin Kott.

CHELSEA HOTEL (222 W. 23RD STREET, NYC) A legendary Manhattan hotel first opened in 1884, the Chelsea Hotel (aka Hotel Chelsea or just the Chelsea) hosted countless musicians, writers, artists, and actors through the years, such as Dee Dee Ramone (who wrote a fictionalized account of his experiences here called *Chelsea Hotel Horror*), Johnny Thunders, Iggy Pop, Nico, Tom Waits, Patti Smith, John Cale, Bob Dylan (who wrote songs for his 1966 album *Blonde on Blonde* in Room 211), Madonna, Thomas Wolfe, Leonard Cohen (whose sexual encounter with Janis Joplin in Room 222 inspired "Chelsea Hotel #2"), Chet Baker, Dylan Thomas, Jack Kerouac,

Allen Ginsberg, William S. Burroughs, Gregory Corso, Brendan Behan, and Arthur C. Clarke (who reportedly wrote the screenplay for *2001: A Space Odyssey* while residing here), among many others. In addition, Andy Warhol and Paul Morrissey filmed the experimental underground film *Chelsea Girls* here in 1966.

Tragically, Room 100 in the Chelsea served as the site where Nancy Spungen, girlfriend of former Sex Pistols bassist Sid Vicious, was found stabbed to death on October 12, 1978. Vicious was charged with the crime

The legendary Chelsea Hotel in Manhattan hosted many punk rockers over the years such as Dee Dee Ramone, Johnny Thunders, Patti Smith, and (most notoriously) Sid Vicious. By VELVET, OWN WORK/WIKIMEDIA COMMONS

but died of a heroin overdose before the trial. In his diary entry for that day, Andy Warhol wrote, "The police just arrested Sid Vicious for stabbing his 20-year-old manager-girlfriend to death in the Chelsea Hotel. . . . They just let anybody in over there, that hotel is dangerous, it seems like somebody's killed there once a week." Listed on the National Register of Historic Places, the Chelsea has been designated a New York City Landmark.

JOE STRUMMER MEMORIAL (132 EAST SEVENTH STREET, NYC) The powerful, brightly colored outdoor mural that commemorates the late, great Joe Strummer of the Clash can be viewed at East Seventh Street and Avenue A outside the Niagara, a dive bar in the East Village. Featuring the image of a young Strummer wearing sunglasses, along with the phrase "The Future Is Unwritten," the mural was originally painted in 2003, just one year after Strummer passed away of a heart attack at the age of fifty on December 22, 2002. Then the mural was repainted by the original street artists, Dr.

Revolt and Zephyr, after the original brick façade had to be repaired in front of the Niagara, which Strummer frequented whenever he was in New York City. The Niagara, which first opened its doors in 1997, sells Joe Strummer "Know Your Rights" T-shirts that feature the mural at $30 a pop. "Know Your Rights" refers to the first track on the Clash's 1982 album, *Combat Rock*.

430 KING'S ROAD (LONDON) The storefront that now houses the World's End boutique holds a special place in the history of punk history, fashion, and style. In 1971, Vivienne Westwood and then boyfriend Malcolm McLaren opened their first boutique here called Let It Rock (named after the 1960 Chuck Berry hit), which sold 1950s fashion and Teddy Boy clothes. In subsequent years, each time the couple designed a new collection, they changed the name of the shop: Too Fast to Live, Too Young to Die (honoring legendary 1950s actor James Dean) between 1973 and 1974, SEX between 1974 and 1976, and Seditionaries between 1976 and 1980. World's End opened in 1980 and remains a part of Westwood's global fashion empire.

It was during the SEX phase of the business (the store then featured fetish and bondage wear) when the idea for the Sex Pistols began to take shape. Future Sex Pistols bass player Glen Matlock even worked as a shop assistant for a time, and members of what later became the Bromley Contingent—such as Siouxsie Sioux—hung out there regularly. In August 1975, nineteen-year-old John Lydon informally auditioned for the Sex Pistols by singing along to Alice Cooper's "I'm Eighteen" on the store's jukebox.

ST. MARK'S PLACE (NYC) Dubbed "America's coolest street" by the *Guardian*, St. Mark's Place is located between Third Avenue and Avenue A along bustling Eighth Street in the East Village. St. Mark's Place became something of a punk gathering spot with the arrival of such quirky stores as Manic Panic. Considered the first punk store in the United States, Manic Panic was opened by Tish and Snooky Bellomo, punk-rock pioneers and former backup singers in Blondie, in 1977. Manic Panic sold vintage clothing, platform shoes, studded accessories, black leather, Dr. Martens, and hair dye, as well as records and fan zines. Other St. Mark's Place hangouts popular with the punk crowd included the St. Mark's Bar & Grill, Manitoba's punk bar (owned by "Handsome Dick" Manitoba of the Dictators), and Gem Spa, a newspaper magazine and tobacco store prominently featured on the back cover of the New York Dolls' self-titled debut album in 1973.

JOEY RAMONE PLACE (EAST SECOND STREET, NYC)   Two years after Joey Ramone passed away from lymphoma at the age of forty-nine and one year after the Ramones were inducted into the Rock and Roll Hall of Fame, a block of East Second Street in New York City was officially renamed Joey Ramone Place on November 30, 2003. Ideally located near the former site of CBGBs, it is also the block where Joey (born Jeffrey Hyman in Forest Hills, Queens) and bandmate Dee Dee Ramone once lived in the Bowery. In 2010, the Associated Press reported that the "Joey Ramone Place" sign was the most stolen sign in New York City. To discourage such activity, the sign was moved to a height of twenty feet from the ground. In addition, several songs have been written honoring Joey over the years, including "Hello Joe" by Blondie, "You Can't Kill Joey Ramone" by Sloppy Seconds, and "I Wanna Be Your Joey Ramone" by Sleater-Kinney.

100 CLUB (100 OXFORD STREET, LONDON)   Although its days of hosting punk-rock bands are long behind it, the venerable 100 Club has been featuring live musical acts in one form or another since first opening its doors as Feldman Swing Club in 1942. In September 1976, the 100 Club hosted the first international punk festival, which featured the likes of the Sex Pistols, Buzzcocks, the Clash, Siouxsie and the Banshees, the Jam, the Damned, and the Stranglers. All the bands were unsigned at the time. Other punk bands to take the stage here over the years included the Adicts, UK Subs, Angelic Upstarts, Black Flag, Crass, and Skrewdriver, among others.

315 BOWERY (FORMER SITE OF CBGBS, NYC)   CBGBs began as a former flophouse then biker bar that was taken over by entrepreneur

Hilly Kristal in 1973. Kristal's initial vision was to host country, bluegrass, and blues acts. However, CBGBs quickly morphed into a punk/new-wave mecca by hosting such acts as Television, the Ramones, Talking Heads, Blondie, Patti Smith, Johnny Thunders and the Heartbreakers, and many others. A rent dispute led to CBGBs closing its doors for good in 2006 (Kristal passed away a year later). Today, the fashionable John Varvatos boutique occupies the former site of the legendary dive bar. Varvatos contains various artifacts from CBGBs on its walls that pay tribute to the club's rich musical heritage and hosts live rock concerts in its "Bowery Live" series.

GG ALLIN'S GRAVE   For many years following the death of infamous punk-rock musician GG Allin from a heroin overdose in 1993, hardcore fans of the singer would make pilgrimages to his gravesite in Saint Rose Cemetery in Littleton, New Hampshire, and (rather appropriately, considering his debauched legacy) shit, piss, vomit, and pour beer all over his tombstone. In addition, the headstone was frequently replaced and removed. However, recent reports indicate that the grave has been permanently removed, so any fans dedicated enough to make the pilgrimage will have to do some online sleuth work to discover the exact location of Allin's gravesite.

DARBY CRASH FINAL RESTING PLACE   After self-destructive lead singer of the Germs Darby Crash committed suicide via an intentional heroin overdose on December 7, 1980, he was buried at Holy Cross Cemetery in Culver City, California. His epitaph reads "Beloved Son & Brother/Jan Paul Beahm/Darby Crash/1958–1980." Holy Cross Cemetery also serves as the final resting place for an eclectic array of celebrities such as Bing Crosby, John Candy, Rita Hayworth, Bela Lugosi, Chris Penn, Lawrence Welk, Sharon Tate, Jimmy Durante, John Ford, Al Martino (Johnny Fontane in *The Godfather*), Mary Astor, Jack Haley (the Tin Man from *The Wizard of Oz*), and others.

NANCY SPUNGEN GRAVESITE   Punk-rock groupie and girlfriend of Sid Vicious, Spungen was stabbed to death on October 12, 1978, in

Room 100 at the Chelsea Hotel in New York City. Vicious was charged with the murder. Spungen was laid to rest at King David Memorial Park in Bensalem, Pennsylvania. Her epitaph reads, "Your Odyssey is Over—Rest in Peace." According to rumor, Vicious's mother scattered his ashes over Spungen's grave after the former bass player for the Sex Pistols died of a heroin overdose on February 2, 1979.

JOHNNY RAMONE STATUE   An eight-foot-tall, $100,000 bronze memorial statue of Johnny Ramone with guitar in hand lies in the Garden of Legends at Hollywood Forever Cemetery in Los Angeles, California, just a few yards away from his bandmate Dee Dee Ramone's grave. A plaque on the memorial reads, "If a man can tell if he's been successful in his life by having great friends, then I have been very successful." The statue was sculpted by artist Wayne Toth. Johnny (real name: John Cummings) passed away of prostate cancer at the age of fifty-five on September 15, 2004. His wife, Linda, coordinated an unveiling ceremony on January 14, 2005, that featured a variety of the punk rocker's friends and former bandmates as speakers, such as Rob Zombie, Nicolas Cage, Eddie Vedder, Vincent Gallo, John Frusciante, Seymour Stein, Peter Yorn, Tommy Ramone, and C. J. Ramone. The Johnny Ramone Tribute gathering at Hollywood Forever Cemetery has since become an annual event. Hollywood Forever Cemetery also serves as the final resting place for the likes of Burt Reynolds, Bugsy Siegel, Judy Garland, Mickey Rooney, Tyrone Power, Peter Finch, Hattie McDaniel, Rudolph Valentino, Darren McGavin, Scott Weiland, and Toto from *The Wizard of Oz*.

An eight-foot-tall bronze statue of Johnny Ramone lies in the Hollywood Forever Cemetery in Los Angeles within a few yards of bandmate Dee Dee Ramone's final resting place. By Katie-Round, Own work/Wikimedia Commons

ROCK 'N' ROLL HIGH SCHOOL FILMING SITES   Starring the Ramones—
Joey, Dee Dee, Johnny, and Marky—this 1979 cult movie produced
by Roger Corman and directed by Allan Arkush was filmed in
various locales around Los Angeles—including the defunct Mount
Carmel High School in South Central (the school's actual demolition was featured at the end of the film). Mira Costa High School
in Manhattan Beach and Van Nuys High School (also used for
Fast Times at Ridgemont High in 1982) in Van Nuys were also used
as filming sites. The concert scenes featuring the Ramones were
filmed at the Roxy, the legendary nightclub on the Sunset Strip in
West Hollywood (with portions also shot at the nearby Whisky a Go
Go). However, the venue's exterior was shot at the landmark 1927
Mayan Theatre in downtown Los Angeles.

The 1979 cult film *Rock 'n' Roll High School*, which starred the Ramones, was filmed
in various locales around Los Angeles such as legendary rock clubs the Roxy and
Whisky A Go Go. New World/Photofest

31

People Who Died
Punk-Rock Casualties

Ain't it fun when you know that you're gonna die young.
—"Ain't It Fun," Rocket from the Tombs

Visionary poet William Blake once wrote, "The road of excess leads to the palace of wisdom." Nearly two hundred years later, Neil Young sang, "It's better to burn out than fade away." Many punk rockers over the years have taken such adages to heart with tragic results. Nirvana's Kurt Cobain even used Young's "burn out" line in his 1994 suicide note when he joined the ever-growing "27 Club" of musicians that includes Jimi Hendrix, Janis Joplin, and Jim Morrison, among many others. In fact, the very nature of punk itself drives devotees not only to go against the grain but also to pursue what French symbolist poet Arthur Rimbaud referred to as "an immense, long, deliberate derangement of all the senses."

ROBERT QUINE (1942–2004) Best known as the highly talented guitarist for Richard Hell and the Voidoids, Quine ranked no. 80 on *Rolling Stone*'s list of the "100 Greatest Guitarists of All Time." He died of an intentional heroin overdose at the age of sixty-one on May 31, 2004. Quine was apparently in a state of depression after his wife Alice had died less than a year before.

LESTER BANGS (1948–1982)   A true iconoclast, rock critic Lester Bangs (Leslie Conway Bangs) died of an accidental drug overdose on April 30, 1982, at the age of thirty-three in his New York City apartment. According to various reports, the Human League's third studio album, *Dare!*, was spinning on his turntable. Bangs's ashes were scattered in the Pacific Ocean. His biographer, Jim DeRogatis, called him "the great gonzo journalist, gutter poet, and romantic visionary of rock writing—it's Hunter S. Thompson, Charles Bukowski and Jack Kerouac all rolled into one."

WENDY O. WILLIAMS (1949–1998)   Known for her outrageous onstage antics (like chain-sawing guitars and blowing up cars), the lead singer of the Plasmatics, who had been struggling with depression for years, died of a self-inflicted gunshot wound to the head at the age of forty-eight on April 6, 1998, in a wooded area near her Storrs, Connecticut, home. Upon hearing the news, Joey Ramone

Known as the "Queen of Shock Rock," Wendy O. Williams died of a self-inflicted gunshot wound to the head at the age of forty-eight in 1998. PHOTOFEST

remarked, "You would never have thought she'd be the type of person to turn a gun on herself."

The "Queen of Shock Rock" had previously attempted suicide in 1993 (by hammering a knife into her chest) and 1997 (with an overdose of ephedrine). Her suicide note read,

> I don't believe that people should take their own lives without deep and thoughtful reflection over a considerable period of time. I do believe strongly, however, that the right to do so is one of the most fundamental rights that anyone in a free society should have. For me, much of the world makes no sense, but my feelings about what I am doing ring loud and clear to an inner ear and a place where there is no self, only calm.

BILLY MURCIA (1951–1972)   The original New York Dolls drummer, Billy Murcia died on November 6, 1972, at the age of twenty-one in London during the band's brief tour of England. Although commonly believed to have died of a drug overdose, it turns out Murcia passed away of asphyxiation during ill-advised attempts to revive him that included placing him in a bathtub and force-feeding him coffee. He was replaced by Jerry Nolan. New York Dolls bandmate Johnny Thunders paid tribute to Murcia by penning the song "Billy Boy," which appeared on his 1985 solo album, *Que Sera Sera*.

DEE DEE RAMONE (1951–2002)   According to Legs McNeil of *Punk* magazine fame in his introduction to Dee Dee Ramone's 2000 memoir, *Lobotomy*, Dee Dee "epitomizes the quintessential punk rocker. The guy was a rock star. He had the look, the hair, and the sneer. We knew him. We understood when he said, 'Fuck it.'" Shortly after being inducted into the Rock and Roll Hall of Fame as part of the Ramones, Dee Dee was found dead of heroin toxicity in his Hollywood home on June 5, 2002, at the age of fifty. He is buried at Hollywood Forever Cemetery in Los Angeles. His epitaph reads, "O.K. . . . I gotta go now."

PETER LAUGHNER (1952–1977)   The founder of legendary Cleveland, Ohio, underground proto-punk-rock band Rocket from the Tombs, Laughner was also involved with starting up the avant-garde band

Pere Ubu and even wrote album reviews for *CREEM* magazine. After struggling with severe drug and alcohol abuse, Laughner died of acute pancreatitis at the age of twenty-four on June 22, 1977. He is buried at Sunset Memorial Park in North Olmsted, Ohio, and his epitaph reads, "Play On Beloved Son."

JOHNNY THUNDERS (1952–1991)   The charismatic and self-destructive former member of both the New York Dolls and the Heartbreakers died under rather mysterious circumstances at the age of thirty-eight in Room 37 at St. Peter's Guest House (now known as the Inn on St. Peter) in New Orleans, Louisiana, on April 23, 1991. He is buried in Mount Saint Mary's Cemetery in Flushing, New York. Duff McKagan of Guns N' Roses once referred to Thunders as a "sloppy heroin addict." However, according to the New Orleans coroner's report, Thunders died from an overdose of cocaine and methadone. Although Thunders's family urged the New Orleans police to reinvestigate his death, no efforts have been made to find out what really happened to Johnny Thunders.

MALCOLM OWEN (1955–1980)   The lead singer for the Ruts died of a heroin overdose in the bathroom of his parents' house on July 14, 1980, at the age of twenty-five. Best known for their reggae-influenced hit, "Babylon's Burning," the band also featured guitarist Paul Fox, bassist John "Segs" Jennings, and drummer Dave Ruffy. The Ruts' track "H-Eyes" off their 1980 album, *Grin & Bear It*, served to foreshadow Owen's demise: "You're so young, you take smack for fun/It's gonna screw you head, you're gonna wind up dead." The Damned recorded a tribute to Owen titled "The Limit Club."

ROGER ROGERSON (1955–1996)   The original bass player for the Circle Jerks died of a heroin overdose at the age of forty-one on August 8, 1996. In 2017, J. Hunter Bennett published *The Prodigal Rogerson: The Tragic, Hilarious, and Possibly Apocryphal Story of Circle Jerks Bassist Roger Rogerson in the Golden Age of LA Punk, 1979–1996*.

GG ALLIN (1956–1993) Throughout his short, turbulent life, shock rocker Allin reveled in hardcore self-destruction fueled by massive amounts of drugs and alcohol. He was born in a log cabin in New Hampshire without electricity, and his actual birth name was (allegedly) Jesus Christ Allin. Notorious for defecating onstage, throwing feces at the audience, and other revolting escapades, Allin and his band, the Murder Junkies (which also featured his brother Merle), rarely completed a gig.

Somewhat predictably, Allin's stable of raunchy material was full of such song titles as "Drink, Fuck and Fight," "Gimme Some Head," and "Pussy Summit Meeting." For years, Allin had been promising to kill himself onstage. Allin was reportedly arrested over fifty times and served a three-year prison stint for "assault with intent to do great bodily harm less than murder." In the ensuing years, Allin proved to be great talk-show fodder for the likes of *The Morton Downey Jr. Show*, *The Geraldo Rivera Show*, and *The Jerry Springer Show*.

In his 2008 memoir, *I Have Fun Everywhere I Go*, Allin's friend and occasional collaborator Mike Edison refers to him as "a skid mark on the boxer short of the music business." According to Edison, after another failed gig (this time at the Gas Station Club), "GG was last seen tumbling down Avenue B in the East Village, buck naked (except for his combat boots), covered in his own filth. . . . Later he went to a party and snorted a bunch of heroin. He woke up dead." The date was June 28, 1993, and Allin was just thirty-six years old.

Director Todd Phillip brilliantly captures the total insanity of Allin's disturbing life and music career in his 1993 documentary, *Hated: GG Allin and the Murder Junkies* (definitely watch at your own risk!). Also, if you have a masochistic desire to read about all the sordid details of Allin's final U.S. tour, grab a copy of *I Was a Murder Junkie*, written by his former roadie, Evan Cohen.

IAN CURTIS (1956–1980) Right before Joy Division was set to embark on a U.S. tour, the band's lead singer and songwriter, Ian Curtis, hanged himself at his Manchester, England, home at the age of twenty-three on May 18, 1980. The band's critically acclaimed second and final album, *Closer*, was released exactly two months later on July 18, 1980, and featured the poignant track, "Love Will Tear Us Apart" (which *NME* once declared "the greatest single of all time").

Curtis is buried at Macclesfield Cemetery in Macclesfield, Cheshire. His epitaph reads, "LOVE WILL TEAR US APART." *Control*, an acclaimed biopic on Curtis based on his widow Deborah's book *Touching from a Distance*, was released in 2007.

CHUCK WAGON (1956–1981)   The multi-instrumentalist for the Dickies, Chuck Wagon (Robert "Bob" Davis) died of a self-inflicted gunshot wound to the head on June 6, 1981, at the age of twenty-four. He was reportedly deeply despondent over the end of his relationship with his girlfriend.

SID VICIOUS (1957–1979)   A self-destructive heroin addict who has become an enduring icon of the punk subculture, Sid Vicious once casually remarked, "I've only been in love with a beer bottle and a mirror." That is apparently until he hooked up with perennial groupie Nancy Spungen, a former Times Square stripper and troubled junkie. For example, Spungen once casually revealed that she had slept with every member of the New York Dolls—except Arthur "Killer" Kane. In his 2017 memoir *Punk Avenue*, Phil Marcade of the Senders called Spungen "the reject of a society made up of society's rejects." According to Sex Pistol manager Malcolm McLaren, "When Nancy Spungen came into my shop it was as if Dr. Strangelove had sent us this dreaded disease."

Both Vicious and Spungen soon became full-blown heroin addicts. On October 12, 1978, Vicious was arrested for allegedly stabbing Spungen to death with a hunting knife while in a drug-induced stupor in Room 100 at the Hotel Chelsea in Manhattan. Spungen was just twenty years old. Out on bail, Vicious was rearrested in November 1978 after cutting Patti Smith's brother Todd in the face with a broken beer bottle. Shortly after being released from a fifty-five-day jail stint at Riker's Island, Vicious died of a heroin overdose on February 2, 1979.

In a 2000 interview, Lemmy of Motorhead remarked, "I got quite upset when [Vicious] died. He never had a chance. He was trying to be all the people he admired and it was impossible for him. But that fucking Nancy Spungen . . . I'd have strangled her if he hadn't have knifed her. She was the Courtney Love of her day." In Mikal Gilmore's *Night Beat*, John Lydon is quoted as saying, "Poor Sid. The only way he could live up to what he wanted everyone to believe about him was to die. That was tragic, but more for Sid than anyone else. He really bought his public image."

Vicious's ashes were allegedly either scattered at Spungen's grave at King David Memorial Park in Bensalem, Pennsylvania, or possibly scattered throughout Heathrow Airport by Sid's mother. The Ramones wrote a song about Vicious and Spungen called "Love Kills" that appears on the band's ninth studio album, *Animal Boy* (1986). Sung by Dee Dee Ramone, it features the lyrics: "Sid was a punk rock king/Nancy was a broken queen/Their lives were so glamorous/Sid and Nancy were a mess."

DARBY CRASH (1958–1980) As part of a supposed suicide pact, notoriously self-destructive Germs lead singer Darby Crash and

The gravestone of the Germs' notorious lead singer, Darby Crash, can be found at Holy Cross Cemetery in Culver City, California. By IllaZilla, Own work/Wikimedia Commons

his girlfriend Casey took potentially lethal doses of heroin on the morning of December 7, 1980, at Casey's mother's bungalow at 173 North Fuller Avenue in Hollywood. However, Crash died, while Casey somehow survived. He was just twenty-two years old. Crash's death was significantly overshadowed by the murder of John Lennon by Mark David Chapman outside the Dakota in New York City the following day.

DIMWIT (1958–1994)   Best known as the drummer for Vancouver hardcore punk band D.O.A., Ken "Dimwit" Montgomery died of a heroin overdose on September 27, 1994, at the age of thirty-six. Considered one of the founders of hardcore punk and known for its outspoken political stances, D.O.A. also featured lead singer/guitarist Joey "Shithead" Keithley, Brian "Wimpy Roy" Goble, and bassist Randy Rampage.

BOB STINSON (1959–1995)   A founding member and the original lead guitarist of Minneapolis-based alternative rock band the Replacements (who was forced out of the group in 1986 allegedly for substance abuse problems), Stinson died of organ failure at the age of thirty-five on February 18, 1995.

DAVE RUBINSTEIN (1964–1993)   Also known as Dave Insurgent, Rubinstein was the cofounder and lead singer of New York City–based hardcore-punk band Reagan Youth. Rubinstein committed suicide on July 3, 1993, at the age of twenty-eight shortly after being affected by two tragedies: first, his girlfriend Tiffany Bresciani was murdered by serial killer Joel Rifkin on June 24, and second, his mother died in a freak accident after being run over by a car driven by his father on June 30.

KRISTEN PFAFF (1967–1994)   Best known as the bassist for Hole, Pfaff died on June 16, 1994, of a heroin overdose in her Seattle apartment at the age of twenty-seven, just several months after her bandmate Courtney Love's husband Kurt Cobain committed suicide on April 5. She is buried at the Forest Lawn Cemetery in Buffalo, New York.

JASON THIRSK (1967–1996) The bassist for California punk band Pennywise (named for the evil clown monster in Stephen King's 1986 horror novel *It*), Thirsk died of a self-inflicted gunshot wound at the age of twenty-eight on July 29, 1996. The band continued performing and dedicated their performances to Thirsk during Warped Tour 1996.

CARL CRACK (1971–2001) Born Karl Bohm, Carl Crack of German band Atari Teenage Riot overdosed on pills and alcohol in his Berlin apartment at the age of thirty on September 6, 2001.

32

We Outnumber You

The Enduring Impact
of Punk Culture

> Punk rock was a liberation, a smashing of the dull, the
> mundane, the formulaic. —Tim Robbins

Punk is alive and well—at least as it relates to the copious amounts
of punk-related projects that continue to be churned out year after
year, proving that there is an endless fascination with the so-called
"golden age" of punk rock. So long as the spirit of rebellion exists,
punk will never die. Below are some of the coolest developments in
punk over the past few years:

THE ART OF PUNK (2013)   A series of documentaries available for
viewing on YouTube, *The Art of Punk* was created by MOCAtv,
the video channel of the Museum of Contemporary Art in Los
Angeles. Scripted, directed, and executive-produced by *Fucked Up
+ Photocopied* author Bryan Ray Turcotte (*Kill Your Idols*) and Bo
Bushnell (*The Western Empire*), the series explores the roots of the
punk movement and the renowned artists behind the iconic logos
of punk bands. Episodes include Black Flag and Raymond Pettibon, who designed the band's iconic four-bar symbol; an inside look
at the world of English anarcho-punk band Crass; the art behind
legendary San Francisco punk band Dead Kennedys, featuring in-
depth analysis of their album covers and gig flyers; and much more.

The 2018 album, *Dr. Demento Covered in Punk*, features Weird Al Yankovic's version of the Ramones' "Beat on the Brat," which *Rolling Stone* hailed as "a blistering, accordian-tinged cover." PHOTOFEST

DR. DEMENTO COVERED IN PUNK **(2018)**   Billed as "a mind-blowing compilation," this two-hour "audio oddity" pays tribute to radio icon Dr. Demento with punk covers of "mad music and crazy comedy songs." The album features guest appearances from the Misfits, Joan Jett, Fred Schneider of the B52's, "Weird Al" Yankovic, William Shatner, and the late Adam "Batman" West. Highlights include "Beat on the Brat" (Yankovic), "The Cockroach That Ate Cincinnati" (Misfits), "Lydia, the Tattooed Lady" (Dead Milkmen), "I Love Beans" (the Meatmen), and "Garbageman" (William Shatner).

TOO FAST TO LIVE, TOO YOUNG TO DIE (2019)   A special exhibit at the Museum of Arts and Design (MAD) in New York City that took place between April 9 and August 18, 2019, Too Fast to Live, Too Young to Die explored the world of punk graphics from 1976 to 1986 with hundreds of memorable graphics, including remixes of reappropriated images and texts, as well as punk-rock flyers and DIY zines.

PISTOL (2022)   Based on *Lonely Boy: Tales from a Sex Pistol*, the 2016 memoir of Sex Pistols guitarist Steve Jones, this FX drama series made its debut in May 2022. Renowned English director Danny Boyle (*Trainspotting*) executive-produced and directed the six-part series, which stars Toby Wallace as Jones, Louis Partridge as Sid Vicious, Anson Boon as John Lydon, Jacob Slater as Paul Cook, Christian Lees as Glen Matlock, and Emma Appleton as Nancy Spungen. The real Lydon lost a court case trying to prevent the usage of Sex Pistols songs in the series.

I SLEPT WITH JOEY RAMONE (2023)   Netflix and STXfilms have announced the development of this new biopic, which will be directed by Jason Orley (*Big Time Adolescence*) and star Pete Davidson as Joey Ramone. The film will be based on the 2009 book *I Slept with Joey Ramone: A Family Memoir*, by Joey's brother, Mickey Leigh. According to an official release from Adam Fogelson, chairman of STXfilms,

> When you share a bed with someone—and not just a bed, but a childhood, a family, and a lifetime—you know that person better than anyone else. Mickey Leigh not only collaborated with his big brother's band—he has irreplaceable memories of and insights into Joey Ramone, having supported him when no one else would and witnessed him overcome adversity in the most dramatic way. *I Slept with Joey Ramone* is a great rock anthem that will make an equally great rock biopic, set apart by a universal story of family.

33

No More Heroes
Whatever Happened to . . .

GAYE ADVERT   One of punk-rock's first female icons, the bassist for the Adverts quit the music business entirely after the band broke up in 1979 and became a manager for the UK social services, as well as a renowned stained-glass and jewelry artist. Advert appears in the 2010 documentary *She's a Punk Rocker UK*.

VIV ALBERTINE   Best known as the guitarist for the Slits, Albertine embarked on a new career as a freelance director for the BBC and British Film Institute after the band's demise in 1982. In 2012, she returned to the studio to record a solo album, *The Vermilion Border*. In addition, Albertine has published two memoirs: *Clothes, Clothes, Clothes. Music, Music, Music. Boys, Boys, Boys* (2014) and *Throw Away Unopened* (2018). In a 2020 interview with *The Guardian*, Albertine remarked, "I've done everything bad I wanted to do. There's only boring stuff left."

ADAM ANT   In 2013, the charismatic singer-songwriter, who has struggled with mental illness, released his sixth solo studio album, *Adam Ant Is the Blueblack Hussar in Marrying the Gunner's Daughter*, which reached no. 25 on the UK charts. Ant brought his "Friend or Foe Tour" to North America and the United Kingdom in 2019, followed by his "Antics Tour" in 2022.

BILLIE JOE ARMSTRONG   The energetic Green Day front man starred in the 2016 comedy-drama *Ordinary World* about the aging lead singer of a punk band called the Skunks. In 2020, Armstrong released a solo compilation album of cover songs, *No Fun Mondays*, which features such classics as "You Can't Put Your Arms around a Memory" (Johnny Thunders), "Corpus Christi" (Avengers), "Not That Way Anymore" (Stiv Bators), "Gimme Some Truth" (John Lennon), "Manic Monday" (the Bangles/Prince), "Whole Wild World" (Wreckless Eric), and "Kids in America" (Kim Wilde), among others. Also in 2020, Green Day released its thirteenth studio album, *Father of All Mother Fuckers* (aka *FOAMF*), to mixed reviews.

CHRIS BAILEY   The cofounder and lead singer of pioneering Australian punk-rock band the Saints, Bailey has released six solo albums, the latest being *Bone Box* (2005), an acoustic collection of both Saints and solo material. In 2012, the Saints released their fourteenth studio album, *King of the Sun*.

LESTER BANGS   The influential rock critic (born Leslie Conway Bangs), who wrote extensively for *Creem* and *Rolling Stone* magazines, died of an accidental prescription overdose at the age of thirty-three on April 30, 1982. His collected writings appeared in 1988 as *Psychotic Reactions and Carburetor Dung: The Work of a Legendary Critic*. By the way, the Ramones referenced Bangs in their 1981 song "It's Not My Place (in the 9 to 5 World)," which features the lyrics "Hangin' out with Lester Bangs you all/And Phil Spector really has it all."

STIV BATORS   The legendary lead singer and guitarist for both the Dead Boys and the Lords of the New Church, Bators (born Steven John Bator) died of traumatic brain injury after getting hit by a car in Paris, France, at the age of forty on June 4, 1990. Bators's girlfriend, Caroline Warren, allegedly complied with his wishes to have his ashes scattered at the grave of Doors front man Jim Morrison at Pere LaChaise Cemetery (she also reportedly snorted a portion of his ashes!). Directed by Danny Garcia, the documentary *Stiv: No Compromise, No Regrets* was released in 2019.

ROBERTA BAYLEY   The renowned photographer of the New York City punk scene for *Punk* magazine during the 1970s who shot the famous cover of the 1976 Ramones self-titled debut album, Bayley coauthored *Patti Smith: An Unauthorized Biography* (1996) and authored *Blondie Unseen* (2006). Her rock photographs have been exhibited in New York City, Los Angeles, Paris, London, Amsterdam, Hong Kong, Tokyo, Sydney, and Mexico City. Bayley still lives in NYC's East Village.

JELLO BIAFRA   The former lead singer and songwriter of Dead Kennedys and cofounder of the record label Alternative Tentacles—who penned such punk classics as "California uber alles" and "Nazi Punks Fuck Off"—continues his work as a tireless social activist and spoken-word artist. In addition, his band Jello Biafra and the Guantanamo School of Medicine released its third album, *Tea Party Revenge Porn*, in 2020. Biafra also appeared in a cameo as a tour guide in the critically acclaimed 2019 film *The Last Black Man in San Francisco*.

RODNEY BINGENHEIMER   The pioneering Los Angeles radio DJ who has been dubbed "punk rock's biggest cheerleader" was the subject of a 2003 documentary, *Mayor of the Sunset Strip*. In 2017, Bingenheimer retired after forty-one years as the host of his immensely popular "Rodney on the ROQ" radio show on LA's KROQ-FM. Bingenheimer summed up his programming philosophy in the late 1970s as "anti-Eagles, anti-beards. Within a few months I was playing four solid hours of punk."

CHUCK BISCUITS   Often described as a "punk journeyman," the highly regarded Canadian drummer (born Charles Montgomery) has been variously associated with such notable punk bands as D.O.A., Black Flag, the Circle Jerks, Danzig, and Social Distortion, among others. Biscuits has been keeping a low profile since 1999, and a false report of his death even surfaced in 2009. However, the question remains—what the hell ever happened to Chuck Biscuits?

JOHNNY BLITZ   A native of Cleveland, Ohio, Blitz (real name: John Madansky) served as the drummer for both Rocket from the Tombs and the Dead Boys. Blitz is also remembered for a notorious altercation in Manhattan's East Village on April 19, 1978, that resulted in him getting stabbed five times. A "Blitz Benefit" was held at CBGBs (with none other than John Belushi filling in for Blitz on drums!) to raise money for his medical care. In 2017, Blitz and fellow Dead Boy Cheetah Chrome reunited with a new lineup for a fortieth-anniversary tour that also featured a rerecording of their debut album titled *Still Snotty: Young, Loud and Snotty at 40*.

DAVID BYRNE   Formerly the lead singer, principal songwriter, and founding member of Talking Heads, Byrne has received three Grammy Awards (*Storytelling Giant*, *Everything That Happens Will Happen Today*, *American Utopia*), an Academy Award (Best Original Score, *The Last Emperor*), a Golden Globe Award (Best Original Score, *The Last Emperor*), and a Tony Award (*American Utopia on Broadway*). In 2022, Byrne launched his new project, *Theater of the Mind*, billed as "an immersive journey inside how we see and create our worlds."

DEZ CADENA   Best known as the third lead singer for Black Flag and as guitarist for the Misfits between 2001 and 2015, Cadena has most recently recorded and performed with Jon Caspi and the First Gun.

JOHN CALE   A founding member of the Velvet Underground, as well as a prolific singer-songwriter and producer, Cale has released sixteen solo albums, the latest being *M:FANS* (2016). He has also scored the soundtracks for such films as *American Psycho* (2000), *The King's Daughter* (2000), *Y Mabinogi* (2003), *Paris* (2003), *Process* (2004), *A Burning Hot Summer* (2011), and *Paul Sanchez Is Back!* (2018), among others.

JIM CARROLL   Best known for penning the critically acclaimed 1978 memoir *The Basketball Diaries* and fronting the Jim Carroll Band ("People Who Died"), Carroll died of a heart attack at the age of

Known for his critically acclaimed 1978 autobiographical work, *The Basketball Diaries*, Jim Carroll also penned the popular 1980 song "People Who Died." BY DAVID SHANKBONE, OWN WORK/WIKIMEDIA COMMONS

sixty in his Manhattan home on September 11, 2009. He is buried in St. Peters Cemetery in Haverstraw, New York. His epitaph reads, "When the Spirit Grows Too Large for the Body, Both Are Called Home."

LEEE BLACK CHILDERS The legendary rock photographer, writer, and manager of Johnny Thunders and the Heartbreakers died on April 6, 2014, from undisclosed causes at the age of sixty-eight in Los Angeles. *Drag Queens, Rent Boys, Pick Pockets, Junkies, Rockstars and Punks*, a fascinating collection of Childers's photographs, was published in 2012.

CHEETAH CHROME The former guitarist for both Rocket from the Tombs and the Dead Boys, Chrome (born Eugene Richard O'Connor) published his autobiography, *Cheetah Chrome: A Dead Boy's Tale from the Front Lines of Punk Rock*, in 2010. A cofounder of Nashville's Plowboy Records, Chrome released his first-ever studio collection of solo material, *Solo*, a seven-song EP, in 2013. In 2017, Chrome took part in the Dead Boys reunion tour to promote the fortieth anniversary of *Young, Loud and Snotty*.

KURT COBAIN   In 2014, Cobain was posthumously inducted into the Rock and Roll Hall of Fame as a member of Nirvana, along with bandmates Krist Novoselic and Dave Grohl. Directed by Brett Morgen, the critically acclaimed documentary *Kurt Cobain: Montage of Heck* premiered at the 2015 Sundance Film Festival.

PAUL COOK   The former Sex Pistols drummer has been associated with various other bands over the years, such as the Professionals, Chiefs of Relief, Man Raze, and Vic Godard and Subway Sect. He is married to Jeni Cook (former backing singer for Culture Club) and the father of reggae singer Hollie Cook.

ELVIS COSTELLO   A true Renaissance man, Costello has dabbled in everything from punk and pop to country and classical music with no signs of slowing down. Along the way, he has collaborated with the likes of Johnny Cash, Paul McCartney, Tony Bennett, Burt Bacharach, Ruben Blades, Brian Eno, Madness, and others. In the summer of 2022, Elvis Costello & the Imposters embarked on "The Boy Named If & Other Favorites Tour" of the United Kingdom.

JAYNE COUNTY   As the vocalist for proto-punk band Jayne County & the Electric Chairs, the first openly transgender rock star was a regular fixture on the early Max's Kansas City and CBGB's punk scene. The tireless performer and artist held a retrospective visual art show titled *Paranoia Paradise* in New York City in 2018 and released a reissued autobiography, *Man Enough to Be a Woman*, in 2021.

DARBY CRASH   The notoriously self-destructive lead singer and his Los Angeles punk band the Germs served as the subject of a biopic titled *What We Do Is Secret*, which premiered at the 2007 Los Angeles Film Festival. In addition, a tribute to Crash—"Thunderclap for

Bobby Pyn"—appeared on Sonic Youth's final studio album, *The Eternal* (2009).

IAN CURTIS   The brilliant and troubled front man of Joy Division, who committed suicide in 1980, was portrayed by Sean Harris in *24 Hour Party People* (2002), which showcased the rise and fall of Factory Records. In addition, Sam Riley of the band 10,000 Things portrayed Curtis in a critically acclaimed 2007 black-and-white biopic titled *Control*.

GLENN DANZIG   Founder of the bands Misfits, Samhain, and Danzig, Danzig owns Evilive Records, as well as Verotik, an adult-oriented comic-book publishing company. In 2017, Danzig appeared on an episode of *Portlandia* ("Weirdo Beach"). The band Danzig released its twelfth studio album, *Danzig Sings Elvis*, in 2020.

HOWARD DEVOTO   Known as the front man for pioneering Manchester bands Buzzcocks and Magazine (which released their final studio album, *No Thyself*, in 2011), Devoto briefly reunited with Buzzcocks during their "Back to Front Tour" in 2012.

CHUCK DUKOWSKI   A founding member of Los Angeles hardcore-punk band Black Flag, Dukowski (born Gary Arthur McDaniel) formed his own band, the Chuck Dukowski Sextet, in 2002. The band, which also features his wife Lora Norton and stepson Milo Gonzalez, has released three albums: *Eat My Life* (2006), *Reverse the Polarity* (2007), and *Haunted* (2012). He also collaborated with Santa Cruz–based punk band Blast on their EP *For Those Who've Graced the Fire* in 2015.

IAN DURY   The lead singer of both Kilburn and the High Roads and Ian Dury and the Blockheads whom *The Guardian* dubbed as "one of few true originals of the English music scene," Dury died of metastatic colorectal cancer at the age of fifty-seven on March 27, 2000. A well-received biopic of Dury starring Andy Serkis titled *Sex & Drugs & Rock & Roll* was released in 2010.

FAT MIKE Best known as the lead singer and bassist for Los Angeles punk band NOFX, Fat Mike (Michael John Burkett) is also a member of punk-rock supergroup/cover band Me First and the Gimme Gimmes along with Spike Slawson, Joey Cape, and Dave Raun. NOFX has released fourteen studio albums, the latest being *Single Album* in 2021.

DANNY FIELDS As publicist for Elektra Records, Fields was instrumental in recommending that the label sign both the MC5 and the Stooges. In the mid-1970s, Fields discovered the Ramones at CBGBs, became their comanager, and helped get them signed to Sire Records. The song "Danny Says" from the Ramones' 1980 album, *End of the Century*, refers to Fields. The subject of a 2015 documentary, *Danny Says*, Fields has written several biographies, including *Dream On* (1996, about Warhol actress Cyrinda Foxe, who was once married to both David Johansen and Steven Tyler) and *Linda McCartney: A Portrait* (2000).

GREG GINN Best known as the founder and primary songwriter of Black Flag, Ginn has also collaborated with such bands as Confront James, Gone, Mojack, and October Faction, among others. Black Flag has released seven studio albums, the latest being *What The . . .* in 2013. Ginn ranked no. 99 on *Rolling Stone*'s list of the "100 Greatest Guitarists of All Time."

KIM GORDON The cofounder and driving force behind alternative-rock band Sonic Youth, Gordon published a 2015 memoir, *Girl in a Band*, and a visual anthology of her life titled *No Icon* in 2020. She also appeared in a small role in the 2018 comedy-drama *Don't Worry, He Won't Get Far on Foot* (based on the critically acclaimed memoir of cartoonist John Callahan), and hosted her first North American museum solo exhibition, *Kim Gordon: Lo-Fi Glamour*, at the Andy Warhol Museum in 2019.

BILL GRUNDY The well-respected English broadcaster and journalist will unfortunately always be primarily remembered for his notorious *Today* show interview with the Sex Pistols on December 1,

1976. During the expletive-laden exchange, Steve Jones of the Sex Pistols called Grundy a "dirty bastard," "dirty fucker," and "fuckin' rotter." Grundy died of a heart attack at the age of sixty-nine on February 9, 1993, at a nursing home in Stockport, England.

H.R. The renowned frontman for pioneering Washington, DC, hardcore-punk band Bad Brains, H.R. (Paul Hudson) served as the subject of the 2016 film *Finding Joseph I: The HR from Bad Brains Documentary*, which highlights his fascinating life and career, as well as his struggles with schizophrenia.

KATHLEEN HANNA The lead singer of punk band Bikini Kill and a pioneer of the feminist punk Riot Grrrl movement, Hanna was the subject of the 2013 documentary *The Punk Singer*. She is married to Adam Horovitz of the Beastie Boys.

DEBBIE HARRY A prolific singer-songwriter and actress, Harry was inducted into the Rock and Roll Hall of Fame as a member of Blondie in 2006. In 2017, Blondie released their eleventh studio album, *Pollinator*, which reached no. 4 on the UK charts. Harry published a well-received memoir titled *Face It* in 2019.

NICKY "TOPPER" HEADON Known as the "Human Drum Machine," the former drummer for the Clash left the band in 1982 right before the Combat Rock Tour due to his struggles with heroin addiction (which forced him to drive a mini cab and busk with bongos on the London Underground to support his habit during the late 1980s). Headon was interviewed extensively for the 2000 documentary *The Clash: Westway to the World*. He has reportedly stayed clean of addiction since 2004 and still performs sporadically.

RICHARD HELL Since the late 1980s, Hell (best known for his pioneering work with Television, the Heartbreakers, and Richard Hell and the Voidoids) has focused primarily on writing, publishing such works as *Massive Pissed Love: Nonfiction 2001–2014* (2015). He also served as the film critic of *BlackBook* magazine from 2004 to 2006 and appeared in such eclectic films as *Blank Generation*

(1980), *Smithereens* (1982), *Geek Maggot Bingo* (1983), *Desperately Seeking Susan* (1985), *What about Me* (1993), and *Blind Light* (1998), among others.

JOHN HOLMSTROM   The founding editor of *Punk* magazine, Holmstrom also illustrated the covers of the Ramones albums *Rocket to Russia* (1977) and *Road to Ruin* (1978). A renowned underground cartoonist and writer, he later served as the publisher of *High Times* magazine.

CHRISSIE HYNDE   A founding member, lead vocalist, and primary songwriter for the Pretenders (which were inducted into the Rock and Roll Hall of Fame in 2005), Hynde released her debut solo album, *Stockholm*, in 2014, followed by *Valve Bone Woe* in 2019. The latter reached no. 1 on the UK Jazz and Blues chart.

BILLY IDOL   In 2014, Idol released both his eighth studio album, *Kings & Queens of the Underground*, and an autobiography, *Dancing with Myself*. In 2018, he became a U.S. citizen, while also retaining his British citizenship. Idol embarked on a tour of the United Kingdom and Europe in 2022.

LUX INTERIOR   The lead singer and founding member of psychobilly pioneers the Cramps died of aortic dissection at the age of sixty-two on February 4, 2009. He was survived by his wife of thirty-seven years, Kristy Mariana Wallace (aka Poison Ivy).

POISON IVY   Cofounder of the Cramps with her husband, Lux Interior (see entry above), Ivy currently resides in Glendale, California, and has kept a relatively low profile since the death of Interior in 2009. In a December 23, 2001, interview with *Guitar World*, Ivy remarked, "It was easier for me to consider playing guitar because I was such a misfit. For me, anything was fair game."

BRIAN JAMES   A founding member of both the Damned and Lords of the New Church, James has released five solo albums, the latest being *The Guitar That Dripped Blood* (2015). He has also

collaborated with the likes of the Dripping Lips and the Rack-
eteers, which also featured Wayne Kramer (MC5), Duff McKagan
(Guns N' Roses), Stewart Copeland (the Police), and Clem Burke
(Blondie).

JOAN JETT   Known as the "Queen of Rock 'n' Roll," Jett ranked no.
87 on *Rolling Stone*'s list of the "100 Greatest Guitarists of All
Time." In 2015, Joan Jett & the Blackhearts were inducted into the
Rock and Roll Hall of Fame. Jett was the subject of a documentary,
Bad Reputation, which premiered at the 2019 Sundance Film Festi-
val. She also voiced the character of Camille in the 2020 animated
TV series *Kipo and the Age of Wonderbeasts*.

DAVID JOHANSEN   Best known as the lead singer/songwriter of the
New York Dolls, as well as for his lounge singer persona Buster
Poindexter ("Hot Hot Hot") and his performance as the Ghost of
Christmas Past in *Scrooged* opposite Bill Murray, Johansen is the
only surviving member of the Dolls. Acclaimed director Martin
Scorsese (*Goodfellas*) has announced plans to direct a documentary
on Johansen.

MICK JONES   After getting booted by the Clash in 1983, Jones was a
cofounder of General Public before starting up Big Audio Dynamite
in 1984. In the early 2000s, Jones formed the group Carbon/Silicon
with Tony James (formerly of Generation X and Sigue Sigue Sput-
nik). He also has collaborated with Gorillaz, the Justice Tonight
Band, the Wallflowers, Rachid Taha, the Flaming Lips, and the
Avalanches.

STEVE JONES   The former Sex Pistols guitarist later created the Professionals with his ex-Pistols bandmate Paul Cook and collaborated
with the likes of Iggy Pop, Johnny Thunders, Thin Lizzy, and Bob
Dylan. In 1995, Jones formed the supergroup Neurotic Outsiders
with Duff McKagan and Matt Sorum of Guns N' Roses and John
Taylor of Duran Duran. *Rolling Stone* ranked Jones no. 97 on its list
of the "100 Greatest Guitarists of All Time."

ARTHUR "KILLER" KANE   The New York Dolls bassist struggled with alcoholism for years before deciding to join the Church of Jesus Christ of Latter-Day Saints in 1989. In 1998, Kane began working as a librarian at the church's Family History Center in Los Angeles. Shortly after reuniting with former New York Dolls bandmates David Johansen and Sylvain Sylvain as part of the Meltdown Festival at the Royal Festival Hall in London in 2004, Kane was diagnosed with leukemia. He died just twenty-two days later at the age of fifty-five on July 13, 2004. Kane's fascinating life and career was documented in the 2005 film *New York Doll*.

LENNY KAYE   The guitarist for the Patti Smith Group and compiler of the outstanding 1972 album *Nuggets: Original Artyfacts from the First Psychedelic Era 1965–1968*, Kaye replaced "Handsome Dick" Manitoba as night DJ on *Little Steven's Underground Garage* on SiriusXM in 2018.

WAYNE KRAMER   Cofounder of pioneering Detroit rock band MC5, Kramer has released eleven solo albums, the latest being *More Dangerous Missions* (2004). In 2018, Kramer embarked on the MC50 tour to celebrate the fiftieth anniversary of "Kick Out the Jams." The lineup also consisted of Kim Thayil and Matt Cameron of Soundgarden, Brendan Canty of Fugazi, Billy Gould of Faith No More, and Don Was. In 2021, Kramer contributed to the Alice Cooper album *Detroit Stories*.

HILLY KRISTAL   The eccentric owner/founder of New York City punk mecca CBGBs died from complications of lung cancer at the age of seventy-five on August 28, 2007, less than one year after the "birthplace of punk rock" closed its doors.

PETER LAUGHNER   Music critic Richie Unterberger has called Laughner (1952–1977) of Rocket from the Tombs and Pere Ubu as "probably the single biggest catalyst in the birth of Cleveland's alternative rock scene in the mid-1970s." Since Rocket from the Tombs never recorded an album during their first incarnation, the 2002 CD *The Day the Earth Met the Rocket from the Tombs* serves as the only real document of the band's creative prowess during that period.

LYDIA LUNCH Always both provocative and confrontational, Lunch cofounded Teenage Jesus and the Jerks and helped pioneer the avant-garde no-wave movement in New York City during the late 1970s. In 1997, Lunch published her autobiographical work, *Paradoxia*. Over the years, she has released several solo albums, the latest being *Urge to Kill* (2015) as Lydia Lunch Retrovirus.

JOHN LYDON The legendary front man of both the Sex Pistols and Public Image Ltd (PiL), John Lydon has released ten studio albums with the latter band (the latest being *What the World Needs Now* (2015). In 2020, Lydon published the memoir, *I Could Be Wrong, I Could Be Right*.

SHANE MACGOWAN Former lead singer of the Pogues and legendary hell-raiser, MacGowan was the subject of a 2020 documentary, *Crock of Gold: A Few Rounds with Shane MacGowan*. In 2022, MacGowan published a new book full of his unpublished writing, illustrations, and handwritten lyrics titled *The Eternal Buzz and the Crock of Gold*.

IAN MACKAYE The front man for two classic Washington, DC–based hardcore bands, Minor Threat and Fugazi, MacKaye is also founder of Dischord Records and advocate of the straight-edge lifestyle. Since 2001, MacKaye has played in the Evens, a duo with Amy Farina (formerly of the post-hardcore band the Warmers).

"HANDSOME DICK" MANITOBA Between 2004 and 2018, the charismatic lead singer of the Dictators hosted "The Handsome Dick Manitoba Radio Program" on Little Steven Van Zandt's Underground Garage channel on SiriusXM Radio. In 2019, he started his own podcast, *You Don't Know Dick*, and released his first solo album, *Born in the Bronx*.

GLEN MATLOCK   The original bassist/songwriter for the Sex Pistols, who was fired from the band and replaced by Sid Vicious in 1977, Matlock went on to form the Rich Kids, a short-lived new-wave band that released one studio album, *Ghosts of Princes in Towers*, in 1978. In 1990, Matlock published his autobiography, *I Was a Teenage Sex Pistol*. He later rejoined the Sex Pistols for reunion tours in 1996 (Filthy Lucre Tour), 2003 (North American Piss Off Tour), and 2007–2008 (Europe Combine Harvester Tour). In addition, his band Glen Matlock & the Philistines, has released six studio albums, the latest being *Good to Go* in 2018.

MALCOLM MCLAREN   The legendary manager of the Sex Pistols died of peritoneal mesothelioma in a Swiss hospital at the age of sixty-four on April 8, 2010. He is buried in Highgate Cemetery in North London. His epitaph reads, "Better a spectacular failure, than a benign success."

LEGS MCNEIL   Along with John Holmstrom and Ged Dunn, McNeil was one of the three founders of *Punk* magazine. He later published *Please Kill Me: The Uncensored Oral History of Punk* (1996, with Gillian McCain) and *The Other Hollywood: The Uncensored Oral History of the Porn Film Industry* (2006, with Jennifer Osborne and Peter Pavia).

KEITH MORRIS   The front man for both Black Flag and Circle Jerks, Morris later led the bands Bug Lamp and Midget Handjob and joined hardcore-punk supergroup Off! In 2016, he published his highly entertaining autobiography, *My Damage: The Story of a Punk Rock Survivor*.

A front man for both Black Flag and the Circle Jerks, Keith Morris published a critically acclaimed autobiography called *My Damage: The Story of a Punk Rock Survivor* in 2016. MERCURY/PHOTOFEST

STERLING MORRISON Founding member and guitarist for the Velvet Underground, Morrison died of non-Hodgkin's lymphoma at the age of fifty-three on August 30, 1995. The following year, the Velvet Underground was inducted into the Rock and Roll Hall of Fame. Band members Lou Reed, John Cale, and Maureen Tucker performed the song "Last Night I Said Goodbye to My Friend" in tribute to Morrison.

NICO Nico (Christa Paffgen), who famously collaborated with the Velvet Underground on their 1967 debut album, *The Velvet Underground & Nico*, died of a cerebral brain hemorrhage at the age of forty-nine on July 18, 1988, after getting injured in a bicycle accident in Ibiza, Spain.

JERRY NOLAN The former New York Dolls and Heartbreakers drummer suffered a stroke and died on January 14, 1992, at the age of forty-five. He is buried at Mount Saint Mary's Cemetery in Flushing, New York. A biography of Nolan titled *Stranded in the Jungle: Jerry Nolan's Wild Ride* by Curt Weiss was published in 2017.

JOHN PEEL The legendary English DJ (born John Robert Parker Ravenscroft) and promoter of punk bands (especially the Undertones!), Peel died of a heart attack at the age of sixty-five on October 25, 2004. He is buried in the graveyard of St. Andrew's Church in Great Finborough, Suffolk. Peel's epitaph reads, "Teenage dreams so hard to beat," a line from the Undertones' 1978 hit single "Teenage Kicks."

AMOS POE One of the first punk filmmakers and pioneer of the no-wave movement in New York City, Poe directed *The Blank Generation* (1976) and *The Foreigner* (1977). More recently he wrote the screenplay for the 2008 film *The Guitar*. His filmography also includes *Steve Earle: Just an American Boy* (2003), *When You Find Me* (2004), *Empire II* (2007), *Ladies & Gentlemen* (2012), *A Walk in the Park* (2012), and *Happiness is a Warm Gun* (2015), among many others.

IGGY POP   The so-called "Godfather of Punk" shows no signs of slowing down! In 2019, the former Stooge won a Grammy Lifetime Achievement Award the same year he released his eighteenth studio album, *Free*, and appeared as a zombie in the Jim Jarmusch comedy horror film *The Dead Don't Die*, alongside Bill Murray, Steve Buscemi, Tom Waits, Chloe Sevigny, Danny Glover, Rosie Perez, and Adam Driver.

DEE DEE RAMONE   After quitting the Ramones in 1989, Dee Dee embarked on a short-lived rap career as "Dee Dee King." He also continued to write songs for the Ramones until the band broke up in 1996. In addition, Dee Dee wrote several books, including *Lobotomy*, *Legend of a Rock Star*, and *Chelsea Horror Hotel*. In *Legend of a Rock Star*, Dee Dee wrote, "It's not too bad being an old rock and roll star. It's like having a tear in your eye and a smile on

In addition to embarking on a thankfully short-lived rap career as "Dee Dee King," Dee Dee Ramone published several books, including *Lobotomy* and *Chelsea Horror Hotel*. PHOTO: MICK ROCK/PHOTOFEST

your face at the same time." Dee Dee struggled with drug addiction most of his life. Shortly after being inducted into the Rock and Roll Hall of Fame as an original member of the Ramones, Dee Dee died of heroin toxicity at the age of forty-nine in his Hollywood home on June 5, 2002. He is buried at Hollywood Forever Cemetery in Los Angeles. His epitaph reads, "OK . . . I gotta go now."

JOEY RAMONE   Described as "tall, languid and mysterious" by *Punk* magazine, the Ramones lead singer passed away from acute lymphoma on April 15, 2001, at the age of forty-nine at New York-Presbyterian Hospital while listening to U2's "In a Little While." He is buried at Hillside Cemetery in Lyndhurst, New Jersey. In 2003, a block at East Second Street in New York City was renamed "Joey Ramone Place."

JOHNNY RAMONE   On September 15, 2004, Johnny died in his Los Angeles home after a five-year battle with prostate cancer at the age of fifty-five. He is memorialized with an eight-foot-tall bronze statue near Dee Dee Ramone's gravesite at Hollywood Forever Cemetery.

MARKY RAMONE   In 1978, Marc Bell of Richard Hell and the Voidoids replaced Tommy Ramone as drummer for the Ramones and became Marky Ramone. In 2015, he released his autobiography, *Punk Rock Blitzkrieg: My Life as a Ramone*. Since 2005, Marky has hosted a show on Sirius XM called *Punk Rock Blitzkrieg*. He also boasts his own line of pasta sauce, "Marky Ramone's Brooklyn's Own Pasta Sauce."

TOMMY RAMONE   After leaving the Ramones in 1978, Tommy continued to work as a successful record producer, musician, and songwriter. He died of bile duct cancer on July 11, 2014, at the age of sixty-five.

LOU REED   Dubbed "rock's answer to Charles Baudelaire" and "a street-smart, sexually ambiguous paradigm of cool" by *The Outlaw Bible of American Literature*, the Velvet Underground singer-songwriter died of liver failure at the age of seventy-one on October

27, 2013. He was survived by his wife, the performance artist and singer Laurie Anderson.

JAMIE REID   The renowned English artist who designed the famous *Never Mind the Bollocks* album cover for the Sex Pistols, Reid is currently represented by the John Marchant Gallery in London. His works can be found in the collections of the Victoria and Albert Museum in London and the Museum of Modern Art in New York City, among others.

HENRY ROLLINS   The former Black Flag front man maintains a busy schedule as a singer, actor, spoken-word artist, and human rights activist. In addition, Rollins has his own publishing company called 2.13.61 (the date of his birth), which has published not only his books but also works by Nick Cave, Exene Cervenka, and Iggy Pop, among others.

RAT SCABIES   Born Christopher John Millar, Rat Scabies served as the drummer for the Damned until his departure in 1995. Since then, he has collaborated with numerous musical acts, such as the Mutants, the Spammed, Urban Voodoo Machine, Jane Horrocks, Chris Goss, the Members, Donovan, Nosferatu, Neville Staple, and Dave Catching of Eagles of Death Metal.

CAPTAIN SENSIBLE   Cofounder and guitarist for the Damned, Captain Sensible (Raymond Ian Burns) left the band in the 1980s to focus on a solo career that featured the release of six studio albums, starting with *Women and Captains First* (1982) and ending with *Mad Cows and Englishmen* (1996). In addition, the Damned has regrouped on and off over the years, with their latest release being *Evil Spirits* in 2018.

PETE SHELLEY   The cofounder of Buzzcocks with Howard Devoto in 1976, Shelley embarked on a successful solo career in 1981. He died of a suspected heart attack at the age of sixty-three on December 6, 2018.

PAUL SIMONON   The bassist for the Clash most recently collaborated with the English art-rock supergroup the Good, the Bad & the Queen, which also featured Damon Albarn of Blur and Gorillaz, guitarist Simon Tong of the Verve, and drummer Tony Allen of Fela Kuti. Simonon is also a renowned visual artist.

SIOUXSIE SIOUX   The lead singer of Siouxsie and the Banshees, Siouxsie Sioux (Susan Janet Ballion) later formed the Creatures and released four studio albums: *Feast* (1983), *Boomerang* (1989), *Anima Animus* (1999), and *Hai!* (2003). In 2007, she released her debut solo album, *Mantaray*, which reached no. 39 on the UK charts. Her song "Love Crime" was featured in the finale of the TV series *Hannibal* in 2015.

PAT SMEAR   A founding member of Los Angeles hardcore-punk band the Germs, Smear (born Georg Albert Ruthenberg) later became touring guitarist for Nirvana between 1993 and 1994, and joined the Foo Fighters (with former Nirvana drummer Dave Grohl as front man). He has also collaborated with the likes of the Martyrs, 45 Grave, Twisted Roots, Vagina Dentata, Tater Totz, Gary Celebrity, Deathfolk, Skull Control, and Paul McCartney.

FRED "SONIC" SMITH   The guitarist for Detroit pioneering rockers MC5 married "punk poetess" Patti Smith in 1980. On November 4, 1994, Smith died of heart failure at the age of forty-six. The band Sonic Youth took its name from Smith's nickname. In 2003, *Rolling Stone* ranked Smith no. 93 on its list of the "100 Greatest Guitarists of All Time."

MARK E. SMITH   An English singer-songwriter, Smith was the one constant member of the band the Fall, which recorded an astounding thirty-one studio albums (the latest being *New Facts Emerge* in 2017) and featured approximately sixty musicians over the years. On January 24, 2018, Smith died of lung and kidney cancer at the age of sixty.

PATTI SMITH   The "punk poet laureate" was inducted into the Rock and Roll Hall of Fame in 2007. In 2010, she received the National Book Award for her critically acclaimed memoir, *Just Kids*. In 2012, Smith released her most recent studio album, *Banga*, which includes a cover of Neil Young's "After the Gold Rush."

NANCY SPUNGEN   Before hooking up with Sid Vicious, Spungen was "a go-go dancer and a groupie for the Heartbreakers," according to Dee Dee Ramone in his 2000 memoir *Lobotomy*. "Everybody slept with Nancy once, and then dumped her. Then no one wanted her around at all. She could really get to you." On October 12, 1978, Spungen was stabbed to death in Room 100 of the Chelsea Hotel, and Sid Vicious was charged with her murder. The tragedy served as the subject of the 2010 documentary *Who Killed Nancy?*

CHRIS STEIN   Cofounder and lead guitarist of Blondie, Stein was diagnosed with a rare autoimmune disease called pemphigus vulgaris in 1983 and cared for by his then girlfriend Debbie Harry. In 2006, he was inducted into the Rock and Roll Hall of Fame as a member of Blondie. Stein is also an accomplished photographer and the author of *Negative: Me, Blondie, and the Advent of Punk* (2014).

BOB STINSON   A founding member and lead guitarist of legendary Minneapolis-based rock band the Replacements, Stinson was reportedly forced out of the band in 1986 due to his struggles with alcoholism. He died of organ failure at the age of thirty-five on February 18, 1995.

JOE STRUMMER   The renowned rhythm guitarist/vocalist for the Clash, Strummer died on December 22, 2002, from an undiagnosed heart defect at the age of fifty. The Clash were inducted into the Rock and Roll Hall of Fame a year later.

POLY STYRENE   The highly energetic lead singer of X-Ray Spex released three solo albums: *Translucence* (1980), *Flower Aeroplane* (2004), and *Generation Indigo* (2011). Styrene died of metastatic breast cancer at the age of fifty-three on April 25, 2011. Recently, she has been the subject of both a 2018 biography (*Day Glo: The Poly Styrene Story*) and a 2021 documentary (*Poly Styrene: I Am a Cliché*).

SYLVAIN SYLVAIN   The former New York Dolls guitarist died of cancer at the age of sixty-nine on January 13, 2021. In a January 16, 2021, interview with *Rolling Stone*, Sylvain's bandmate David Johansen remarked, "If it hadn't been for him, the band would have sounded crappy. He knew what he was doing and he could play the guitar. He came up with really great rhythms. He was very accomplished. He was a natural player. He loved playing."

JOHNNY THUNDERS   The 2014 documentary *Looking for Johnny: The Legend of Johnny Thunders* offers insights into the life and career of the former New York Doll and Heartbreaker, who died of an apparent drug overdose in New Orleans on April 23, 1991, at the age of thirty-eight.

ARI UP   Founding member and lead singer for the Slits, Ari Up (Ariane Daniele Forster) was the stepdaughter of Sex Pistol Johnny Rotten (Lydon). She passed away of breast cancer at the age of forty-eight on October 20, 2010.

DAVE VANIAN   The lead singer of the Damned and a goth style icon, Vanian (born David Lett) formed the band Dave Vanian and the Phantom Chords in the 1990s. In 2009, he composed the soundtrack for the film *The Perfect Sleep*.

TOM VERLAINE   The former front man of Television has released ten solo albums, the latest being *Around* in 2006. In addition, Verlaine (born Thomas Miller) is a member of the Million Dollar Bashers, a supergroup featuring Lee Ranaldo and Steve Shelley of Sonic Youth, Nels Cline of Wilco, bassist Tony Garnier, guitarist Smokey Hormel, and keyboardist John Medeski. The group contributed several tracks to the soundtrack for the Bob Dylan biopic *I'm Not There* in 2007.

SID VICIOUS In 2006, Vicious, who died of a heroin overdose on February 2, 1979, at the age of twenty-one, was posthumously inducted into the Rock and Roll Hall of Fame as a member of the Sex Pistols. The surviving band members refused the honor and did not show up at the ceremony.

LEE VING Best known as the front man for Los Angeles punk band Fear, Ving has also cultivated somewhat of an acting career that includes memorable appearances in *Flashdance* (1983), *The Wild Life* (1984), *Streets of Fire* (1984), *Dudes* (1987), *Endless Bummer* (2009), and *Death Rider in the House of Vampires* (2021).

ANDY WARHOL The "Pope of Pop" died from complications following a gallbladder operation at the age of fifty-eight on February 22, 1987. He is buried at Saint John the Baptist Catholic Cemetery in Castle Shannon, Pennsylvania. Warhol's grave is typically covered with Coca Cola bottles and Campbell's Soup cans by overzealous fans of the artist.

VIVIENNE WESTWOOD Known for collaborating with Sex Pistols manager Malcolm McLaren (her onetime boyfriend) and extending the influence of the punk subculture into fashion during the 1970s, Westwood was featured in the 2018 documentary *Westwood: Punk, Icon, Activist*.

WENDY O. WILLIAMS Known variously as the "Queen of Shock Rock," "Dominatrix of Decibels," "High Priestess of Metal," and "Evel Knievelette," the Plasmatics lead singer died of a self-inflicted gunshot wound at the age of forty-eight on April 6, 1998.

JAH WOBBLE The original bass player for Public Image Ltd (PiL), Wobble (John Joseph Wardle) published his autobiography, *Memoirs of a Geezer: Music, Mayhem, Life*, in 2009. He continues to record and perform with his band, Jah Wobble & the Invaders of the Heart.

34

Should I Stay or Should I Go

A Comprehensive Punk Timeline

1965

- The Velvet Underground form in New York City with singer/ guitarist Lou Reed, multi-instrumentalist John Cale, guitarist Sterling Morrison, and drummer Angus MacLise (soon to be replaced by Moe Tucker).

1967

- The Velvet Underground release the landmark album *The Velvet Underground & Nico*, which sells approximately only thirty thousand copies in its first five years (but "everyone who bought one of those 30,000 copies started a band," according to British musician Brian Eno).

1968

- Legendary proto-punk band the Stooges (originally known as the Psychedelic Stooges) form in Detroit, Michigan. Original band members include Iggy Pop (James Newell Osterberg Jr.), Ron Asheton, Scott Asheton, and Dave Alexander.

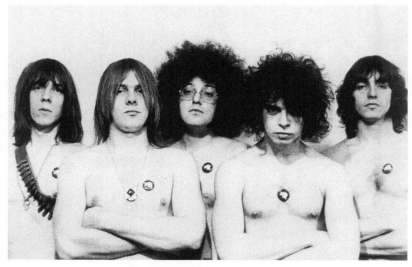

In 1969, Detroit proto-punk rockers MC5 released their highly influential debut album, *Kick Out the Jams*, which peaked at No. 30 on the U.S. charts. PHOTOFEST

1969

- Detroit rockers MC5 release their debut album, *Kick Out the Jams*, which was recorded live at the Grande Ballroom the previous year. The original MC5 lineup consists of Rob Tyner, Wayne Kramer, Fred "Sonic" Smith, Michael Davis, and Dennis Thompson.
- The Stooges release their self-titled debut album, which features such classics as "I Wanna Be Your Dog" and "1969." However, the album stalls at no. 106 on the U.S. charts.
- Glam rocker David Bowie releases the single "Space Oddity," which reaches no. 5 on the UK charts.

1970

- The Stooges release their second album, *Fun House*, which both Joey Ramone and Henry Rollins later declare as their favorite album of all time.

1971

- Rock critic Dave Marsh uses the phrase *punk rock* to describe the eclectic sound of Question Mark and the Mysterians ("96 Tears") in a *CREEM* magazine review.
- Malcolm McLaren and Vivienne Westwood open Let It Rock boutique at 430 King's Road in London.
- The New York Dolls make their inauspicious stage debut on Christmas Day at an "old welfare hotel." The original Dolls lineup consists of David Johansen, Johnny Thunders, Rick Rivets, Arthur "Killer" Kane, and Billy Murcia.

1972

- The MC5 perform their final show at Detroit's Grande Ballroom on New Year's Day.
- Alice Cooper releases the rock anthem "School's Out," which reaches no. 7 on the U.S. charts.

1973

- A landmark in the glam/glitter rock movement, David Bowie's album *Ziggy Stardust & the Spiders* from Mars reaches no. 5 on the UK charts and no. 75 on the U.S. charts.
- Later dubbed the "Birthplace of Punk Rock," CBGB & OMFUG (Country, Bluegrass, Blues and Other Music for Uplifting Gormandizers) opens its doors at 315 Bowery in New York City.
- Iggy and the Stooges release their highly influential third studio album, *Raw Power*, which features the classic tracks "Search and Destroy" and "Gimme Danger."
- The New York Dolls release their self-titled debut album, which reaches only no. 116 on the U.S. charts, but features such enduring hits as "Personality Crisis," "Trash," and "Jet Boy."
- The New York Dolls perform on *The Old Grey Whistle Test*, a British TV music show, whose host (Bob Harris) deems the band "mock rock."

1974

- Television takes the stage for their first-ever gig against an actual backdrop of televisions at the Townhouse Theater in NYC on March 2.
- The Ramones play their first-ever gig at the Performance Studio in New York City.
- Malcolm McLaren and Vivienne Westwood open SEX boutique in London.
- The Ramones play their first gig at CBGBs on August 16 with reportedly just six people in the audience.
- Patti Smith releases her debut single, "Hey Joe," with the proto-punk classic "Piss Factory" as the B-side.
- Beat Generation legend William S. Burroughs takes up residence near CBGBs in "The Bunker" (222 Bowery), where he entertains such guests as Andy Warhol, Lou Reed, Patti Smith, Debbie Harry, and many other NYC punk scene regulars.

1975

- Plagued by drug and alcohol abuse among their ranks, the New York Dolls split up for good.
- UK glam rock band Sweet releases "Ballroom Blitz," which reaches no. 5 on the U.S. charts.
- Patti Smith releases her critically acclaimed debut album, *Horses*, which is produced by John Cale, former member of the Velvet Underground. It reaches no. 47 on the U.S. charts.
- The Sex Pistols form and play their first gig at Saint Martin's School of Art in London (as the opening act for Bazooka Joe).
- John Holmstrom publishes the first issue of the highly influential *Punk* magazine.
- The Ramones release their first single, "Blitzkrieg Bop," which fails to chart but becomes one of the band's most recognized songs.

1976

- The Ramones release their debut album, *Ramones*, on April 23. It stalls at no. 111 on the U.S. charts.
- Stiff Records is created in London by Dave Robinson and Jake Riviera. The label eventually signs such pivotal acts as the Damned, the Adverts, Richard Hell and the Voidoids, Ian Dury, Elvis Costello, the Pogues, Nick Lowe, Madness, Wreckless Eric, and Lene Lovich, among many others.
- The Runaways release their self-titled debut album, which features their moderate hit "Cherry Bomb."
- The Ramones make their triumphant London debut, opening for the Flamin' Groovies (with the Stranglers appearing third on the bill) at the Roundhouse on July 4 in front of two thousand fans, including Rat Scabies of the Damned and Gaye Advert of the Adverts.
- The Clash play their first gig opening for the Sex Pistols at the Black Swan in Sheffield on July 4.
- Mark Perry publishes the first issue of *Sniffin' Glue*, a punk fanzine named after the Ramones' song "Now I Wanna Sniff Some Glue" that will become highly influential.
- The Modern Lovers release their self-titled debut album featuring proto-punk classics "Roadrunner" and "Pablo Picasso." The album doesn't even chart.
- Malcolm McLaren helps organize the two-day 100 Club Punk Festival in London on September 20–21, which features a who's who of the early UK punk scene, including the Sex Pistols, the Clash, the Damned, Vibrators, Subway Sect, Siouxsie and the Banshees, and Stinky Toys, among others.
- The Sex Pistols sign a two-year contract (that actually lasts only three months) with EMI on October 8.
- The Damned release their classic song "New Rose," considered the first British punk single.
- The Sex Pistols release their first single, "Anarchy in the UK," which barely breaks into the top 40 at no. 38 on the UK charts.
- The Sex Pistols and several members of the so-called Bromley Contingent appear live on the *Today* show hosted by Bill Grundy on December 1 and cause quite a stir during a profanity-laced

interview, causing the *Daily Mirror* to print the notorious headline "The Filth and the Fury!"

- The Sex Pistols (with support from the Clash, the Damned, and Johnny Thunders and the Heartbreakers) embark on the infamous Anarchy Tour of the UK.
- Blondie releases their self-titled debut album, which features such songs as "X Offender," "In the Flesh," and "Rip Her to Shreds." It fails to chart in either the United States or United Kingdom.
- Generation X (fronted by future superstar Billy Idol) takes the stage at the Central College of Art and Design for the band's first-ever gig on December 10.

1977

- Following two months of adverse publicity generated by the Sex Pistols, EMI terminates the band's recording contract on January 6.
- Buzzcocks release their EP *Spiral Scratch* on January 29, featuring the hit single "Boredom."
- The Damned release the first UK punk album, *Damned Damned Damned*, via Stiff Records on February 18.
- Australian punk-rock band the Saints release their debut album, *(I'm) Stranded.*
- On February 28, Glen Matlock is fired as bassist for the Sex Pistols (for purportedly liking the Beatles!) and quickly replaced by Sid Vicious.
- Television releases its debut album, *Marquee Moon*, which fails to chart in the United States, but reaches no. 28 on the UK charts.
- The Clash release their debut single, "White Riot," off their landmark self-titled debut album.
- Iggy Pop releases his debut solo album, *The Idiot*, which is produced by David Bowie.
- A&M Records terminates the Sex Pistols' recording contract on March 16.

- The Damned become the first English punk band to embark on a U.S. tour—playing gigs at such legendary clubs as CBGBs in New York City and the Rat in Boston.
- The Adverts release their debut single, "One Chord Wonders," on April 22.
- On May 13, the Sex Pistols sign a three-album deal with Virgin Records. In a Virgin press release, Johnny Rotten states, "Everyone is so fed up with the old way. We were constantly being dictated to by musical old farts out of university who've got rich parents."
- On May 27, the Sex Pistols release their second single, "God Save the Queen," which is banned by BBC Radio, but nevertheless reaches no. 2 on the UK charts.
- The Sex Pistols release their third single, "Pretty Vacant," on July 2. It reaches no. 6 on the UK charts.
- During a July 16 Capital Radio show titled *The Punk and His Music*, Johnny Rotten plays some of his favorite songs—an eclectic selection that includes Neil Young's "Revolution Blues," Tim Buckley's "Sweet Surrender," Captain Beefheart's "The Blimp," Nico's "Janitor of Lunacy," and Peter Tosh's "Legalize It."
- T. Rex singer-songwriter and glam-rock pioneer Marc Bolan dies in a car crash at the age of twenty-nine on September 16.
- The Heartbreakers release their debut album, *LAMF* (aka "Like a Mother Fucker") on October 3, featuring such classic tracks as "Born to Lose," "Chinese Rocks," and "One Track Mind."
- On October 28, the Sex Pistols release their only studio album, *Never Mind the Bollocks, Here's the Sex Pistols* in the UK through Virgin Records, and it reaches no. 1 on the UK charts (but peaks at only no. 106 on the U.S. charts).
- The Clash release their self-titled debut album through CBS Records. It reaches no. 12 on the UK charts.
- On November 4, the Ramones release their third album, *Rocket to Russia*, which features such classic tracks as "Rockaway Beach," "Sheena Is a Punk Rocker," and "Teenage Lobotomy," as well as covers of Bobby Freeman's "Do You Wanna Dance?" and the Trashmen's "Surfin' Bird."

- The Roxy opens in London as a punk nightclub with the Clash taking the stage.
- Richard Hell and the Voidoids release their debut album, *Blank Generation*.
- The Jam release their debut album, *In the City*, which reaches no. 20 on the UK charts.
- Wire releases its debut album, *Pink Flag*, which Henry Rollins of Black Flag later calls "a perfect album."

1978

- The Sex Pistols end their disastrous U.S. tour on January 14 with a notorious performance at the Winterland Ballroom in San Francisco that ends with a disgruntled Johnny Rotten famously asking the audience, "Ever get the feeling you've been cheated?"
- An episode of the TV comedy show *C.P.O. Sharkey* (which stars Don Rickles) titled "Punk Rock Sharkey" features Los Angeles punk band the Dickies performing "Hideous."
- Buzzcocks release their debut album *Another Music in a Different Kitchen*, which reaches no. 15 on the UK charts.
- The Rock Against Racism rally takes place on April 30 in Victoria Park with performances by the Clash, X-Ray Spex, Tom Robinson Band, and others.
- The Cramps perform an incredibly bizarre show at the Napa State Mental Hospital in Napa, California, with a set that includes "Love Me," "Human Fly," "Domino," and "TV Set."
- Devo releases their debut album, *Q: Are We Not Men? A: We Are Devo!* It reaches no. 12 on the UK charts and no. 78 on the U.S. charts.
- The Cars release their debut single, "Just What I Needed," which rises to no. 27 on the U.S. charts.
- Sid Vicious is charged with murdering girlfriend Nancy Spungen in Room 100 at the Chelsea Hotel in New York City on October 12.
- Black Flag founder/guitarist Greg Ginn forms SST Records, which goes on to release albums from not only Black Flag but also Meat Puppets, the Dicks, Dinosaur Jr., DC3, Descendents,

Minutemen, Husker Du, Sonic Youth, and the Stains, among others.

- The Boomtown Rats score a no. 1 single in the UK with "Rat Trap."
- Siouxsie and the Banshees release their debut album, *The Scream*, which peaks at no. 12 on the UK charts.
- Public Image Ltd (featuring a post–Sex Pistols Johnny Lydon) releases their debut album, *First Issue*, which reaches no. 18 on the UK charts.
- X-Ray Spex releases their debut album, *Germ Free Adolescents*, which reaches no. 18 on the UK charts.

1979

- Ex–Sex Pistol bassist and punk icon Sid Vicious dies of a heroin overdose on February 2 at the age of twenty-one.
- Virgin Records releases the posthumous album of Sid Vicious titled *Sid Sings*, featuring eclectic interpretations of Johnny Thunders's "Born to Lose," the Stooges' "I Wanna Be Your Dog," the New York Dolls' "Take a Chance on Me," and, of course, Frank Sinatra's "My Way," among others.
- Blondie hits no. 1 in both the United States and UK with their single "Heart of Glass."
- The Cure release their debut album, *Three Imaginary Boys*, which reaches no. 44 on the UK charts and features the single "Boys Don't Cry."
- Joy Division releases its critically acclaimed debut album, *Unknown Pleasures*, which peaks at no. 71 on the UK charts.

In 1979, Virgin Records released a posthumous album of Sid Vicious titled *Sid Sings*, which featured a cover of Frank Sinatra's "My Way." Photofest

- The Ramones (Joey, Dee Dee, Johnny, and Marky) star in the cult musical comedy *Rock 'n' Roll High School.*
- Best known for their hit single "Teenage Kicks," the Undertones release their self-titled debut album.
- The disastrous "Disco Demolition Night" takes place between games at a White Sox doubleheader in Chicago and nearly leads to a riot after fans rush the field and run amok.
- The B-52's release their debut single, "Rock Lobster," which peaks at no. 22 on the UK charts and no. 71 on the U.S. charts.
- Gang of Four releases their debut album, *Entertainment!,* which climbs to no. 45 on the UK charts.
- The Slits release their debut album, *Cut,* which reaches no. 30 on the UK charts.
- The Clash release their third studio album, *London Calling,* which reaches no. 11 on the UK charts and no. 27 on the U.S. charts. The album eventually goes on to sell more than five million copies.
- The UK Subs release their debut album, *Another Kind of Blues.* It reaches no. 21 on the UK charts.
- The Germs release their first and only album, *GI,* which is produced by Joan Jett.
- Stiff Little Fingers release their debut album, *Inflammable Material,* which Paul Morley of the *NME* calls "the classic punk rock record."
- The Ruts release their debut album, *The Crack,* which contains the hit singles "Babylon's Burning" and "Something That I Said."

1980

- The Pretenders release their single "Brass in Pocket," which reaches no. 1 on the UK charts. The band's self-titled debut album also reaches no. 1 on the UK charts.
- The Ramones release their fifth album, *End of the Century,* which is produced by Phil Spector. It reaches no. 14 in the UK and no. 41 in the United States.
- Blondie scores another no. 1 hit in both the United States and UK with their single "Call Me."

- Joy Division lead singer Ian Curtis commits suicide by hanging himself on May 18 at the age of twenty-three. The song "Love Will Tear Us Apart" from the band's second album, *Closer*, reaches no. 13 on the UK charts. The surviving band members go on to form New Order.
- The Ruts lead singer Malcolm Owen dies of a heroin overdose on July 14 at the age of twenty-six.
- The Dead Kennedys release their debut album, *Fresh Fruit for Rotting Vegetables*. It reaches no. 33 on the UK charts.
- An unintentionally hilarious episode ("Next Stop, Nowhere") of the TV show *Quincy, M.E.*, starring Jack Klugman in the title role, warns of the dangers of punk-rock music after a teenager gets murdered with an ice pick at a punk show: "Whoever killed that boy was listening to words that literally cried out for blood."
- Killing Joke releases its self-titled debut album, which peaks at no. 39 on the UK charts.
- X releases their debut album, *Los Angeles*, which is produced by former Doors keyboardist Ray Manzarek. The album fails to chart.
- The Jam release the single "Going Underground," which reaches no. 1 on the UK charts.
- Virgin Films releases the British mockumentary featuring the Sex Pistols titled *The Great Rock 'n' Roll Swindle*, which music critic John Strausbaugh calls "[Malcolm] McLaren's stunningly ugly ode to himself" and "quite possibly the very, very worst rock 'n' roll movie ever made."
- The Wipers release their debut album, *Is This Real?* Legendary DJ John Peel later lists it among his twenty favorite albums of all time.
- Directed by Penelope Spheeris, the seminal documentary *The Decline of Western Civilization* is released, showcasing the gritty Los Angeles punk scene with interviews and performances by Black Flag, Germs, Fear, Circle Jerks, X, Alice Bag Band, and Catholic Discipline.
- Germs lead singer Darby Crash commits suicide with an intentional heroin overdose on December 7 at the age of

twenty-two—one day before John Lennon is murdered by a deranged fan outside his Dakota apartment in New York City.
- The Clash release the triple album *Sandinista!*, which includes thirty-six tracks. It reaches no. 19 on the UK charts and no. 24 on the U.S. charts.

1981

- Adam and the Ants release their second album, *Kings of the Wild Frontier*, which reaches no. 1 on the UK charts and no. 44 on the U.S. charts.
- Henry Rollins (Garfield) joins Los Angeles–based hardcore-punk band Black Flag as lead singer.
- The Dead Kennedys release the anti-racism anthem "Nazi Punks Fuck Off."
- MTV makes its debut on August 1 with the Buggles' music video "Video Killed the Radio Star."
- The Adolescents release their self-titled debut album (aka *The Blue Album*), which features such classic tracks as "Kids of the Black Hole" and "Amoeba."
- Bow Wow Wow releases its debut album, *See Jungle! See Jungle! Go You're your Gang Yeah, City All Over! Go Ape Crazy!*, which contains the hit single "Go Wild in the Country," as well as an MTV-friendly cover of the Strangeloves' "I Want Candy."
- Los Angeles punk band Fear causes a stir on *Saturday Night Live* when slam-dancing fans (including *SNL* legend John Belushi!) run amok and trash the set.
- The Replacements release their debut album, *Sorry Ma, Forgot to Take Out the Trash*.
- Canadian hardcore-punk band D.O.A. releases the pioneering album *Hardcore '81*, which features classic tracks such as "I Don't Give a Shit," "001 Loser's Club," and "Smash the State."

1982

- Former Runaway Joan Jett scores a no. 1 hit in the United States with "I Love Rock 'n' Roll."

- The Go-Go's reach no. 2 on the U.S. chart with their hit single "We Got the Beat."
- Descendents release their debut album, *Milo Goes to College*.
- Legendary rock critic Lester Bangs dies of an accidental overdose on April 30 at the age of thirty-three.
- Adam Ant releases his incredibly successful solo debut album, *Friend or Foe*, which reaches no. 5 on the UK charts and features the no. 1 UK single "Goody Two Shoes."
- The Misfits release their debut album, *Walk Among Us*, which contains such classics as "Night of the Living Dead," "Skulls," and "Mommy, Can I Go Out and Kill Tonight?"
- Bad Brains releases its self-titled debut album (aka "The Yellow Tape"), which features the legendary track "Pay to Cum."
- Fear release their debut album, *The Record*, which includes such signature tracks as "I Love Livin' in the City" and "Let's Have a War."

1983

- The Clash score their only no. 1 hit in the United States with "Rock the Casbah" from their fifth album, *Combat Rock*.
- The Pretenders release their hit single "Back on the Chain Gang," which reaches no. 5 on the U.S. charts.
- Mick Jones gets kicked out of the Clash and soon forms the band Big Audio Dynamite.
- San Francisco–based punk band Avengers release a self-titled compilation album that includes a quirky cover of the Rolling Stones' classic "Paint It Black."
- Featuring former band members from Joy Division, New Order releases the single "Blue Monday," which reaches no. 9 on the UK charts.
- The Violent Femmes release their self-titled debut album, which includes their signature track, "Blister in the Sun."
- Suicidal Tendencies release their self-titled debut album, which features the hit single "Institutionalized."

1984

- Echo & the Bunnymen release the single "The Killing Moon," which reaches no. 9 on the UK charts.
- The Smiths release their self-titled debut album, which reaches no. 2 on the UK charts, but stalls at no. 150 on the U.S. charts. It contains the hit single "What Difference Does It Make?"
- Husker Du release their critically acclaimed double album *Zen Arcade*, which later ranks no. 4 on *Spin* magazine's list of "Top 100 Alternative Music Albums."
- Minutemen release their third album, *Double Nickels on the Dime*, a double album containing forty-five songs. It later ranks no. 7 on *Rolling Stone*'s list of the "40 Greatest Punk Albums of all Time."

1985

- The Jesus and Mary Chain release their debut album, *Psychocandy*, which reaches no. 31 on the UK charts.
- The Clash release their final (and worst!) album, *Cut the Crap*.
- Philadelphia punk band the Dead Milkmen release their debut album, *Big Lizard in My Backyard*.

1987

- Pop-art maverick Andy Warhol dies at the age of fifty-eight on February 22 of a cardiac arrhythmia following gallbladder surgery.
- Big Black releases its second album, *Songs about Fucking*, which *Pitchfork* later ranks no. 54 on its list of the "Top 100 Albums of the 1980s."

1988

- Sonic Youth releases its critically acclaimed fifth studio album, *Daydream Nation*, which features the enduring classic "Teenage Riot."

- Bad Religion releases its critically acclaimed third album, *Suffer*, which fails to chart.

1989

- Dee Dee Ramone quits the Ramones, embarks on a short-lived rap career as "Dee Dee King," and releases his first solo album, *Standing in the Spotlight*.
- The B-52's release their single "Love Shack," which charts at no. 3 in the United States and no. 2 in the UK.
- The Ramones release their eleventh album, *Brain Drain*, the last to feature Dee Dee Ramone.

1990

- Led by Ian MacKaye, Washington, DC–based hardcore-punk band Fugazi release their debut album, *Repeater*.

1991

- Johnny Thunders dies of an apparent overdose on April 23 at the age of thirty-eight in New Orleans.
- The first Lollapalooza Festival takes place with performances by Jane's Addiction, Siouxsie and the Banshees, Living Colour, Nine Inch Nails, Ice-T and Body Count, Butthole Surfers, Henry Rollins Band, Violent Femmes, and Fishbone.
- Nirvana releases their phenomenally successful second studio album, *Nevermind*, which reaches no. 1 in the United States and eventually sells thirty million copies.

1992

- Green Day releases its second studio album, *Kerplunk*, which is the band's first album to feature Tre Cool on drums.

1993

- Beat legend William S. Burroughs and Kurt Cobain of Nirvana collaborate on the album *The "Priest" They Called Him*.
- Guns N' Roses releases an album of covers titled *The Spaghetti Incident?* which includes the likes of "New Rose" (the Damned), "Raw Power" (the Stooges), "Down on the Farm" (UK Subs), "Human Being" (New York Dolls), "Attitude" (Misfits), "Black Leather" (the Professionals), "You Can't Put Your Arms around a Memory" (Johnny Thunders), and "I Don't Care about You" (Fear).
- Bikini Kill releases their debut studio album, *Pussy Whipped*, which helps to define the Riot Grrrl sound with such signature tracks as "Rebel Girl."

1994

- Green Day release their most successful album, *Dookie*, which goes on to sell ten million copies. It reaches no. 2 on the U.S. charts and no. 13 on the UK charts.
- Bad Religion releases its eighth studio album, *Stranger Than Fiction*, which peaks at no. 87 on the U.S. charts.
- Kurt Cobain of Nirvana dies of a self-inflicted gunshot wound on April 8 at the age of twenty-seven.
- NOFX releases its fifth album, *Punk in Drublic*, which fails to chart but eventually sells over one million copies worldwide.
- Woodstock '94 (aka "Mudstock") celebrates the twenty-fifth anniversary of the original Woodstock festival in 1969 with performances

Green Day's most successful album, *Dookie*, reached No. 2 on the U.S. charts and eventually sold ten million copies. PHOTOFEST

by Bob Dylan, Nine Inch Nails, Aerosmith, Metallica, Henry Rollins Band, Collective Soul, Violent Femmes, Cypress Hill, Blind Melon, Red Hot Chili Peppers, and the Cranberries, among many others.

- The Offspring release their third album, *Smash*, which contains such hit singles as "Gotta Get Away," "Come Out and Play," and "Self Esteem."
- Rancid releases its second album, *Let's Go*, which reaches no. 97 on the U.S. charts.

1995

- The Rock and Roll Hall of Fame opens its doors in Cleveland, Ohio.
- Rancid releases its third album, . . . *And Out Came the Wolves*, which contains the hit singles "Roots Radicals," "Time Bomb," and "Ruby Soho." The album's title was taken from a poem in punk poet Jim Carroll's *The Basketball Diaries*.
- Green Day releases its fourth album, *Insomniac*, which peaks at no. 2 on the U.S. charts and contains the hit single "Brain Stew."

1996

- The surviving members of the Sex Pistols reunite for a reunion tour (dubbed "Fat, Forty, and Back") and release a live album, *Filthy Lucre Live*.
- The Ramones break up after approximately 2,200 live shows.
- The Velvet Underground—Lou Reed, John Cale, Sterling Morrison, and Maureen "Moe" Tucker—are inducted into the Rock and Roll Hall of Fame.
- John Lydon, former lead singer of the Sex Pistols, appears in a Mountain Dew commercial.

1997

- British anarcho-punk band Chumbawamba score an unlikely hit with "Tubthumping," which reaches no. 19 on the UK charts and no. 6 on the U.S. charts.
- Sleater-Kinney releases their third album, *Dig Me Out*, which *Rolling Stone* later ranks 189 on its list of the "500 Greatest Albums of All Time."
- Green Day releases its fifth album, *Nimrod*, which features the hit single, "Good Riddance (Time of Your Life)."

1998

- The Offspring release their fifth album, *Americana*, which generates three hit singles: "Pretty Fly (for a White Guy)," "Why Don't You Get a Job?" and "The Kids Aren't Alright."

1999

- Marred by violence, sexual assault, vandalism, fires, and looting, Woodstock '99 goes down in history—for all the wrong reasons. The eclectic lineup of performers includes the Offspring, Korn, Bush, James Brown, Godsmack, Sheryl Crow, Insane Clown Posse, Fatboy Slim, and Willie Nelson, among many others.
- Blink-182 releases their third album, *Enema of the State*, which features such hits as "What's My Age Again?" "All the Small Things," and "Adam's Song." The album sells over fifteen million copies.

2001

- Pennywise release their sixth album, *Land of the Free?*, which peaks at no. 67 on the U.S. charts and spawns the hit single "Fuck Authority."

2002

- The Ramones and Talking Heads become the first punk bands to be inducted into the Rock and Roll Hall of Fame.
- Dee Dee Ramone dies on June 5 at the age of forty-nine from a heroin overdose.
- Joe Strummer of the Clash dies of a heart attack on December 22 at the age of fifty.
- Gainesville, Florida, punk band Against Me! releases its debut album, *Reinventing Axl Rose*.

2003

- The Clash—Joe Strummer, Mick Jones, Paul Simonon, Topper Headon, and Terry Chimes—are inducted into the Rock and Roll Hall of Fame.
- AFI releases its sixth album, *Sing the Sorrow*, which peaks at no. 5 on the U.S. charts.

2004

- Johnny Ramone dies on September 15 at the age of fifty-five following a five-year battle with prostate cancer.

2005

- The Dropkick Murphys release their fifth album, *The Warrior's Code*, which includes the hit single "I'm Shipping Up to Boston" (written by Woody Guthrie and featured on *The Departed* soundtrack).

2006

- CBGBs closes its doors for good on October 31 with a final concert by "punk poetess" Patti Smith.
- The Sex Pistols are inducted into the Rock and Roll Hall of Fame but refuse the honor.

- "I Wish I Was a Punk Rocker (with Flowers in My Hair)," the debut single from Scottish singer-songwriter Sandi Thom, reaches no. 1 on the UK charts.

2007

- Patti Smith is inducted into the Rock and Roll Hall of Fame.

2010

- The Stooges—Iggy Pop, Ron Asheton, Scott Asheton, James Williamson, and Dave Alexander—are inducted into the Rock and Roll Hall of Fame.

2013

- Lou Reed dies of liver disease at the age of seventy-one in his East Hampton, New York, home.

2015

- Green Day—Billie Armstrong, Tre Cool, and Mike Dirnt—is inducted into the Rock and Roll Hall of Fame.
- Lou Reed is posthumously inducted into the Rock and Roll Hall of Fame.

2018

- Vivienne Westwood is featured in the documentary *Westwood: Punk, Icon, Activist*.
- Mark E. Smith of the Fall dies of lung and kidney cancer at the age of sixty on January 24.

2020

- Green Day releases its thirteenth studio album, *Father of All Mother Fuckers*.

2021

- The Go-Gos are inducted into the Rock and Roll Hall of Fame.

2022

- Based on the memoir of Sex Pistols guitarist Steve Jones titled *Lonely Boy: Tales of a Sex Pistol*, the FX drama series *Pistol* makes its debut.

Selected Bibliography

Acker, Kathy. *Blood and Guts in High School*. New York: Grove Press, 1994.

Antonia, Nina. *The New York Dolls: Too Much Too Soon*. New York: Omnibus Press, 1998.

Ball, Hugo. *Flight Out of Time: A Dada Diary*. Berkeley: University of California Press, 1996.

Ballard, J. G. *High-Rise*. New York: Liveright, 1975.

Bangs, Lester. *Psychotic Reactions and Carburetor Dung*. New York: Alfred A. Knopf, 1987.

Benoit, Tod. *Where Are They Buried?* New York: Black Dog & Leventhal, 2003.

Bockris, Victor. *With William Burroughs: A Report from the Bunker*. New York: St. Martin's Press, 1996.

Boot, Adrian, and Chris Salewicz. *Punk: The Illustrated History of a Music Revolution*. New York: Penguin Books, 1996.

Bovey, Seth. *Five Years Ahead of My Time: Garage Rock from the 1950s to the Present*. London: Reaktion Books, 2019.

Bronson, Fred. *The Billboard Book of Number 1 Hits*. New York: Billboard Books, 2003.

Buckley, Jonathan, and Mark Ellingham, eds. *Rock: The Rough Guide*. London: Rough Guides, 1996.

Bukszpan, Daniel. *The Encyclopedia of New Wave*. New York: Sterling, 2012.

Burroughs, William S. *The Wild Boys: A Book of the Dead*. New York: Grove Press, 1994.

Carroll, Jim. *The Basketball Diaries*. New York: Penguin Books, 1987.

Castle, Alison, ed. *The Stanley Kubrick Archives*. Cologne, Germany: Taschen, 2005.

Clarke, Victoria Mary, and Shane MacGowan. *A Drink with Shane Mac-Gowan*. New York: Grove Press, 2001.

Cogan, Brian. *The Encyclopedia of Punk*. New York: Sterling, 2008.

Covach, John. *What's That Sound? An Introduction to Rock and Its History*. New York: W. W. Norton, 2009.

DeCurtis, Anthony, and James Henke. *The Rolling Stone Album Guide*. New York: Random House, 1992.

Doe, John, with Tom DeSavia. *More Fun in the New World: The Unmaking and Legacy of LA Punk*. New York: Da Capo Press, 2019.

Draper, Jason. *A Brief History of Album Covers*. New York: Flame Tree Press, 2017.

Drexler, Rosalyn. *Starburn: The Story of Jenni Love*. New York: Simon and Schuster, 1979.

Edison, Mike. *I Have Fun Everywhere I Go*. New York: Faber and Faber, 2008.

Epting, Chris. *Led Zeppelin Crashed Here: The Rock and Roll Landmarks of North America*. Santa Monica, CA: Santa Monica Press, 2007.

Gaines, Donna. *A Misfit's Manifesto: The Spiritual Journey of a Rock & Roll Heart*. New York: Villard Books, 2003.

Gilmore, Mikal. *Night Beat: A Shadow History of Rock & Roll*. London: Picador, 1998.

Gimarac, George. *Punk Diary: 1970–1979*. New York: St. Martin's Press, 1994.

Gold, Jeff. *101 Essential Rock Records: The Golden Age of Vinyl from the Beatles to the Sex Pistols*. Berkeley: Gingko Press, 2012.

Grecco, Michael. *Punk, Post Punk, New Wave: Onstage, Backstage, in Your Face, 1978–1991*. New York: Abrams, 2020.

Grogan, Jake. *Origins of a Song: 202 True Inspirations behind the World's Greatest Lyrics*. Kennebunkport, ME: Cider Mill Press, 2018.

Hannon, Sharon, M. *Punks: A Guide to an American Subculture*. Westport, CT: Greenwood Press, 2009.

Harris, John. *Hail! Hail! Rock 'n' Roll*. London: Sphere, 2009.

Hell, Richard. *Massive Pissed Love*. New York: Soft Skull Press, 2015.

———. *The Voidoid*. New York: 38th Street, 2009.

Herman, Gary. *Rock 'n' Roll Babylon*. New York: Perigee Books, 1982.

Heylin, Clinton. *From the Velvets to the Voidoids: The Birth of American Punk Rock*. Chicago: A Cappella Books, 2005.

Holmstrom, John, and Bridget Hurd, eds. *Punk: The Best of Punk Magazine*. New York: HarperCollins, 2012.

Hooley, Terri, and Richard Sullivan. *Hoolyegan: Music, Mayhem and Good Vibrations*. Belfast, Ireland: Blackstaff Press, 2010.

Hoskyns, Barney. *Waiting for the Sun: Strange Days, Weird Scenes and the Sound of Los Angeles*. New York: St. Martin's Press, 1996.

Hurchalla, George. *Going Underground: American Punk 1979–1989*. Oakland, CA: PM Press, 2016.

Ingram, Chris, and Daniel Lane. *The Book of Metal*. New York: Thunder's Mouth Press, 2002.

Jancik, Wayne, and Tad Lathrop. *Cult Rockers*. New York: FIRESIDE, 1995.

Katz, Mike, and Crispin Kott. *Rock and Roll Explorer Guide to New York City*. Lanham, MD: Globe Pequot, 2018.

Kaufman, Alan, Neil Ortenberg, and Barney Rosset. *The Outlaw Bible of American Literature*. New York: Thunder's Mouth Press, 2004.

Kristal, Hilly. *CBGB & OMFUG: Thirty Years from the Home of Underground Rock*. New York: Abrams, 2005.

Krivine, Andrew. *Too Fast to Live Too Young to Die: Punk & Post Punk Graphics 1976–1986*. London: Pavilion, 2020.

Lunch, Lydia. *Paradoxia: A Predator's Diary*. New York: Akashic Books, 2007.

Lydon, John. *Rotten: No Irish, No Blacks, No Dogs*. New York: St. Martin's Press, 1994.

Manitoba, Handsome Dick, and Amy Wallace. *The Official Punk Rock Book of Lists*. New York: Backbeat Books: 2007.

Marcade, Phil. *Punk Avenue: Inside the New York City Underground 1972–1982*. New York: Three Rooms Press, 2017.

Marcus, Greil. *Lipstick Traces: A Secret History of the Twentieth Century*. Cambridge: Harvard University Press, 1990.

Marks, Craig, and Rob Tannenbaum. *I Want My MTV: The Uncensored Story of the Music Video Revolution*. New York: Dutton, 2011.

McCain, Gillian, and Legs McNeil. *Please Kill Me: The Uncensored Oral History of Punk*. New York: Grove Press, 1996.

Miller, James. *Flowers in the Dustbin: The Rise of Rock and Roll, 1947–1977*. New York: Simon & Schuster, 1999.

Morgan, Ted. *Literary Outlaw: The Life and Times of William S. Burroughs*. New York: Henry Holt, 1988.

Morris, Keith. *My Damage: The Story of a Punk Rock Survivor*. New York: Da Capo Press, 2017.

Parsons, Tony. *Hail! Hail! Rock 'n' Roll*. London: Sphere, 2009.

Peary, Danny. *Guide for the Film Fanatic*. New York: Simon & Schuster, 1986.

Popoff, Martin. *Punk Tees: The Punk Revolution in 125 T-Shirts*. New York: Sterling, 2016.

———. *Satisfaction: 10 Albums that Changed My Life*. Iola, WI: Krause, 2019.

Ramone, Dee Dee. *Chelsea Hotel Horror*. Boston: Da Capo Press, 2016.

———. *Lobotomy: Surviving the Ramones*. New York: Thunder's Mouth Press, 2000.

Resh, Jon. *Amped: Notes from a Go-Nowhere Punk Band*. Chicago: Viper Press, 2006.

Reynolds, Simon. *Retromania: Pop Culture's Addiction to Its Own Past*. New York: Farrar, Straus and Giroux, 2011.

———. *Rip It Up and Start Again: Postpunk 1978–1984*. New York: Penguin Books, 2006.

Riordan, John. *Music's Cult Artists*. New York: Dog 'n' Bone Books, 2020.

Robb, John. *Punk Rock: An Oral History*. Oakland, CA: PM Press, 2012.

Robbins, Ira A., ed. *Trouser Press Record Guide*. New York: Collier Books, 1991.

Roberts, David, ed. *Rock Chronicles*. Buffalo: Firefly Books, 2019.

Rombes, Nicholas. *A Cultural Dictionary of Punk 1974–1982*. New York: Continuum International, 2009.

Sabin, Roger. *Punk Rock: So What?* New York: Routledge, 2009.

Savage, Jon. *England's Dreaming: Anarchy, Sex Pistols, Punk Rock, and Beyond*. New York: St. Martin's Press, 2001.

Schinder, Scott, and the Editors of Rolling Stone Press. *Rolling Stone's Alt-Rock-A-Rama*. New York: Dell Publishing, 1996.

Sex Pistols. *1977: The Bollocks Diaries*. New York: Hatchette, 2012.

Shaffer, Andrew. *Literary Rogues*. New York: Harper Perennial, 2013.

Smith, Patti. *Just Kids*. New York: Ecco, 2010.

Spicer, Al. *The Rough Guide to Punk*. London: Penguin, 2006.

Strausbaugh, John. *Rock til You Drop: The Decline from Rebellion to Nostalgia*. New York: Verso, 2002.

Sugerman, Danny. *Wonderland Avenue: Tales of Glamour and Excess*. London: Abacus, 1989.

Szatmary, David. *A Time to Rock: A Social History of Rock 'n' Roll*. New York: Shirmer Books, 1996.

Thompson, Dave. *Alternative Rock*. San Francisco: Miller Freeman Books, 2000.

Walker, Matt. *Gainesville Punk: A History of Bands & Music*. Charleston: The History Press, 2016.

Walsh, Gavin. *Punk on 45: Revolutions on Vinyl 1976–79*. London: Plexus, 2006.

Weldon, Michael. *The Psychotronic Encyclopedia of Film*. New York: Ballantine Books, 1983.

Wide, Steve. *A Field Guide to Punk*. Melbourne, Australia: Smith Street Book, 2020.

Index